Shocked But Connected

Shocked But Connected

Notes on Laughter

Michael Roemer

ROWMAN & LITTLEFIELD PUBLISHERS, INC.
Lanham • Boulder • New York • Toronto • Plymouth, UK

Published by Rowman & Littlefield Publishers, Inc.
A wholly owned subsidiary of The Rowman & Littlefield Publishing Group, Inc.
4501 Forbes Boulevard, Suite 200, Lanham, Maryland 20706
www.rowman.com

10 Thornbury Road, Plymouth PL6 7PP, United Kingdom

British Library Cataloguing in Publication Information Available

Library of Congress Cataloging-in-Publication Data
Roemer, Michael, 1928–
  Shocked but connected : notes on laughter / Michael Roemer.
     p. cm.
  ISBN 978-1-4422-1756-0 (cloth : alk. paper) — ISBN 978-1-4422-1758-4 (electronic)
  1. Comic, The. 2. Wit and humor—Philosophy. 3. Laughter. I. Title.
  B105.C456R84 2012
  152.4'3—dc23   2012017675

∞™ The paper used in this publication meets the minimum requirements of American National Standard for Information Sciences—Permanence of Paper for Printed Library Materials, ANSI/NISO Z39.48-1992.

Printed in the United States of America

For our children—David, Jonathan, and Ruth—and
for their children, Samuel and Noah

Contents

Preface

In 1939, a quirk of fate and my mother's willingness to let her children go sent us to a Jewish boarding school in England. We would as obediently have boarded a train for Poland.

Nothing in my privileged life since then has allowed me to believe that I deserved my survival any more than millions of others deserved their suffering and death.

Cast up on the shores of New England after the war, neither the optimism of my fellow Americans nor my own strenuous efforts could persuade me that my will is free or my own. Indeed, I have become ever more convinced that whatever I am, do, or have is owed to others, who may be as little in charge of their lives as I have been of mine.

Though this may seem discouraging, once I admitted it, I felt freer and no less able to act than I was during the many years I spent trying to prove the opposite.

Laughter is so deeply rooted in the human condition that thinking about it without thinking about our existence seems pointless. Moreover, we laugh for so many reasons that any attempt to corral them into a unified field theory is doomed.

All this book attempts is a synthesis, built largely on the insights of others, that might be useful in our time.

I could never have written it or anything else without the courage, kindness, generosity, and faith in life of my wife, Barbara.

If, at the outset, my own life had been presented to me like a menu with the cost of each item clearly marked, and if I had been free, I might have chosen a different course.

As it is, all I can do is acknowledge my gratitude to someone who is no longer living but who is with me still.

I am deeply indebted to the work of Edward Edinger and Loretta Paulson; to my friend, Stimson Bullitt; to the painters Frank Auerbach and Leon Kossoff; to the confidence and support of Stanley Plotnick; to my colleagues at the Yale School of Art; to the editorial help of Van Truong; and to my companion and friend, Judy Rudiakov.

CHAPTER ONE

Surprised

A

We assume we know what will and won't happen but remain dimly aware that even the next moment isn't guaranteed.

During the London Blitz, the war correspondent David Schoenbrun came out of an air-raid shelter and, in an after-effect of the bombing, saw the entire front of a building fall away. With all the apartments exposed to view, a man was standing in a first-floor bathroom and laughing hysterically. When Schoenbrun asked him why, the man said that just as he pulled the chain on the toilet, the whole front of the house came tumbling down.

When America entered World War I, Teddy Roosevelt asked to see President Woodrow Wilson and offered to lead a brigade of volunteers to Europe. Wilson had no use for the leader of the Rough Riders, and turned him down. After the meeting, a deeply disappointed Roosevelt said to the president's chief of staff, "All I did was offer to die for my country." Colonel Edward House replied, "Did you make that quite clear to the president?"[1]

Charlie Chaplin was asked whether he would let the audience see the banana peel before a man slipped on it. He said he would, but that he would have the man see it as well—and then let him step carefully across it into an open manhole.

The comic happens suddenly. Most jokes, comic stories, and funny incidents surprise us. We *crack* jokes, and many have punch lines.

Though the popular arts, like our institutions and belief systems, serve largely to reassure us, surprise is central to all the arts. Artists and entertainers confound our expectations, just as opponents in warfare and competitive games do.

Surprises in painting spring from the instantaneous impact of the whole, while in narrative and music, they happen in time. If we are unfamiliar with a play by Shakespeare, the next line is impossible to predict, and even the next word often comes as a surprise.

John Coltrane said when he was playing with Thelonious Monk, "I always had to be alert . . . because if you didn't keep aware all the time . . . you'd suddenly feel you'd stepped into an open elevator shaft."[2]

When Sergei Diaghilev commissioned Jean Cocteau to design a ballet, he said, "I want you to astonish me." We never know what Fred Astaire, Ray Bolger, or Bojangles Robinson will do next, and even if we have seen the performance before, their grace and skill have a sensory effect that makes it new.

Art works through the senses. A piece of music may be familiar, but a cymbal crash—like cold water—surprises us every time.

Most stories are adventures into the unknown, encounters with the unfamiliar and unexpected. In fiction, hearing or seeing what we already know is of little interest to us until the foregone ending. What the figures want and expect is queered by events beyond their control, and what they do has unforeseen, often unintended consequences.

Though we know the outcome of most stories, the path taking the characters there has unexpected turns. We know before the movie begins that Bonnie and Clyde will die, but not how it will come about, just as the myths that structure Greek tragedy were familiar to the audience, but not how they would be enacted in a particular play.

Ernest Hemingway said if he knew the story, he wouldn't have to tell it. Storytellers themselves are often surprised by what happens. Unless they are working in a genre structure with its reassuring conventions, the events lie ahead of them, uncertain and confusing—just as in life we may think we know what's coming only to find ourselves playing catch-up.

The storyteller's motto might well be *Discover and Bury*. He finds out what is really going on—which is not often what he first assumed—then buries it, so that we, the audience, may discover it on our own and be surprised or disconcerted, as we so often are by life.

At the end of *Grandma's Boy*, Harold Lloyd, who has been cowardly and incompetent throughout, wins the hand of the girl he loves. In the last shot, he proudly carries her across a shallow brook, stepping carefully from stone to stone. But the last stone turns out to be the back of a pig cooling off in the water. It stands up and tumbles them into the brook.

Surprises are a mild shock. The difference is one of degree. I'm surprised if it happens to you, but shocked if it happens to me. Harold's fall shocks him, but comes as a pleasurable surprise to us.

B

The appearance and behavior of the comic figure are often ridiculous and the situations absurd. In *The Gold Rush*, Charlie Chaplin wanders through the snow in a threadbare outfit that would leave him dead in minutes. What happens is patently unreal, yet the surprises Chaplin springs have an immediate *physical* effect on us, and may convulse us with laughter.

In most stories, we share the adventures of the figures because they *might* happen. But the comic actually *does* happen—to us. When a bear attacks Charlie, we are attacked by the surprise: the fictive has become immediate and physically real. Though we don't *believe* what is happening to him, our bodies clearly believe what is happening to *us*, for we are shaking with laughter. Charlie merely *appears* to face harm to his body, but we have briefly lost control over our own.

Surprise is the fulcrum, the point at which we ourselves become startled and disconcerted. We don't laugh because the comic figure has stepped into an open manhole, but because—psychologically—we have.

It is *we* who become the fall guy, or victim. Our laughter breaks us up. It catches us unaware. We don't know when it will come or what will trigger it. *Surprised* means "seized, overtaken." We have in effect been seized, taken over, become vulnerable. We are no longer in command of ourselves, can't help laughing, and sometimes can't stop. As René Girard says, "The loss of autonomy and self-possession that is present in all forms of the comic must be present, somehow, in laughter itself."[3]

Though jokes are artificial verbal constructs and reach us primarily through the mind, the surprises they spring affect us on a gut level. They invade us and go directly, often deeply, into us. In the arts, only music and horror stories have a comparable immediate and physical effect.

Since the surprise must strike suddenly, we cannot be forewarned. Speed is essential; all comic theories stress brevity. Comedians speak and move quickly. So do visual gags.

The figures and action in most comedies are sketched economically, in their essentials, for we must perceive and understand them quickly. Caricature is the most abstract comic form and the most rapidly read.

If we have to think about a joke, it can't take us by surprise.

> Shmuel ran into a fellow Jew on the train and asked him where he was going. When his friend said he was going to Lemberg, Shmuel got angry: "You know perfectly well if you *tell* me you're going to Lemberg, I'll *think* you're going to Minsk. But I happen to know you *are* going to Lemberg—so why d'you lie to me?"

The joke is brilliant but too subtle to have a sudden impact. Once we get it, we are apt to smile at its intricacy, but we won't burst out laughing. If the comic requires mental processing, it diffuses the startling quasi-physical effect that breaks us up.

> An Indian maharajah offered his daughter and throne to anyone who could teach his favorite elephant English— but since the penalty for failure was death, no one came forward. Finally, a man appeared at the palace and said he would try. He made just one condition: he would need five years. When his friends heard what he had done, they told him he was crazy.
>
> "Maybe," he said. "But in five years the maharajah may be dead—I could die—or perhaps the elephant will learn English."

> Two men were out walking. When they passed a large toad, one said to the other, "I bet you a dollar I can swallow that toad." His friend took the bet, and the man stuck the toad into his mouth. He nearly vomited but managed to get it down, and so his friend gave him a dollar.

A while later they happened on an even larger toad, and now the loser said, "I bet you a dollar I can swallow *this* toad." His friend shook his head. "Believe me—you'll die trying!"

The man picked up the huge toad, stuck it into his mouth, and after almost choking, managed to swallow it, and won back his dollar.

They walked on for a while. Then one said to the other, "Can you tell me why we swallowed those toads!?"

The very meaning of these jokes—their "wisdom"—may give us pause and stop us from laughing out loud.

The comic depends on speed, but our eyes move so rapidly over print that reading rather than hearing a joke may keep us from laughing. Tension must build between the setup and the punch line—a stretch of time our fast-moving eye collapses to almost nothing on the page.

Conversely, some jokes are more effectively told in print.

President Lincoln and Secretary of State William Seward were out walking on Pennsylvania Avenue when Lincoln noticed a sign advertising the name *T. R. Strong*. He turned to Seward and said, "Coffee are stronger."

The joke is too refined for ears like ours, no longer attuned to auditory verbal subtlety.

Though the effect of the comic is usually simple, the reasons we laugh are often complex.

At a roast for Lucille Ball, Milton Berle, who was known for off-color jokes, assured his audience that since they had come to celebrate a lady, they wouldn't hear a single dirty word.

He continued, "It is quite an honor to serve as roastmaster for the great comedian and actress Lucille Testicle."[4]

The substitution of a scientific term for the innocent *Ball* shocks us into recognizing its "dirty" possibilities. Moreover, Lucille, with its old-fashioned, ladylike ring, combines fortuitously with *testicle*; without making us fully aware of it, the three L's in her name invoke the now sullied *Ball*, like a line of alliterative poetry.

C

Surprises can be frightening. We take out insurance policies against them.

Discontinuities and incongruities entertain us in a text, but in life they are often disturbing. A gap or disconnect in the physical world may be the missing step in a stairway that breaks your neck.

No news is best, and even good news has been known to set off heart attacks. The nighttime newscast ends with the weather so we can go to sleep, but when the weather is threatening it becomes a headline.

Surprises make us vulnerable and open us up to something we may know or sense but prefer to ignore. The instant we walk into a surprise party, we tense up. The rug has been pulled from under us, leaving us startled and disconnected. Not until a moment later, when we have recovered our orientation and balance, are we free to laugh with both relief and pleasure.

Like a surprise party, the comic often begins as *funny-peculiar* and ends as *funny-haha*.

Our identity, sense of security, and our relationships to each other and to society depend on predictability. We have to believe that we, and those we trust, have a measure of control over what happens next, and it is a central function of the community to make us and our lives as unsurprising as possible.

Within our institutions, cause and effect generally apply. But as Friedrich Nietzsche points out, they are mere assumptions. Even the most familiar realm is riven by nonsequiturs—unforeseen and unforeseeable events that make a hash of dependable sequences and connections. All too often, the story we have been told or tell ourselves becomes discontinuous. We live in a fiction we call reality—disrupted by natural disasters, violence, accidents, illness, and sudden death.

The largely suppositional picture we have of our world is a necessary illusion. We could not survive without it, just as, from moment to moment, we cannot help taking our lives for granted. We stay in the comfort zone of our assumptions, and when we have to leave it, carry what Nietzsche calls our *enveilment* with us. But, deep down, we know that at any moment something could happen that would change our lives radically.

The gift of consciousness that makes us human comes twinned with an awareness of uncertainty—an uncertainty we can afford to face only in stories that claim to be untrue. Any extended exposure to the reality of our situation would implode us.

As William Butler Yeats says, "The knowledge of reality is always a secret knowledge. It is a kind of death."[5] Or, as a friend once said, "God is the only realist. The rest of us can't afford it."

D

We need to perceive what happens to and around us in a preexisting format, and can only make sense of things with a blueprint.[6]

Our experience is prestructured, and our perception is predicated on essential but often unwarranted assumptions. We see largely what we have learned and expect to see, skipping over anomalies and conforming the unexpected to the familiar.[7]

Like the Talmud student who burst out of his study, shouting, "I have the most wonderful answer! Will someone please tell me the question?" our answers may stop us from actually *hearing* the questions. Remaining deaf to them allows us to live in relative calm, but it often keeps us from being alert to changes, dangers, and opportunities.

We remain blind to anything that doesn't fit our scheme of things unless it asserts itself forcefully. Much of the time believing *is* seeing.

If there were ghosts in the room, we would likely not see them, since we don't believe they exist.

Today, moreover, so much is coming at us that we barely have time to process the familiar, never mind the anomalous.

Dostoevsky said that if he had to choose between Jesus and the truth, he would choose Jesus. I was startled until I realized that I, too, cling to certain beliefs even though they fly in the face of what science and reason tell me.

Like most of us, I believe what I need to keep going.

E

It is often said that in art we suspend our disbelief. But what we actually suspend is our *belief*—our picture of the world and ourselves.

In stories, we expect to face the very anomalies and riddles that would create havoc in daily life and undermine our confidence and ability to act.

We come to art and entertainment *for* surprises, and are disappointed if we can outguess them.[8] Although our lives are structured by reassuring repetition, in fiction the familiar and certain is of little interest. Once the uncertainty that underlies the narrative resolves into certainty, the story, joke, or riddle is over.

Not many of us would go to football games if we knew the outcome beforehand, or enjoy sporting events between ill-matched teams and players.

If Goliath had killed David—as the onlookers surely expected—we wouldn't be reading about it.

Buster Keaton said he always wanted the audience to outguess him so he could double-cross them.

Artists avoid the familiar not only because it has often ceased to be true but because we *expect* the surprising.

In stories, we are interested in unpredictable people or the ordinary person who has been forced out of his routine by unusual circumstances. In a setting that is absolutely safe, we come for the pleasure of *not* knowing and the thrill of anxiety. In yarns and melodrama, plot generates the uncertainty, while in more complex stories it may derive from contradictions in the central figure or in our reactions to them. King Lear and Charles Foster Kane leave us with ambivalent feelings.

We live in an anxious age, but since uncertainty has always been central to narrative, our core experience may be less different from that of earlier generations than we assume.

F

Comedians and those who think about the comic agree that we laugh when a hidden truth emerges suddenly. Sigmund Freud observed that many of his patients laughed when they recalled something true, particularly if it was painful.

The truth is often kept out of view and comes as a surprise when brought to our attention.

> In response to the old charge that the Jews killed Christ, Leon Wieseltier said, "We only killed him for a couple of days."[9]

The joke at once dismisses the charge and implies that since the crucifixion and resurrection hold the core meaning of their religion, Christians should feel indebted to Jews instead of persecuting them.

Often, what happens in a joke is not credible or "real."

> The stand-up comedian Kerry Awn was doing a bit about tattoos, when a woman in the audience announced she had

Tweety Bird tattooed on her thigh. Kerry invited her up on-
stage and raised her skirt. There was no tattoo. "So where's
Tweety Bird?" Kerry asked. The woman shrugged and said,
"I guess my pussy ate it."[10]

Though the situation and punch line are entirely artificial, we
laugh because a hidden body part has appeared in the open. Significantly, it is the surprise and not, necessarily, what it reveals that is
"real" or "true" and makes us laugh. By disrupting our equanimity, it
allows us to acknowledge, in the safe arena of fiction, what we hide
or avoid in life.

The surprise ending of many jokes and riddles appears to join the
fragments into a whole, but the connection is as often artful as credible or true.

In art, the familiar and predictable is less persuasive than the surprising or new. Surprises create a sense of spontaneous, unscripted life.
They render what we *might* see and hear if we could perceive and survive reality without a familiar, oversimplified, often invalid blueprint.

Yet even in art the most radical rendering of our experience rests on
a set of shared assumptions. We can never start from scratch. There
is always a limiting and reassuring structure that allows us to see and
hear, and we cannot get far beyond it without losing our bearings.

Like all art, the comic can do no more than defamiliarize the blueprint. Even surprises depend on the known coordinates of our assumptions and expectations.

G

Since the comic can get us to face shocking facts without having us
turn away, it may be the most realistic form of narrative, despite its
obvious *un*reality.

The accidents and coincidences that drive and resolve many comedies don't strike us as arbitrary. They confirm what we have sensed or
feared—that we are not in command of our fate. This is so disconcerting that it must be framed in a story that is patently absurd—one we
need not believe.[11]

Coincidences are a metaphor for the role of chance in our lives. Significantly, they determine the action in comedy far more often than in tragedy.[12]

Just as the promise of a happy ending permits the fairy tale to render frightening and even gruesome aspects of our existence without distressing us, the exaggerated appearance and behavior of comic figures allow us to witness unpleasant and painful situations without discomfort, and indeed with pleasure.

As the most improbable form of the comic, jokes can invoke the most disturbing realities.

> On a USO tour Bob Hope entered a ward of paraplegic soldiers and called out, "Don't get up!"

> In his nightclub act, Lenny Bruce once held up a newspaper with the headline, "Six million Jews found in Argentina."

The men in the hospital roared at Hope's greeting; they laughed at their own fate, as they had often done among themselves. But one wonders where Bruce could go after invoking the Holocaust for an audience that could hardly laugh at the death of millions.

H

Just as teenagers go to horror movies to be terrified, we expect stories to put us under tension—to be frightened, invaded, even overwhelmed. If a story or joke doesn't make us tense, we are disappointed.

Though much of the time we are barely aware of it, tension—like surprises—is not an aesthetic convention but an inescapable part of our existence, and stories that fail to make us tense don't seem altogether real to us.

Though we try to avoid or minimize stress in life just as we do surprises, we expect and enjoy it in fiction. We come to stories as we go on roller coasters, and laugh at comic surprises much as we scream when our stomachs drop away on a sudden, steep decline in the track. As Aristotle says, we can enjoy in art the very things that disturb or terrify us in life.

Usually we are surprised at the same instant as the comic figure. But sometimes we are *in* on a comic situation and look forward to seeing it unfold. Storytellers often hint that something untoward is about to happen, and the tension of anticipating it is pleasurable.

In *The Gold Rush*, Charlie repeatedly hurls himself against a door that is frozen shut. We know what he doesn't—that it opens on an abyss—and the impending disaster delights us, just as we look forward to the fatal encounter between Captain Ahab and Moby Dick. It makes no difference that Charlie survives and Captain Ahab doesn't. Both induce a state of pleasurable suspense.

Practical jokes put us in the privileged position of being in on the joke without removing the element of suspense, since we don't know how the victim will react.

> In an installment of *Candid Camera*, a car with its engine removed was rolled downhill into a gas station. The driver asked the attendant to check the oil, and we anticipated watching his reaction when he opened the hood. Of course, the driver claimed to be as bewildered as the attendant by the utter disruption of the world as they knew it.

I

Stories and jokes often resemble riddles.[13] Ancient in origin, they are as true to our experience as surprises and, like them, they render the uncertainty of our existence. The oracle of Apollo gave ambiguous or riddling answers, for the gods were deemed unpredictable in their relationship to us.

Like our ancestors, we try to resolve the riddle of reality with our assumptions, but we find ourselves on continually shifting ground. As long as we lived in small, homogeneous communities, we knew the people we met, their histories, and their families. They could keep few secrets from us, and lies about matters of consequence were pointless. But today we don't know most of the people we meet and often find that we don't really know those we *thought* we knew. Moreover, in our need to keep up with continually changing circumstances, we don't always know who we are ourselves.

But we cannot get through the day without the set of assumptions we call trust. We need to believe that as long as we stay in our familiar realm we are safe and can foresee the consequences or effects of our actions. Yet an old rule of storytelling—effects before causes—is deeply rooted in our experience. Much of the time, we don't understand an event until it is past, and we often don't know *why* we do what we do until we look back.

As G. W. F. Hegel says, the owl of Minerva flies at dusk—imparting wisdom or awareness when it is too late to make a difference.

Many stories derive from riddlelike situations, and solving riddles in myths, fairy tales, and comedies is often a matter of life and death. Oedipus must guess the riddle of the Sphinx or be eaten, the princess has to discover Rumpelstiltskin's name or lose her child, and Charlie Chaplin and Buster Keaton face one dangerous, riddlelike problem after another.

Likely many figures in fairy tales and myths, Bluebeard's wife feels compelled to open a forbidden door. We understand and side with her, for the hidden may constitute a threat. We enjoy the risk she takes, though in life we leave opening doors on the unknown to those who thrive on danger or brave it for the rewards it may bring.

Buster and Charlie continually find themselves in riddlelike situations that appear to offer no solution or escape. Often they are not even aware of the danger they are in. During a hurricane in *Steamboat Bill, Jr.*, Buster is standing with his back to a large building when the entire facade tears loose and swats down on him. We wonder how he can possibly survive, but a small window on the top floor is open and lands exactly where he stands.

Much of the time, the comedian's ingenuity or dexterity solves the puzzle. In *Sherlock Jr.*, Buster has been locked onto the roof of an apartment building by the villain, who drives off on the street below, with nothing to stop him from getting to the captive heroine and having his way with her. Buster appears to be helpless on the roof—until he suddenly leaps onto an upright crossing barrier we hadn't noticed and swings down into the rear seat of the villain's convertible. In a single graceful move, he solves the riddle-situation, closes the gap between himself and the man he is pursuing, and turns failure into success by having the villain chauffeur him, unknowingly, to their final confrontation.

Like Keaton's unexpected leap, the solution to a riddle is often a surprise that makes us laugh, and many jokes take the form of a riddle:

> An old man tells a friend that he has found a medication to prevent memory loss.
> "Wonderful! What is it?"
> "You know those flowers—the ones that prick your fingers?"
> "You mean, roses?"
> "Yeah! Hey, Rosie—what's the name of that new medicine?"

> "What should you do if a pit bull humps your leg?"
> "Fake an orgasm."

In a familiar anecdote, when Willie Sutton was asked why he robbed banks, he said, "Because that's where the money is." Like the unexpected solution to many riddles, his response makes us laugh. He deliberately misinterprets the gist of the question, yet his answer makes perfect sense.[14]

J

In his discussion of jokes, Freud assigns no special importance to surprise.[15] He does, however, point to the *gap* in them.

> After a dig in Israel, an archaeologist returned to Jerusalem in a state of great excitement and told his colleagues, "I found the skeleton of a man four thousand years old who died of a heart attack."
> "How could you tell?" they asked.
> "He was holding a piece of parchment that said, 'A hundred shekels on Goliath.'"[16]

When I asked a friend where he would most like to be, he said, "In my wife in Venice."

After a screening of *Ninotchka*, Ernst Lubitch came across an audience response card that said, "Funniest film never saw. I laughed so hard, I peed in my girlfriend's hand."[17]

The gap in a story, comic or not, constitutes a break in the expected continuity and allows us to make a surprising connection.

A man riding to a friend's house at night lost his way in a forest, and was relieved to see a light shining through the trees. It turned out to be a chapel so small he could look through the window without getting off his horse. Inside, he saw four cats carrying a tiny coffin to an open tomb, and on the coffin lay a golden crown.

When he arrived at his friend's house and reported his strange experience, the instant he mentioned the golden crown, the cat that had been dozing by the fireplace jumped up. As it leaped through the open window, they could hear it cry out, "Then I am king!"

Freud observes that "the joke says what it says . . . in too few words." So does the riddle. Both present us with a gap and ask us to bridge it.

An old man tells his son, "Every time I go to the bathroom at night, the light goes on as soon as I open the door, and when I go out the light goes off again!"

"Sure, Dad. You've been peeing into the refrigerator."

In *The Immigrant*, Charlie—unable to pay his bill in a restaurant and threatened with a brutal beating—spots a coin on the floor. Fearful that the huge waiter waiting for payment will find it, he comes down hard on it with his foot. Since the film is silent, we don't hear the impact of his shoe, but the musicians at the rear stop playing and look in his direction. We make the connection and laugh, whereas, in a sound film, there would have been no gap to bridge and no reason to laugh.

> A Vermont friend hired a man to help him clean out the debris under his barn. During their lunch break, the hired man noticed that my friend was about to eat a tangerine and said, skeptically, "Never seen one of those." My friend urged him to try it and he did.
>
> Back at work, they came on a dead sheep wedged under the barn and tried to pull it out, but it was so decomposed that half of it fell away, releasing a sickening stench. Both men stumbled out into the open, where the hired man vomited up his lunch.
>
> When he was done, he turned to my friend and said, "Must'a been that tangerine!"

He ingeniously created a gap where none existed, and bridged it with a false connection that mocked his presumed simplemindedness.

K

Like riddles and magic, the comic thrives on misleading us. It plays on our misperceptions and misunderstandings.

In the world of Buster Keaton, what we see often turns out to be an illusion, and we delight in watching the unexpected truth emerge from a deceptive or false surface.

Gaps and omissions are crucial components in all the arts. Henri Matisse says painting is not what you include, but what you leave out. As in the erotic, the hidden and incomplete draw us in. The omitted or obscured engages us, prompting us to connect and complete the picture.

Like Bluebeard's wife, we may well be drawn to the unseen by anxiety. It prompts us to ascertain what dangers or opportunities hide within it.

All stories, whether fiction, newspaper accounts, or jokes, take us behind the scenes. They reveal what we don't know, have failed to notice, or have deliberately ignored. The darkest of them bring us news we would rather not hear or see.

In many fictions, the central figure is searching for the missing piece in a puzzle—tries to solve a crime, expose a plot, or uncover events in the past that have brought about a troubled present. Inevitably, when the hidden is revealed, it comes as a surprise.

Secrets are at the core of many stories. It is the evildoer in fairy tales, melodrama, and high comedy who hides his intentions. Villains know what they want and keep it to themselves, although few are as hard to read as Iago, who not only hides his intentions from others but fails to understand them himself. He keeps shifting from motive to motive, and if he has found his secret at the end, he doesn't tell us—perhaps because it has shattered him.

Hamlet's situation *forces* him to hide his intentions. But, like Iago and Mother Courage, he also harbors a secret from himself. Bertolt Brecht makes sure *we* understand what Mother Courage fails to see—that the death of her children is directly linked to the war that supports her family. But the source of Hamlet's dilemma remains ambiguous. We may, with Freud, find it in the contradictory pressures on and within him, but Shakespeare, who seldom leaves us in doubt about anything critical, doesn't spell it out. The secrets that both Iago and Hamlet keep from themselves not only define and determine them but may have driven Shakespeare to tell their stories. Perhaps he felt impelled to discover them.

We all have secrets. Living with other people obliges us to be less than truthful, and those who don't curb or disguise their own needs and feelings and fail to adapt their "authentic" core to the needs and expectations of others find themselves alone.

In stories, however, we welcome the very figures who violate the rules that govern us. On occasion, we may even find ourselves partial to a villain because—in a world of pretenders and self-deceivers—he doesn't lie to himself or us.

When the Marx Brothers were about to shoot their first film, Groucho was told that unless he used a hair mustache instead of a painted one, the audience wouldn't believe him. "The audience doesn't believe us anyhow," he said, and went right on using grease-paint.

In the world of the Marx Brothers, everyone is fraudulent and everything, including the physical settings, are fake. Only their own, openly displayed fraudulence and their delight in trashing all communal conventions and structures—including the very movie we are watching—are genuine.

Margaret Dumont's sincerity, her persistent refusal to recognize situations and relationships as sham, and her operatic devotion to Groucho despite his open disdain for her—"I can see you right now, bending over a hot stove, but I can't see the stove"[18]—make her the biggest fraud of all, though she deceives no one but herself.

L

Neil Simon says comedy is "shared secrets." But the secrets we share in his skillfully crafted plays are secrets we confess gladly. The truth of entertainment lies close to the surface and seldom disconcerts us. We can be sure that a movie called *The Awful Truth* will tell us no such thing, just as television sitcoms deal with embarrassing but never truly disturbing situations.

Urbanization initiated the manufacture and proliferation of popular entertainments, and if there were many stories before the nineteenth century that served solely to distract the audience, few have survived. The vast increase in our leisure time exposes us to an emptiness that might overwhelm us if it were left unfilled, and our need for distraction has become urgent. Moreover, since we are confined to physical passivity in situations that once allowed us to be active and so gave us a semblance of autonomy, the action and movement of figures on the screen, the playing field, or in video games substitute for our own lack of meaningful activity.

The Enlightenment empowered us as a species and endowed us with the confidence—indeed the expectation—that reason could account for everything. But our faith in the ability to control our lives has eroded even as the belief systems that once allayed our fears and uncertainties have lost their hold. Today we are so urgently in need of reassurance that we seek certainty even in the safe arena of fiction, where we could once afford to face psychological risks.

This may account for the popularity of utterly predictable genre narratives that frame the unknown and unexpected in known, reassuring structures. They run on television twenty-four hours a day, and offer us an escape from the surprises, changes, and distressing news that reach us instantaneously from faraway places. There is little we can do with the information bombarding us; it merely reinforces our sense of helplessness, and it prompts many people to confine their interest and attention to local news.

The outcome of fictive stories has always been known, even in times and places that appear less haunted by anxiety than our own. The darkest tragedy or tale of horror cannot truly violate our expectations, for every story is over before it begins, and we know the ending from the start. The preclusive structure of narrative ordains that the figures *must* do what they do; their path is predetermined and leaves them no freedom. But while the foreclosed narrative is limiting and forbidding, like all structures it also shelters us, for we know what to expect.

Since ultimately both art and popular entertainment serve to reassure us, the boundaries between them seem to blur. But there is a difference between the dangers facing the figures in myths, fairy tales, and tragedies and the often laughable disasters that threaten the heroes and heroines of melodrama—between the physical and psychological risks taken by Chaplin and Keaton and the kindly ribbing to which Neil Simon subjects his characters and audiences. Our laughter in *The Gold Rush* and *Steamboat Bill, Jr.* is a response to fears and dangers that are wholly absent in *The Odd Couple*. We laugh with Charlie and Buster because they and we have *survived*, even if we, in the audience, were only threatened with losing our psychological balance and not our very existence.

Yet even the greatest comedians only *touch* on truly devastating secrets. The forbidding reality of our situation must remain hidden, or just barely admitted to our awareness, if it is to make us laugh instead of annihilating us.

George Bernard Shaw said that if you tell people the truth, you better make them laugh, or they'll kill you. They'll kill you in self-defense, for the truth may wipe them out.

At court, only the jester could tell the truth without risking his neck, and even he claimed to be just fooling.

CHAPTER TWO

Freud

A

Often the most disturbing surprises and secrets emerge from within us. The truth we are least willing to face is the truth about ourselves. We hide it not just from the eyes of others but from our own.

As we mature, most of us acquire and maintain a controlled, predictable surface, but the inner realm remains unpredictable. We are expected to keep it locked away, and are allowed open access to it only in communally sanctioned, carefully circumscribed situations.

Art can be seen as a substantiated rendering of the inner world. It uses correlatives of our physical existence to give tangible, accessible form to the inchoate and chaotic. Crisis situations compel both comic and tragic figures in fiction to live out the irrational impulses that are, in life, displayed only by sociopaths and badly behaved adolescents.

At first glance, the comic, like all art, appears to be a safe arena. The situations are unlikely and, in jokes, often impossible; the comic figure doesn't resemble us in appearance or behavior.

The five-year-old at the circus assumes the clown is utterly unlike her—absurd looking, stupid, and clumsy.[1] But when she laughs, she admits, without knowing it, that not long ago she was herself as clumsy and foolish. Watching him, she finds herself flung back to a time she thought she had left behind and, for an instant, she is frightened. Then she remembers she *isn't* like the clown anymore, and bursts out laughing.[2]

Though Freud claims that the child feels superior to the clown,[3] he recognizes that when we feel superior to a person or situation we are apt to smile rather than laugh. Since the child is laughing, she isn't just feeling superior.[4]

When we took our handicapped son to the circus, he started to cry the moment the clowns came out—no doubt because he recognized himself in them—while his younger sister, after the initial shock, felt sufficiently distant from their pratfalls and self-inflicted indignities to enjoy them.

Surely a reason children in nursery school find toilet references uproarious is that their bodily functions remain a threat to their sense of control. The scary/funny words take them briefly back to an earlier time; then they realize they are no longer in jeopardy and laugh with relief or, indeed, a sense of mastery.

I remember a painful incident in kindergarten when I had an accident in public and became the laughingstock of the other children. I burst into tears at the impending disaster, alerting them even before the evidence of my shame spread across the floor. As the same thing could have happened to them, they had to distance themselves and banished me with jeers and laughter.

In the Old Testament, a goat bearing the sins of Israel is sent into the wilderness, and the butt of a joke is still sometimes called the goat.

Dostoevsky says the Karamazovs have broad souls, and we, too, harbor feelings and thoughts that range from the heroic and altruistic to the abject and destructive. We gladly admit to our virtues, but we try not to show or see our shameful inclinations. When the comic illuminates them like a lightning flash, what we face isn't new to us. We are merely made aware of what we have half-known all along. If comic situations and figures were more credible, we wouldn't find them the least bit funny.

Often when we are laughing at Chaplin we admit that we are seeing a secret, shameful aspect of ourselves.[5]

In *The Kid*, Charlie comes upon an abandoned infant, but once he picks it up from the pavement, he doesn't know what to do with it. He tries to deposit it in a baby carriage with another child, but the outraged mother catches him in the act. After several schemes to get rid of it fail, he sits down on the curb clueless, with the infant in his lap. Then his eyes fall on a sewer, located opportunely at his feet. He lifts the grating and considers dropping the baby into the hole—but foregoes the temptation and, with a shrug, resigns himself to keeping it.

We laugh at Charlie contemplating infanticide not because we would *do* the same thing but because we recognize the impulse. Babies are sacred, but they are also demanding and disruptive. As civilized adults, we don't display our raw impulses and may not even be aware of them; thousands of years of civilization suppress them the very instant they emerge into consciousness. But they persist and can assert themselves tragically: time and again we read of enraged parents and stepparents who injure or kill the children in their care.

Some of the games that even loving parents play with their offspring—like dropping them suddenly or tossing them high into the air—threaten danger and death. Since the child is sure of a safe landing, he enjoys falling or flying, but if the game didn't arouse his fear, he wouldn't be laughing with relief once he is back in his parent's arms.[6]

Monique Melinaud's observation that "what makes one laugh is on the one hand absurd, and on the other familiar" could be read to mean that the *action* is absurd, but the *impulse* is familiar.[7]

At the end of *The Gold Rush*, Charlie has become a millionaire. Sailing home from the Klondike in style, he enters his first-class cabin and takes off an expensive fur coat—only to reveal a second coat under it. Wearing two coats is clearly absurd; few of us would let the fear of not having enough push us into acting it out graphically. But the impulse is familiar to anyone who has suffered physical or emotional deprivation.

In life, stories about people who have lost control over their impulses are a source of tragic headlines. But in the realm of fiction, comedians enact our darkest impulses. Only Greek myths display them more nakedly.

The comic suspends us between a sense of superiority and a lurking awareness of our inadequacies—a contradictory self-perception that would, in life, make us tense and uncomfortable.

Baudelaire says, "Laughter is the expression of a double, or contradictory, feeling and that is why a convulsion occurs."

In *The Kid*, after the foundling has grown into an undersized but enterprising boy, he and Charlie go off to earn a living. In a well-practiced routine, the Kid runs down the street, throws a rock through a window, and hides around the corner—just as Charlie happens along fortuitously with a glazier's frame on his back and offers to repair the damage. All goes well until a policeman notices the Kid's furtive behavior and watches suspiciously while Charlie replaces the broken glass. Aware of the danger, Charlie hurries off the moment he is paid, and when he turns the corner, the Kid comes running toward him eagerly. Charlie can't let the officer see the two of them together and kicks him away, but the Kid fails to understand and keeps trying to rejoin his dad—only to be rejected brutally every time.

We are unlikely to have ever faced the same dilemma, but we laugh because we are familiar with double-bind situations that can be resolved only by doing violence to our own feelings or the feelings of someone we care about.

Contradictions are at the heart of our experience—indeed, of our being. We might say they define the human. Most of the time they are not the least bit funny. In a tragic version of Charlie's dilemma, a woman who had just arrived at a concentration camp realized that mothers with children were sent directly to their death. Unlike the other women in the transport, she denied that the small girl at her side was her daughter and let her go into the gas chamber alone.

B

Physical comedy—like car chases, boxing matches, and demolition derbies, in which the performers are at risk while we sit safely in the stands—induce a quasi-physiological response in us. Even track-and-field events can leave us with a faint muscular sensation, as though we had ourselves run the hurdles or squeezed over the bar in the pole vault. Our bodies are subjected to an alternating pattern of stress and release.

When Chaplin sits on a hypodermic needle or Keaton barely escapes being squashed between two freight cars, our physiological empathy makes a visual experience seem tactile and kinetic, though we experience the physical threat only in psychological form, as tension.

In *Something about Mary*, a young man's scrotum gets caught in his zipper and he can't extricate himself without excruciating pain. His physical predicament is graphically brought home in a close-up, and generated a palpable quasi-physical response among males in the audience. When I saw the film with my wife, she started laughing hysterically. I was sure she was torn between empathy and glee—a contradiction she could resolve only in the physical convulsion noted by Baudelaire.

Though the comedy of Chaplin and Keaton often engages us physiologically, their work—unlike many slapstick performances—seems persuasive and true because it renders their inner, or psychological, experiences and invokes similar experiences in us. It reaches us much as myth, poetry, and painting do. What they do or have done to them is clearly "untrue," yet comes alive and seems real because their physical performance invokes a state in us that we cannot help believing, since it has happened—or is happening—to *us*. We don't doubt our *own* experience and it, in turn, endows the events on the screen with credibility.

When Dostoevsky describes himself as "a realist in the higher sense of the word," he surely meant that his primary concern was the inner world. We only become aware of the streets and houses in *Crime and Punishment* as Raskolnikov moves through them, just as the artist's brush in an animated cartoon will sometimes sketch a room just before the figure walks into it.

Chaplin, too, is a realist in the "higher sense of the word." We expect the snowbound shacks in *The Gold Rush* to be rendered realistically, but our core experience—though we may not be aware of it—is Charlie's inner world.

The physical situations we find him in and his encounters with others serve largely to make his inner realm palpable, much as the situations and encounters in *Hamlet* serve Hamlet's inner story. Claudius, Gertrude, Ophelia, and Horatio appear on stage when they are needed to crystallize Hamlet's subjective life, and make it visible to us.

Neither Chaplin nor Dostoevsky take the easy path of sentimental storytellers, who tend to violate physical, social, and economic realities to meet the emotional needs of the audience. Charlie is no freer than Raskolnikov of the economic, physical, and psychological facts that limit all of us. Poverty, hunger, and isolation force him to act out his needs, just as Hamlet is forced to reveal who he is by family and power relationships at Elsinore. The rendering of a "higher" or inner reality is not used to justify the violation of "lower," external facts.

Chaplin did his own stunts, and his physical feats are performed in full view. Apart from speeding up the action and the occasional use of a model, he uses no tricks or stunt doubles. When Charlie dreams he is an angel, we see the wires that allow him to be airborne. He doesn't claim he can fly, not even in a dream.

Surprisingly, there is no clash between the realistic settings in his films and the accelerated, highly stylized figures that move through them. Whatever happens *to* Charlie also happens *in* him, and his inner life is as real to us as the cabin in which he is trapped. Though they constitute different orders of reality, one doesn't undermine the other. Like Buster Keaton, Laurel and Hardy, and Mickey Mouse, his is a hyperreality that subsumes the physical surroundings. The settings in his films, even when they depend on an artifice—like the cabin on the abyss in *The Gold Rush*—seem real to us because *he* does: they serve largely as the stage for his inner world.

By virtue of Chaplin's mimetic gift and control over his body, Charlie is rendered with a physical immediacy that allows us to ignore how improbable he is. Our connection with him is so kinetic and visceral, we forget that his body is a metaphor—the physical rendering of a psychological state. What happens to him and how he reacts opens a window on the interior—Charlie's *and* our own.

Compared to the circus clown and the Marx Brothers, he is a credible figure. Though on the surface nothing about his situation, appearance, and behavior corresponds to our own, we connect with him the moment he appears. It is often assumed that "The Little Fellow," as Chaplin sometimes called him, stands for the common man. But surely people everywhere find him instantaneously familiar and funny a century after he first appeared because he plays the little fellow who lives on in all of us—the clumsy, lonely, well-meaning, barely conscious, highly energized and multigifted child.

What happens in comedy is often preposterous, but the skill, energy, and daring of the comedians are undeniably real. Their work seems effortless, though we know it took years of harsh discipline and sacrifice. Like most performers, they are fueled by a need so urgent, it drives them to risk what most of us fear and avoid: public failure and rejection. The same need impels them to perfect their craft and to use it as a way of connecting with us.

C

Often, in comedy, the subtext *is* the text. Whatever happens in Charlie is visible on the surface, just as Basil Fawlty's aggressive-defensive impulses are manifest in everything he says and does. He can't contain or restrain them; they keep leaking or exploding out of him.

In popular stories like melodrama only the villain has a subtext and hides his intentions. The other figures are seen as we prefer to see ourselves—decent folk without dark secrets. If they *had* a subtext, it would presumably be familiar and uninteresting.

But of course it isn't so. We are all potentially "villains" with a far-from-uninteresting subtext of hidden feelings, motives, and vices. What the comedian reveals about us is at first startling, then familiar. Charlie may seem simple but—in the shorts—turns out to be contradictory, sneaky, and even vengeful, just like our own secret selves. The comic lulls us into a false sense of security until our laughter reveals we have recognized ourselves.

In comic stories, we often identify with the ill-mannered and poorly adjusted outsiders. It is the *misfits* in *TAXI*—Louie, Latka, and Iggy—and not their more normal colleagues who keep the scenes alive. We invariably side with the Marx Brothers and not with those they use as punching bags, though that is surely how they would treat us if we were within reach. Bergson points out that in high comedy we connect with the knaves and deceivers, not their victims.[8]

In popular stories, we identify with the pure in heart, and since in art the surface is a metaphor of the interior, the central figures are physically beautiful. But in comedy we connect with those who act out their offensive impulses, and so the comic figure is apt to be ugly or even gross. His misshapen appearance matches the secret image we have of ourselves.[9]

In popular entertainment, not only the world we live in but also the inner realm is benign. Don Lockwood's "vice" in *Singin' in the Rain* is mere conceit, and even the villain, Lina, is just guilty of envy and self-deception.

Jerry Seinfeld says doing stand-up is like going to work in your underwear.[10] But the great comedians work closer to naked. They dig up what we bury and display the darker truth we don't want to show or see.

D

The inner realm serves to contain and manage the biological energies that preserve and perpetuate the species. It may have its origin in a communal imperative.

If our instincts are not to damage the fabric of communal life, they must be carefully channeled, and the most effective way to control them is through the individual. Whether we live in a guilt or shame culture, we are made to feel personally responsible for controlling the biological drives that find expression through us. Even societies that severely restrict individual freedom assign us a measure of free will.

Today many are persuaded that the inner realm has become ir-relevant—the last refuge of religious delusions that have too long imprisoned humankind. But since we are separate biological beings and conscious of it, we remain stuck with an ill-defined inner space that is as essential to human survival as our bodies—the domain of a generic past that can be neither expressed freely nor simply repressed.

We learn early on that unless we inhibit our instincts and im-pulses, the community will reject us. To become masters in our own house, we are asked to undermine or contradict an essential part of ourselves—to internalize the rules and laws of society, and let them govern the creature in us.

It may well be this splitting or self-contradiction that engenders or at least reinforces our consciousness and conscience. It obliges us at an early age to step away from ourselves and, by extension, from everything around us.

The individual could be said to begin with a *"Don't!"*—as human existence does in the myth of Eden. The *"Don't!"* limits and defines us; it prefigures the prohibitions and laws that constitute the price we pay for membership in the community. Though we may rail against them, we know they are the foundation of the social and personal relationships that confer a measure of security and predictability on our lives.

The inhibition of natural impulses may initiate our inner life and our identity.

Perhaps we say that children must be allowed their secrets, for what we hide from others separates us from them and may help to form the core around which our sense of self accrues. Like the *"Don't!"* in Genesis, perhaps it is our forbidden secrets that help us become separate, civilized beings.

Though the inner realm initially serves to contain our drives, it becomes the depository for all feelings and thoughts we keep from others and, often, ourselves.

Relationships and community depend on keeping what might be called the "authentic" out of sight. In life, only children and small animals are free to show themselves as they truly are, for they are not yet strong enough to do any damage. Indeed, their authentic, unpredictable behavior delights rather than threatens us, and leaves us free to laugh at their open display of the very impulses and feelings we must hide as adults.

The process of socialization could be said to turn us into performers and pretenders.

In childhood and adolescence, when we first try to conform to what is expected of us, we camouflage what we really want or feel and claim to be better than we are. But as we mature, pretense becomes "reality": The mask becomes the face, for if we had to live in perpetual conflict with ourselves, we could not be relied upon to meet the expectations of the community. Trying to control our drives consciously in situation after situation would require ceaseless vigilance, and the only way to manage it economically is for the process to become habitual or automatic. Our second or learned nature effectively becomes first nature in us—though, when our survival is at stake, all bets are off.

Relationships are built on compromise and a kind of deception. When we are with others, we are no longer completely or "truly" ourselves. Moreover, we often put on a show for our own benefit to assure us we are who we *claim* to be.

Like authenticity, truth telling in life is apt to be transgressive. It violates expected behavior, disregards the feelings of others, and intrudes on their space. We don't often tell even those close to us what we really think and feel, nor do we much want to know what they really think and feel about us.

Pretense, appearances, deception, and self-deception are quintessential to our existence—as central to the survival of the human community as biological imperatives. The inner realm with its secrets and hidden truths is no truer—or more authentic—than the civilized behavior that camouflages it. Appearance and "reality" are equally "real," and to be human is to be caught in a ceaseless disputation between them—even if our second nature confines us largely to the realm of appearances.

The dualism of an inner and outer reality is essential to us. It defines us, even though the inner realm may be nothing more than an assumption, and may exist—like the self—largely because we have been taught by the community to assume its existence from childhood on.

Though in most of us the biological drives are channeled into sanctioned relationships and activities—like marriage, work, and competitive games—the process of socialization is never complete.

In men, especially, there is often an overflow of aggression and sexuality. The Old Adam keeps rearing up and puts their first and second nature into conflict. But *no one* in communal life can altogether escape the stress generated by the repression and self-division imposed on us at an early age, and today tension is further exacerbated by our blurred identities and the loss of space that once separated us.

The "discontent" that Freud calls an inevitable consequence of civilization must be periodically released if it is not to become destructive or self-destructive. In our highly specialized societies, moreover, stress is an inescapable by-product of most work and forms of play that demand intense attention. *Tension* and *attention* share an etymological root.

In every community, there are people with a surcharge of energy most often fueled by powerful, unmet needs. Sanctioned relationships and activities can't always contain it, and those endowed with—or possessed by—it must find alternate outlets to keep it from blowing them apart. Some harness it to become leaders, mavericks, performers, or artists, while those who are blocked from releasing it productively may become ill or find release in addiction and crime. Joe Cocker said that if he had not found music, he would have become a murderer.

Artists find or make forms that give safe expression to their energies and, for a spell, make them feel whole and connected to everyone else. Their work, in turn, allows the rest of us to discharge tension and frees us briefly of conflict.

In the safe arena of fiction, our own secrets can be published without shame, and we enjoy living out the very impulses we have learned to bottle up. In stories, we expect the hidden to be exposed and the "true" or authentic to show itself. Here physical and emotional violence is welcome, excess is the rule, and compromises, without which no relationship or communal life could survive, are banished.

When a fictive figure—often a comedian or villain—speaks truthfully and cuts through the appearances and conventions that allow the community to function, we forgive him a great deal, though in life we would likely shun him.

Freud calls jokes that allow us to siphon off excess aggression and sexuality "tendentious" to distinguish them from those that hurt or offend no one. *The Joke and its Relation to the Unconscious* was published in 1905, just six years after *The Interpretation of Dreams*, and it is deeply invested in exploring parallels between jokes and dreams that illuminate the working of the unconscious.

At the time, the unconscious was an unfamiliar, highly controversial concept, and Freud's essay may be seen as part of his campaign to establish its existence scientifically. This leads him to draw a sharp distinction between jokes and the comic since, in his view, the comic *isn't* fueled by the aggressive and sexual drives that fuel tendentious jokes.

His study, like most of his therapeutic and theoretical work, is focused on the verbal, and he makes no mention of low comedy, which thrives on physical action. Perhaps he was not familiar with this ancient popular form, though it was very much alive in the theaters and musical halls of Vienna at the end of the nineteenth century.[11]

In 1915, Mack Sennett—who drew directly on the traditions of low comedy and hired performers like Chaplin who embodied it—said that "sex or crime [are] the great feeding ground of funny ideas."[12] His films give open expression to the very aggression and sexuality Freud identified as the covert source of tendentious jokes—and, like them, serve as a safety valve for our repressed biological drives.[13]

Since Freud's insistence on a fundamental difference between jokes and the comic is conditioned by his own agenda, we need not be bound by the distinction and can draw on his insight into jokes in our study of the comic.[14]

E

Like earlier observers, Freud recognizes that laughter serves as a release of tension, but he makes no mention of fear—a primary source of stress and a driving force in low comedy, where injury, death, and disaster threaten the figures without letup.

Fear is a constant of creature life and runs like a subterranean river just under the surface of our existence even when we are not consciously afraid of anything. Nietzsche saw it as the source of our every effort to know and understand. It drives us to discover—or generate—sequences of cause and effect that allow us to predict the future with some confidence, leave us feeling less helpless when we are surprised, and give us a measure or illusion of control.

Consciousness itself could be called a form of fear. Our awareness, or wariness, alerts us to dangers ahead, and prompts us to devise schemes for averting them.

Art at once gives expression to fear and exorcises it.

What Picasso says of painting—that it is "a way of seizing power by giving form to our terrors, as well as our desire"—is true of most stories, and certainly true of physical comedy.

All aesthetics are conditioned by the experience of their time, and middle-class life in Freud's Vienna was likely less fear-driven and subject to constant surprises than our own. Although the poor have always lived on the edge and had to fight for survival, today even the privileged are often haunted by anxiety, if not outright fear.

Since the structures that once sheltered us and made our lives predictable have become frail and porous, we—unlike Freud—are primed to recognize fear as a wellspring of the comic. The extension of our awareness to the furthest reaches of the earth, and the speed at which news from everywhere reaches us, have made surprise, shock, and change constants of daily life. The uncertain future, once remote, is now immediately upon us.

But even if in earlier times our social and religious institutions en-abled us to move forward with greater confidence, deep down we have always known, or sensed, that what lies ahead is neither certain nor subject to our control.

That, indeed, is the burden of traditional stories. *We* know what will happen to Oedipus, Hamlet, Captain Ahab, and Little Red Rid-ing Hood, but *they* don't. Their stories are over before they begin, and nothing they do can avert what they fear or bring about what they want. Though we watch from the vantage point of gods, surely we identify with them because we sense that our own situation may be no different. To initiate any undertaking, we must believe we know what will happen; yet most of us are aware, even if we repress the possibility, that the outcome may be determined by unknown causes and lead to unintended consequences. Our fundamental uncertainty is acknowl-edged by the once common interjection "God willing!"

Though the Enlightenment endowed us with an unprecedented sense of confidence and provided the foundation for two centuries of progress, the exponential increase in our knowledge can do little to allay our insecurity. We may understand the workings of nature but no longer really know most of the people we "know." Our neighbors are apt to be friendly, helpful, and unthreatening, but we glimpse them mostly in passing, and the people we work with all day disappear into the unknown at closing time.

To connect and interact with others, we must be predictable yet malleable enough to adapt to ever-changing circumstances. We adjust and readjust, only to discover, time and again, that what we think, feel, and do is based on incomplete information or invalid assumptions.

Reality has become so complex and uncertain that our comfort zone has shrunk to a small patch, and most of us withdraw into gated communities of one kind or another. Even when there is no fence or wall around us we protect our small, presumably safe realm by shutting out most of the information available to us. No one is an island, but most of us live on one—in the family, the neighborhood, or the community.

While we have always survived by psychologically excluding whatever threatens to undermine us, our awareness was, until recently, bounded by the limitations of our physical reach, and not as glaringly by our fears.

In a context of continuous change, with the familiar transforming rapidly into the strange, it isn't easy to maintain our psychological balance. Yet any show of imbalance, fear, or distress is apt to alarm those around us, since it may make us unpredictable.

Moreover, we sense that the boundaries of our identity, once clearly marked by our social station, have become uncertain. Whatever affects you may contaminate me. Robert Kennedy said we live in a time of psychological infections—surely one reason many of us shrink from contact and relationships.

Since fear makes us vulnerable and potentially dangerous, we learn early on to hide it. If I stumble on the street, the first thing I do, reflexively, is to smile at those who witnessed it. I need to show that I haven't been wounded or made vulnerable and to reestablish myself in the sidewalk community from which I feel briefly exiled by my imbalance.

But hiding our fears, like the repression of our impulses and drives, builds up tension that laughter allows us to vent. It may indeed be the presence of fear at the core of the comic that accounts for the critical role of surprise. For surprises both constitute the unpredictable *and*—in an as-if context—elicit a harmless loss of control that would be deeply disconcerting in life.

Like fear, laughter is infectious and can leave us helplessly enthralled. The psychological and physiological *link* between them may well be the trigger that allows laughter to release the physical grip in which tension, anxiety, and fear hold us.

In life, a close call can make us laugh, sometimes hysterically.[15]

The young child, who has learned he exists by being seen, fears that he ceases to be when no one sees him—a situation peek-a-boo turns into a game. The threat of nonexistence is invoked playfully, then the hidden adult reappears, and the child laughs with relief/delight: he has survived.

If laughter is to discharge our fears, we must, like the child, be sure of a happy ending. For unless we know that the figures will survive, we won't lend ourselves to their situation and enjoy the dangers besetting them.

Though Freud makes no mention of survival as an essential component of the comic, several of his hostile jokes depend on it.

After the marriage broker introduced the young man to a prospective bride, the man said reproachfully, "Why did you bring me here? She's ugly and old, squints, and has a hunchback?!" The broker interrupted him: "You don't have to whisper. She's deaf as well."[16]

Traveling in his domain, a royal personage noticed a young man who bore a striking resemblance to him. He called the man over and said, "Was your mother once in service at the palace?"

   "No," the man replied. "But my father was."[17]

We laugh or smile not just because the jokes allow us to vent hostility—most humor is reductive and so *inherently* hostile—but because the person under pressure survives the attack.

While the threat in a joke is psychological and not, as in low comedy, physical, we laugh for the same reason. The endangered figure—like the hero or heroine of fairy tales and popular movies—survives adversity and, in an unexpected move, bests the aggressor. The marriage broker parries the attack not, as *we* might, by trying to justify himself, but by redirecting the attack toward the woman. He piles on another negative, silences his critic, and surprises us into laughter, just as the man whose family was impugned by the royal personage was able to turn the attack directed at him back against the attacker—a familiar maneuver in the martial arts.[18]

A Civil War general was touring the new headquarters of Mary Baker Eddy's First Church of Christ Scientist with a genteel Boston lady as his guide. When he asked her whether it was permitted to smoke, she said, "It is permitted, but it has never been done."

Occasionally, the joke is on the survivor.

During World War II, an American fighter pilot found himself alone in the sky, facing thirty Japanese planes. Certain that his life was over, he flew right into the middle of them, firing every which way. In the chaos, he took down fifteen enemy planes and made a miraculous escape.

Exhilarated, though barely in command of his plane, he landed on the carrier deck, pulled back the hatch, and yelled down to the flight crew, "Guys, you won't believe it, but I just killed fifteen Japs!"

There was a silence. Then a voice said, "Ah so. But you make one mistake."

F

Low or popular comedy has always involved physical skills and risk. A troupe of comedians in Sparta seven centuries before Christ included jugglers, tumblers, and ropedancers, and from descriptions of circuses and nineteenth-century music halls we know that clowns throughout history were acrobats, equestrians, high-wire and trapeze artists, contortionists, jugglers, and tumblers.[19]

The French "grotesque" Jean-Baptiste Auriol could "run along the tops of a row of bottles without knocking them over . . . then balance atop the last bottle while playing the trumpet." He could somersault out of and back into his slippers and, with the help of a springboard, leap over eight mounted horses or twenty-four soldiers with fixed bayonets.[20]

An English clown, James Boswell, held up an unsupported ladder and climbed it, discarding each rung as he passed over it. Once he reached the top, he dropped one stile of the ladder and performed a headstand on the other. During a performance of this act he had a stroke that killed him when he was thirty-nine.[21]

Comedy that requires extraordinary physical skill and daring continued into the twentieth century, not only in the circus, with clown-acrobats pretending to be dangerously incompetent on the high-wire—or in traveling air shows, where they performed acrobatic horseplay on the wings of a biplane—but in the work of silent movie comedians like Buster Keaton, who insisted on doing his own stunts and suffered serious injury on several occasions.

The risks they took and survived surely embodied the dangers besetting the audience that was, like them, mostly poor and up against it.

Their work carried on a tradition that did not originate in any one place or time but sprang up spontaneously among people everywhere.

G

We noted that in the comic the truth often emerges from an exaggerated or absurd fiction that allows us to laugh. But even when the situations are utterly improbable, the true in humor can be so threatening to our security and self-esteem that we can't afford to become fully aware of *why* we are laughing.

Freud says about tendentious jokes that "we do not in the strict sense know what we're laughing at."[22] If the hostility and sexuality were out in the open, they would distress us. They are, however, far more easily camouflaged in verbal humor than in physical comedy. Words have multiple and sometimes ambiguous meanings that allow us to disguise or evade an unpleasant truth. They transform the direct into the indirect, just as they substitute for action and violence in life, and so make relationships and community possible. Like numbers, they dephysicalize or abstract our experience—allowing us to think of two hundred elephants without parading them past our mind's eye one after the other.

The tendentious jokes cited by Freud depend almost entirely on wordplay. What he calls their "technique"—brevity, condensation, discontinuity, displacement, and misdirection—distracts us from the socially unacceptable impulses that fuel them, and allows us to indulge and enjoy the forbidden under cover of laughing at the unexpected use of language.[23]

> "My mom always said, 'Men are like linoleum floors. Lay them right, and you can walk all over them for 30 years.'"[24]

But physical comedy doesn't—indeed, cannot—camouflage the aggression, fear, and sexuality that drive it. Charlie's motives and intentions are always apparent, Harpo Marx chases young women without inhibition, and the farces of Mack Sennett gleefully indulge violent and vengeful impulses. Though physical comedians, too, use misdirection, brevity, condensation, discontinuity, and displacement, they serve a different purpose. With the forbidden in plain sight, they draw our attention from the essential to the inessential in order to set us up for the gag or surprise.

Since jokes are purely verbal, they can touch on physical realities that more credible forms of the comic avoid. When the boy in Bible class says Solomon had three hundred wives and three hundred porcupines, we are unlikely to visualize the physical implications.

> During a live broadcast of *You Bet Your Life*, a woman told Groucho Marx she had thirteen children. When Groucho asked her why so many, she told him, "I guess I just love my husband."
>
> Without missing a beat, Groucho said, "I love my cigar, too, but I take it out once in a while."[25]

The surprise, or shock, and our convulsive laughter keep the intimate physical moment when the man "takes it out" from our awareness, and obscures that most of the time he *doesn't* take it out. Rather, it slips out in a limp state that renders him temporarily impotent.

The truth isn't always admitted even in less invasive jokes.

> St. Peter grew tired of sitting at heaven's gate, and asked Jesus to take a shift for him. That was fine with Jesus, but he wondered what he would have to do. Peter told him he just needed to talk to everyone who came and decide whether to let the person in.
>
> As soon as Jesus sat down in Peter's chair, someone knocked at the gate. A humble old man in work clothes stood outside, and Jesus asked who he was.
>
> "My name is Joseph, Sir."
>
> "Where are you from, Joseph?"
>
> "A little town, far away."
>
> "What did you do?"
>
> "I was a carpenter, Sir."
>
> Jesus began to suspect the truth.
>
> "Tell me, Joseph—did you have a son?"
>
> The old man bowed his head in shame.
>
> "What is it, Joseph?"
>
> "He came to a terrible end."
>
> "Did he have little holes in his hands and feet?"

The old man looked at him in wonderment—"How did you know?!"

Unable to contain himself, Jesus threw his arms around Joseph and cried out, "Father!"

In a breaking voice and with tears in his eyes the old man said—"Pinocchio!"

Our laughter at the solution of the riddlelike joke allows us to ignore that the all-knowing Son of God has been fooled and believes from the start that his father is a mortal being.

We noted that a surprise first makes us tense, then allows the tension to escape as laughter through the very breach it has struck in our composure. Since we are in the ostensibly unreal domain of art, we can ignore, or skip across, the fault line that the joke or comic situation has exposed in our belief system.

Immanuel Kant calls the comic "an expectation that comes to nothing,"[26] and René Girard says the threat in the comic "must be both overwhelming and nil."[27] Unless something of significance is at stake, it won't make us tense, and unless we are sure it will come to nothing, we won't be free to laugh.

Our laughter shakes us up physically to the point of helplessness and leaves us in no condition to protect ourselves against an uncomfortable truth—while the speed at which the comic happens allows us no time to inquire into its source.

Moreover, only professional comedians *want* to know what makes us laugh. Most of us are glad to enjoy ourselves, just as we enjoy a good meal without asking about the ingredients or their origin.

Though all jokes are verbal, some build on comic situations—like stories—and don't depend simply on wordplay or wit.[28]

Two men, who were shipwrecked on an island, agreed that one would cook until the other started complaining. They drew lots, and the loser did his best to prepare decent meals using their severely limited resources. After a while, he grew tired of the chore and let the quality of his cooking deteriorate, but his companion kept eating what he was served without complaint. Finally, he became so frustrated that he wrapped some excrement in a palm leaf, broiled it, and served it for dinner. His companion bit into it and spat it out. "Tastes like shit!" he said—then quickly added, "But it's awfully good!"

A young woman was walking in the park when she heard someone calling her name. She stopped, but the only creature she could see was a large frog that looked at her with soulful eyes and said, "Please pick me up and take me home!" The young woman hesitated but picked up the frog and carried it home. When she put it on her kitchen table, the frog said, "If you kiss me, I'll turn into a handsome prince and marry you." But the young woman said nothing and went to bed.

When she came into the kitchen the next morning, the frog looked at her mournfully. "Why didn't you kiss me?!"

"I thought about it," the young woman said, "and I'd rather have a talking frog."

Magicians, like comedians, draw attention from the essential to the inessential in order to distract and astonish us, and we laugh not just in delight at their skill, but because, like comedians, they arouse a faint sense of discomfort in us. We have been tricked or deceived, as we often are in life by our own misperceptions or the misdirections of others. Here, too, an as-if situation allows us to enjoy what might, in life, pose a threat to our sense of security.

When a magician saws a young woman in half and identical twins emerge from the two halves of the coffinlike box, we laugh not just at the unexpected variation of a familiar routine but with a trace of relief that the victim has survived and, indeed, multiplied. Though we are watching an illusion with a guaranteed happy end, the performance comes close enough to the grisly so that the fear and suffering the woman presumably endures is rarely made explicit. The young woman shows no hesitation when climbing into the box and doesn't scream when the saw appears to slice through her body. If she claimed to be frightened or in pain, our pleasure in her survival might well be undermined.

H

We try to mute our differences with others, but conflicts are inevitable, and though culture channels our basic drives and keeps them from erupting, just being on guard against anger and impatience is stressful.

We noted that as change and surprise become constants of daily life, tension is exacerbated. We can't fully trust most of the people we meet, and our very identity and integrity are threatened by the fragmentation of contemporary experience.

Moreover, tension has always been critical to our very existence. Just as the single cell maintains its shape and integrity through surface tension, we preserve ourselves as individuals and accountable members of the community by a continuous balancing act. The tension that maintains the single cell has a parallel in the complex psychological equilibration required of the individual by the community. We are forever caught in the contradictory pull between self and others—by our need to be at once separate *and* connected. One might say we are given our definition and identity as individual beings by the very contradictions that threaten to pull us asunder.

If the stress that sustains or contains us were not periodically vented, we would likely explode, and so we learn to discharge it in work and competitive games; by watching violent spectacles; by engaging in active pastimes like gardening, hiking, or painting; and by telling or listening to stories and jokes.

Laughter is clearly a physical release. Ludovic Dugas calls it a *détente*, and Girard says that both laughter and tears expel something we cannot long or comfortably contain.[29]

While recent research suggests that primates use sounds resembling laughter to communicate, only human beings laugh explosively and convulsively.[30] The creature isn't self-contradicted, and since it is *always* "authentic"—it uses stealth only to protect itself against predators and to pursue prey—it is free of the tensions we release in outbursts of hilarity.

For our stress to be discharged, there must be a prior charge—a "psychical damming up."[31] The tension in stories, jokes, races, and games usually builds to a climax before it is released—a discharge that is effected no matter whether the figures win or lose, survive or die.

In fiction, we identify with those under the greatest threat, for though—unlike many fictive figures—we rarely experience imminent danger, our balance and integrity are often at risk.[32] Like the tightrope walker, we must continually adjust and adapt to maintain our equilibrium. His performance is a vivid analog of our psychological experience; we know what it feels like to teeter—to be in danger of losing our balance.[33]

A performance or story without tension will not hold our interest or persuade us of its reality, for even on an uneventful day we live with a low level of stress that is so continuous and familiar that we are barely aware of it. It could be called our default position.

We come to stories, sports events, and the gambling casino primarily *for* the tension that uncertainty and surprises generate. We are physically safe but expect to be psychologically engaged and stressed—one reason spectators bet on horse races and football games. By *hyping* the event, they give themselves a stake in it, and so become tense participants instead of remaining cool observers.

While anyone addicted to gambling or an extreme sport seeks out actual danger, most of us don't voluntarily subject ourselves to stress unless no harm can come to us. But in the safe arena of art, even intense stress is pleasurable, for it relieves us of the more intractable distress of being human.

In stories, jokes, and games the tensions induced by life are expelled along with those that have been induced by artifice.

Though Freud doesn't deal with the stress that tendentious jokes arouse in us, he suggests they give us pleasure by sparing us the distress they *would* inflict if we became aware of their forbidden content.[34] *Tendentious* and *tension* both derive from the Latin *tendo*, "to stretch."

A tendentious joke is often a barely disguised ad hominem attack. When we ourselves are the targets and there are no witnesses, we may feel comfortable enough to laugh. But when it is directed at us in the presence of others, we become the laughingstock and are likely to feel exposed, shamed, and exiled.[35]

The effect of a sexual joke may depend on the absence of the sex at which it is directed. When I screened a Marx Brothers movie for a class of both men and women, the misogynist comments of Groucho made everyone uncomfortable—the women because the aggressive feelings of the men were evident in their choked-back laughter, and the men because they felt guilty about it. At a screening for men only, the laughter was uninhibited.

In a socially secure and sophisticated group, a tendentious joke may actually be enjoyed by the person at whom it is directed.

> A titled lady of Marcel Proust's acquaintance was in the habit of inviting friends to her box at the Paris Opera, but she invariably chatted her way through the entire performance. When she asked a friend to join her for an evening, he said he would be delighted since he had never heard her in *Aida*. She was so pleased with his witticism and felt so entitled to behave without regard for others that she repeated the joke to all her friends.

I

We try to avoid crises in life but expect them in narrative and entertainment.

The crisis in a story or joke is the point at which the pressure on the figures, and so on us, is most intense. The cabin in *The Gold Rush* is on the verge of tipping into the abyss; the villain in melodrama is about to ravish the girl; and Little Red Riding Hood has been swallowed by the wolf. But at the last moment, something happens to change the situation radically—for better or worse. The messenger sent to save Cordelia arrives too late, and Charlie becomes a millionaire at the very instant and place he has barely escaped death.

The fictive figures are in no position to foresee the outcome, but since we have an implicit contract with the storyteller, it comes as no surprise to us. Hearing or seeing the story a second time would hold little interest if the visual or verbal rendering and our empathy with the figures did not make it happen to us psychologically—or quasi-physically—every time.

We feel grateful when a crisis is averted in life, but if it happens in fiction we feel cheated.

> The Second City performed a skit in which two actors, one on each side of the stage, mimed steering the wheels of great ships. Then one called out to the other—
> "What ship be ye?"
> "The *Pequod*."
> "Have you seen anything of a white whale?"
> "Yeah. Two days out. We killed it."
> "Oh shit!"[36]

Most stories—including documentaries that would seem exempt from the "rules" of fiction—intensify and accelerate as they move forward. Short fictions can dispense with acceleration and crisis, but if we sense that a longer piece is going nowhere, we lose interest. Our attention flags as well when the uncertainty that charges the narrative and keeps us alert turns into certainty—when the situation or riddle is resolved and the figures are either married or buried.[37]

During the buildup to a comic crisis, some of our tension may spill as laughter, but it rebuilds immediately. When Charlie, clinging to the sloping icy floor of the cabin by his fingernails, is seized by a coughing spell, the slightest vibration drops him closer to the void, and we laugh in empathetic terror every time he coughs or hiccups. Not until Big Jim pulls him to safety—at the very instant the cabin slides into the abyss—are we free to laugh without drawing in our breath at yet another turn of the screw.[38]

∾

Wondering "What is black and white and re[a]d all over?" won't make us nearly as tense as worrying about Charlie on the edge of the abyss. But riddles, too, could be said to generate and resolve tension. The solution is often unexpected and witty, though it will likely make us smile rather than laugh since a verbal game is not a physical threat.

In comedies, tragedies, thrillers, and horror movies the sudden turn of events at the height of the crisis releases the pressure in us as laughter, tears, or screams. We are overwhelmed by a single involuntary response—become undivided, uncontradicted, and whole. Body, heart, and mind merge into one, and for a brief moment we are free of the inner conflicts and contradictions that are our daily lot.

In a crisis—whether in fiction or life—the secret and hidden come to the surface, the repressed is expressed, and the subtext becomes text.

In the skillfully crafted movie *Back to the Future*, a time machine allows a teenage boy to travel back to the 1950s and meet his own mother as a nubile young woman. While he knows the nature of their relationship, she has no idea that he is her future son, and—for reasons that bewilder her but are perfectly clear to us—she finds herself powerfully attracted to him. It is a situation charged with comic possibilities and tensions: a relationship threatens that is prohibited by a strong taboo in every society, for it countermands the unconscious ties fostered by the protracted stay in our birth families that makes us into human beings. Our fear of it is so deep as to seem inborn.

But after setting up and promising us a forbidden romance between mother and son, the movie backs off and allows their courtship to progress no further than a scene in a parked car, with mom stripped to her slip for some heavy necking. The instant she kisses him, she pulls away and says that it feels just like kissing her brother—a reaction with no basis in physical or psychological fact. It is clearly motivated by the filmmaker's unwillingness to undermine the commercial appeal of his movie by venturing onto dangerous ground. A promising and explosive comic situation has been deflated. Moreover, instead of obeying biological and psychological reality by letting the boy be as helplessly attracted to his mother as she is to him and allowing him to become the rival of the teenager who is destined to become his father, the filmmaker has him scheming to bring his parents back together after they split up. He is ostensibly prompted by the fear that unless he succeeds he won't be born himself—an unpersuasive motive, since his screen existence is never in doubt. Commerce rather than the logic, or psychologic, of the story determines the action.

The movie fails to take the characters right up to the edge and suspend them over it, as Chaplin does in *The Gold Rush*. Instead, it pulls away from the abyss and resolves the situation with a crisis so mild that—though the characters seem distressed—we don't feel the least bit tense. However, it is *our* experience that we came for. Theirs is only a means to it.

Like surprise, the crisis structure of narrative is widely deemed to be an aesthetic convention that satisfies the needs of the audience but in no way reflects life itself. Yet crises—both psychological and physical—are a constant of our experience, and thinking of them as conventions distorts our reality and turns the truth of fiction into an escape.

Not insignificantly, the sexual act resembles and illuminates the structure of narrative. It, too, involves a buildup of tension and, often enough, an element of uncertainty, risk, and fear. Here, too, there are surprises, both those we spring and those sprung on us. Here, too, the tension is pleasurable, and we postpone releasing it as long as possible, much as the storyteller delays resolving his story. Here, too, we pause for moments of rest, like those the comedian allows us before the next onslaught. Here, too, we expect a satisfying resolution and assume our needs will be met. Here, too, we cease being in control and surrender to a paroxysm or crisis that leaves us as helpless as laughter. And here, too, we become undivided—at one not just with the impersonal forces we usually suppress but joined to another being, much as our laughter joins us to those who are laughing all around us.

We seem to have come far afield, but the parallel may take us closer to the source of laughter and the deep needs and longings it meets. It springs from the core of our being, and allows us, briefly, to return to it.

CHAPTER THREE

Different and Scary

A

Given that Freud views aggression as "an original, self-subsisting, instinctual disposition in man, [that] . . . constitutes the greatest impediment to civilization," it isn't surprising that the majority of his tendentious jokes, including many of the obscene, are hostile. Aggression is more broadly destructive of relationships and community than our unmet sexual needs, and must find a safe outlet.[1]

Most of us suppress our feelings of hostility and frustration, and let comedians, prizefighters, and dramatists act them out for us.

Henrik Ibsen once kept a scorpion in an empty bottle on his desk. After several days, he inserted a cork and watched the scorpion attack it ferociously to rid itself of the poison that had accumulated in its body. When he removed the cork, the scorpion began striking itself with its own tail.

The parallel Ibsen noted to his own way of discharging rage in his plays is true of comedians as well.

W. C. Fields once placed an ad in *Variety* that said, "A Merry Christmas to all but three," but he hated a great many more than three. Will Rogers said it was a good thing he wasn't in politics, or the country would be permanently at war.[2]

Mel Brooks's observation that "tragedy is if I cut my finger. Comedy is if you walk into an open sewer and die" makes us laugh not just because it touches on a truth but because the hostility is hard to miss. Comedians are at our mercy, and since their psychological survival may depend on our response, they don't always feel kindly toward us.

In low comedy, aggression is physical, often motiveless, and carried out for the sheer pleasure of it.

The lemonade vendor in *Duck Soup* does nothing to deserve the punishment Chico and Harpo inflict on him, and Laurel and Hardy are caught up in a perpetual orgy of destruction. Their violence is largely directed at property—the cars, houses, and furnishings we are taught to hold sacred from childhood on. They obey the rules of duels and games—with the combatants taking a shot, then waiting for their opponent to take his. But by ritualizing the aggression and lending it a veneer of fair play, they isolate each act of violence and give it greater emphasis.

B

In order to preserve our uncertain sense of self, we need to find ways of equalizing differences in status or power, and humor lets us reduce those in a "higher" place to our own level. It is frequently directed at those in authority—people we fear and resent—or at those who claim to be more or better than we.

Whereas tragedy, music, and the visual arts enhance our image of ourselves, jokes and comic stories are reductive of us and others.

Humor, like laughter, comes from "below," from common ground, often from the body, and much of it originates among the disadvantaged and oppressed, who are obliged to live and work in a physical, gritty, and severely circumscribed setting.

We saw that in Freud's tendentious jokes "inferior" instincts assert themselves by treating the "superior" civilizing forces reductively.

Though his aggressive and sexual jokes are intricate in form and must be filtered through the mind, their source is in baser stuff.

In life, aggressive and reductive behaviors are hard to tell apart. Since most humor is reductive, it is inherently aggressive.

Even jokes that put down no one in particular, or no one in our presence, can help us discharge aggression.

> Lord Rutherford reportedly said, "All science is either physics or stamp collecting."[3]

> After Bernarr Macfadden—a big name in male bodybuilding—was taken to the ballet, he was asked for his reaction. He said he enjoyed it, but couldn't figure out which side was winning.

> Red Smith wrote about an upcoming Harvard-Yale game, "I don't see how either team can win." The teams and their coaches may have been offended, but newspaper readers laughed.

> At a party, Chaplin did an imitation of John Barrymore's celebrated declamation of "To be or not to be." But just before beginning, he discreetly picked his nose, then tried to free his fingers of the sticky stuff throughout the recital.[4]

Reductive jokes strip away the pretension and falsehood in which we cloak much of what we are and do.[5]

> When Wernher von Braun published his autobiography, *I Aim at the Stars*, Mort Sahl suggested a subtitle: *But Sometimes I Hit London.*

On occasion, even brutal humor that is directed at someone in our presence is so well deserved that we laugh, despite the pain it inflicts.

> Jay McInerney describes a performance of *The Diary of Anne Frank* that was so bad, when the fascist police came looking for Anne at the end someone in the audience yelled, "She's in the attic!"[6]

Comedy is reductive of the sacred and has little use for the super-natural. The gods in Aristophanes are ridiculed; the ghost that terrifies Abbott and Costello turns out to be a hat stand; and when a comic figure sees a divine light, it is apt to be a burning bush.

> Mel Brooks, playing a waiter at the Last Supper, asks Jesus and his disciples, "Are you all together, or is it separate checks? Does everyone want soup?"[7]

> It is said that, today, the Ten Commandments have become ten recommendations.

> A man who ordered a pair of pants had to wait seven weeks before they were finished. They fit perfectly, but he couldn't stop himself from saying, "Seven weeks for a pair of pants! God took just seven days to make the whole world."
> "That's true," said the tailor. "But look at the world, and look at this pair of pants!"

England was long governed by a secure, self-assured aristocracy, and has a tradition of reductive verbal exchanges, both in public and private, that would likely lead to a fistfight in the United States.

> Winston Churchill called Clement Attlee, his partner in their wartime government, a sheep in sheep's clothing, and said, when Attlee was commended for his modesty, that he had a great deal to be modest about.

Though sarcasm is a staple of upper-class wit in England and France, it is rare in American humor, perhaps because it implies a superior vantage point.

In war, the comic is used to reduce the enemy to caricatures that make them appear less frightening and easier to kill. As soon as Hitler came to power, Nazi "humor" ridiculed and degraded Jews. In the camps, officers and guards devised activities they found vastly amusing though—or rather because—they ended in the death of their victims.

> It took a community of dehumanized sadists to organize matches that pitted a well-known Jewish boxer against prisoners weakened by starvation. Obliged to fight in order to save his own life, he knew as well as his fellow prisoners that the losers were immediately killed. The Germans around the ring laughed and cheered him on in victory after victory.

> In the 1970s, Mexican soldiers charged with murdering opponents of the government told those they threw blindfolded into the sea from helicopters that they would be sailors and those they dropped into canyons that they would be miners. No doubt they had to distance themselves from their victims to carry out their brutalizing task.

In a very different setting, W. C. Fields and a cohort of his friends took pleasure in traveling around Southern California to cheer on a hopelessly incompetent boxer as he lost fight after fight.

In 1938, German Jews were no longer allowed at the movies, but the woman who took care of us was so addicted to them, she kept sneaking us into theaters with her. One afternoon, to keep my five-year-old sister quiet, she promised she would get to see Mickey Mouse. My sister sat through a program of shorts without complaining, but when a newsreel came on with Joseph Goebbels in one of his screeching rants, she said in a loud, clearly disappointed voice, "Is *that* Mickey Mouse?!"

Terrified, our governess grabbed my sister and fled into the street, but the audience burst into laughter and applause. Even Germans couldn't express themselves without risk and were delighted—in the anonymous dark of a theater—to hear a child's voice reduce an all-powerful figure to a cartoon character. His oversized head, short body, clubfoot, and high-pitched voice made it easy to see how a five-year-old could mistake him for an animated mouse.

During the Watergate hearings, Attorney General John Mitchell was listening to testimony that clearly incriminated him. The television camera was at the back of the room, and when I watched his shoulders shake, I assumed he was weeping. Then a second camera revealed that he was, in fact, laughing. From *his* perspective, anyone who was shocked by what he and the White House had done was naive. In a situation that even politicians with unusually thick hides would find painful, his laughter clearly suggested he had distanced himself from the proceedings and felt superior to all who took them seriously.

Napoleon Bonaparte, who—like many political leaders—was often reductive in private but grandiloquent in public, told the troops he had assembled within sight of the pyramids, "Five thousand years look down upon you!"

General George Patton allegedly said to his soldiers, "You and Napoleon pissed through the same straw."

For Thomas Hobbes, laughter is the expression of a "sudden glory arising from some conception of eminence in ourselves by comparison with the infirmity of others, or with our own, formerly."[8]

Freud agrees that the primary source of tendentious humor is our former unsocialized selves, but rejects the possibility that feelings of "eminence" or superiority contribute to our pleasure. In his view, though "[a] child will laugh out of a feeling of superiority or schadenfreude, adult laughter is less primitive."[9]

But since his focus is primarily on the origin and not the effect of the joke, he ignores the person at whom it is directed. The object or butt of a joke may well feel inferior to the person who made it and to those who are laughing about it.

We listen to jokes and comic stories, as we do to all fiction, from a detached, inherently superior vantage point until the moment they surprise us. Even the pleasure we take in tragedy derives in part from *our* knowledge of the situation and its outcome, while the figures remain ignorant.

In life, too, though we may not readily admit it, seeing others fall or fail can contribute to our own sense of well-being. Even if we are not in direct competition with them, their lesser state may raise our self-esteem. After watching the day's disasters on the evening news, a faint trace of "them—not us" can contribute to our sense of satisfaction as we settle into our beds.

Dame Edna Everage says she was given the priceless gift of enjoying the misfortunes of others.

When we laugh at a naive person, our response is clearly tinged with superiority. But since naive behavior, even when it is rude or obscene, is unintended, the naive person is apt to elicit protective feelings that make him or her endearing.

> George Gershwin said the most amazing thing about his mother was how modest she was about him. He was so confident of his genius and personal magnetism that Oscar Levant asked him, "If you had to do it over, George, would you still fall in love with yourself?"

Surely one reason we enjoy scams in comedies and heist movies is that we are in on the scheme and feel superior to those who are being tricked or manipulated.

I once saw a ventriloquist ask a man and a woman he had invited onstage a series of innocent questions. By casting his voice, he then turned their answers into indecencies. When they tried to deny what they appeared to be saying, he changed their protests into ever more suggestive invitations to each other until they collapsed in hysterical laughter. Of course, the audience was delighted.

Practical jokes are effectively scams, and the pleasure we take in watching them unfold derives in large part from the sense of superiority that our foreknowledge confers. Devising and setting them up can be a power trip.

> Henry, a friend in the same college dorm, used to take long afternoon naps. One day, I acquired a lifelike rubber mask of a very old man and enlisted the help of Henry's roommate, who was studying in their living room. I put on the mask, went into Henry's room, stood at the foot of his bed, and kept repeating, "Henry!" in a quiet but persistent voice until he opened his eyes. As soon as he took in the old man, I left the room.
>
> The first afternoon, Henry merely mentioned that he had had a vivid dream, but the next day he came running out of his bedroom after me and asked whether a very old man had passed through. His roommate told him he had seen no one.
>
> On the third day, Henry was so alarmed by the immediacy of his "dream" that he rushed out into the hallway and looked down the stairs. If he had looked up instead, he would have caught sight of me.

We never told Henry we had manufactured his dream, and I distinctly remember the pleasure I derived from devising and executing it, though I knew it was a bit unsavory.

We attribute a sense of humor to someone who not only sees life in its comic aspect but can look reductively at herself.

Alice Roosevelt Longworth, who was often commended for her youthfulness in old age, said she had discovered the secret of eternal youth: arrested development.

In modern life, we must maintain a measure of importance in our own eyes, since much of what we do—even driving to the store for milk—can impact others. But most of us are spared an exaggerated sense of our own significance. We remain aware of our limitations and spot pretensions and the ridiculous in others and ourselves before they get out of hand.

Even those in whom the community fosters a sense of greater importance in order to spur them on to exceptional effort or risk may use humor to maintain their balance. They periodically reduce themselves to the level of everyone else—or others will do it for them.

On the day Harry Truman was sworn in as president, his friend, Speaker Sam Rayburn, walked him down a Capitol corridor and said, "Now, Harry, a lot of people are going to tell you you're a great man. But you and I know it ain't so."[10]

When General Ulysses Grant said he knew only two tunes—"Yankee Doodle" and one that wasn't—or told an interviewer after traveling to Europe that he enjoyed Venice but would have liked it even better if they had drained the canals, he was putting down both himself and any claim to culture that might separate him from his fellow Americans.

Chaim Weizmann said that during an Atlantic crossing, "Einstein explained his theory to me every day, and by the time we arrived I was fully convinced that he really understands it."[11]

On the day his first book was published, Franz Kafka sat on the terrace of a cafe when a man approached and said, "Aren't you Franz Kafka?" Surprised, Kafka asked how he implored them to spare the old lady. But Grandma raised her hand: "Shh, Kinder—a pogrom is a pogrom!"

In *Pulp Fiction*, Vincent Vega is worried about the dire consequences of letting the wife of his violence-prone gangster boss seduce him. In a scary-hilarious turn, she overdoses on drugs and almost dies on him instead.

Our sexuality, far from being a simple source of pleasure, has been inextricably bound up with fear, disease, and death.

It can, moreover, have us feeling both enthralled and powerless. We think we are having sex, but as Schopenhauer suggests, sex may be having *us*. Like fear and laughter, an instinct can overwhelm us and must be channeled if its raw energy is not to swamp identity and difference on which all relationships and community depend.

Like the uncanny—*das Unheimliche*—our biological drives are the past we think we have overcome. We believe we have them under control only to find that, like Carrie's arm, they keep thrusting up, undefeated and immortal.

Our instincts are embodied in both comic and fear-inspiring figures that recur and repeat. We can no more free ourselves of them than we can will our hearts to stop beating. They are assertions of primordial life, determined to propagate itself and rooted in the beginning of biological time—a highly evolved form of the energy that was released at the beginning of the universe.

Though our instincts depersonalize us and threaten the individual with extinction, they are also the source of rebirth and renewal.

In its instinctual form, love is indeed as strong as death.

The obstacles and complications that men and women face as they try to connect, and often *after* they do, have always been a central concern of narrative. But only brief periods and small communities of the leisured seem to have focused as much attention on them as we do.

knew. When the man told him, "I bought your book," Kafka said, "Oh, it was *you*."[12]

Of course, his wit raised him up even as he put himself down.

Self-deprecatory humor can effectively blunt aggression.

> When someone in the audience yelled at the stand-up comedian, "You stink!" he got in the last word and laugh by yelling back, "You should've seen me last week!"

A scapegoated minority will often include the offending majority in its self-deprecatory humor.

> During the civil rights campaign, a story told of a little black girl who stood in front of a mirror and said:
> "Mirror, Mirror on the wall,
> Who is the fairest of them all?"
> "Snow White—and don't you forget it!"

> Telling a Jewish joke is pointless. The Jews have all heard it, and the goyim don't get it.

Like many anti-Semitic jokes, a definition of anti-Semitism, "Hating Jews more than necessary," is Jewish in origin. It puts down anti-Semites even as it seems to put down know-it-all Jews.

> Debbie Moskowitz took her grandmother to one of the Roman spectaculars at the movie theater. Grandma watched quietly until the Christians were thrown to the lions. Then she started complaining, "Oh, the poor people—the poor people!"
> Debbie tried to reassure her, but Grandma remained distressed until Debbie whispered that all the victims were Christians. That seemed to calm the old lady, but soon she started complaining again.

"What is it now, Grandma?"

"The little one in the corner isn't getting any!"

The priest and the rabbi met after work. After a few drinks, the priest turned to the rabbi. "I've always wondered, my friend—have you ever had ham?"

The rabbi nodded. "I did. Once."

The priest nodded and smiled.

A drink or two later, the rabbi turned to the priest.

"I won't tell anyone, Father—but have you ever had a woman?"

"Yes," the priest said reluctantly. "Once."

Now the rabbi smiled: "Better than ham, wasn't it?"

C

When young children are asked to say something funny, they often mention chopped-off heads. Some burst out laughing when they see a legless man on the street.[13]

Adults, too, sometimes deal reductively with the scary by turning it into a laughing matter. The devil in the Middle Ages was ever-present and frightening, but in comic folk tales and on the puppet stage we get to laugh about him: A clever blacksmith can outwit him, and Punch takes a cudgel to him.

"You must be joking" is a common response to bad news.

Freud calls tendentious jokes wish fulfilling—a definition he extends to all art. But Pablo Picasso's comment that art speaks to our fears as well as our wishes is true for the comic as well.

In the aesthetic realm, wish and fear are often linked, for the enactment of our impulses, even by grossly exaggerated figures in preposterous situations, takes us back to childhood, and further still, to the infancy of the race.[14]

By reducing us to our earlier, uncivilized selves, by casting off restraints and prohibitions, and by erasing boundaries and differences, the comic undermines our hard-won existence as individuals. Though what happens in jokes and comic stories is unreal, it hovers on the edge of the terrifying.

When I showed footage of a brilliant circus clown in class, the great majority of students found him not funny but scary.

With respect to the frightening element in the comic, it is useful to connect Freud's study of the joke with his later essay, "Das Unheim-liche."[15]

The German word *Unheimlich* means "that which is not homelike, not like family." In Freud's essay it constitutes "that class of the frightening which leads back to what is known of old" but has been repressed.[16]

We encounter *das Unheimliche* when we think we have put something behind us, outgrown it, or overcome it rationally—only to rediscover it suddenly right in front of us. It happens frequently in tales of terror and horror movies. We know that the old woman in *Psycho* died years ago, but for one frightening moment she seems to come back to life, just as we are sure, at the end of *Carrie*, that Carrie is dead and buried only to have her arm come thrusting out of the grave.

Discussions of art often mention "the shock of the new." It undermines our confidence in the world as we know it. But the shock of the old can be even more disturbing. As we saw in the child's response to the clown and our own distress when the primitive suddenly reappears from within us, the old—or ancient—can undermine our confidence in ourselves. In both scary *and* comic stories the familiar becomes unfamiliar, surprising, and frightening.

The inner realm is an abode of ghosts. Indeed, civilized life could be said to depend on the ghosts that haunt us—both the commandments of family and community that were imprinted on us in childhood, and our own deepest experiences—like the relationship of our parents to us and each other. What happens to us is determined by specters—unreal only in the material sense—as often as it is by more immediate and tangible events. Though they have no physical reality, they can determine what we feel, think, and do.

When Charlie in *The Gold Rush* steps outside his cabin to greet Georgia, he is hit smack in the face by a snowball. He turns to wipe off his eye, then steps back outside to see who threw it—only to be hit in the face by a second one.

Expected or unexpected repetitions are an intrinsic component of both the comic and the terrifying. The ghosts and apparitions that haunt old stories and their contemporary counterparts—the Freddy Kruegers in horror movies—are repetitions, avatars of the past. Coming upon them has a clear parallel in our comic encounters with an urge we thought we had tamed or buried.

But what happens in scary tales isn't distanced, as it is in the comic. The fearful in horror movies happens *in close-up*, and the comic process is turned upside down: Instead of feeling threatened and then relieved of fear and tension, we are inveigled into thinking we are safe—though of course we know better—then are brought suddenly face to face with the thing we feared.[17]

Laughter and fear are often found in proximity. Many circus acts teeter on the edge of death, and performances in the commedia dell'arte tradition sometimes included executions and scenes of mutilations. Baudelaire describes an English music hall act in which Pierrot was guillotined and his head rolled down to the footlights, with the bloody disk of his neck showing clearly.

When a stage magician turns one thing into another or rejoins what he has sundered, we laugh with delight at the surprising connection or reconnection. But magic was once in the service of religion, and what we now perceive as sleight of hand and deception was deemed proof of the supernatural. It made the invisible visible and filled us with awe and fear.

Rooted in biology, fear is with us until the day we die. It haunts our lives even after aggression and sexuality have abated. In its ubiquitous contemporary form—anxiety—it resembles the witches of old.

It can take any shape and fastens on whatever arouses our sense of uncertainty, or manifests our lack of control. Even when it is allayed or suppressed, it lurks in the unconscious until a chink in our sense of security lets it alight on a new object.

The further our awareness expands, the less secure we are apt to feel. *To apprehend* means both "to understand" and "to be in fear of future evil." Though we think we want to know our situation and future, we are inclined—no doubt by self-preservation—to turn away from information that leaves us feeling powerless. I once asked a class how many of them would want to know the date of their death. One woman raised her hand, while the others looked a bit embarrassed.

We both *want* to know *and* don't. The uncertain and limitless terrifies us. Like many creatures, we prefer caves of one kind or another. We need to feel enclosed or held, and we build walls both to include *and* exclude. Boundaries delimit where we belong and feel connected—the realm within which we are safe, known, knowing, competent, and can be held responsible.

Some, however, are exiled from the connected realm. What Rudolf Nureyev says about dancers—"They pay us for our fear"—is true for many artists.[18] They are fated to live with an exacerbated awareness of uncertainty and a dubious sense of control that only their work can allay—and never for long.

Death, says Walter Benjamin, sanctions all stories.[19] It is an analog of everything beyond our command, and—as the ultimate source of our fears—haunts a great deal of humor.

But whereas, in life, fatal accidents, illness, natural disasters, and death strike suddenly and anywhere, humor invokes them in a separate and safe arena. In a familiar pattern, the joke at once invokes *and* evades them.

> A man who was sentenced to die in the electric chair asked his lawyer what he should do. The lawyer told him, "Don't sit down."

Woody Allen says to a woman, "What are you doing Saturday night?"

"Committing suicide."

"What about Friday night?"[20]

In a cartoon, three cats sit around a restaurant table looking pleased with themselves. One is going over the check, and says, "Who had the canary?"

In another cartoon, Dorothy and Toto are tied to a tree. The Cowardly Lion tells the Tin Man and the Scarecrow, "You can have her heart—you can have her brain—and I'll eat the little dog."

When General Franco lay dying, he heard a great commotion outside the palace and asked what was happening.

"Ten thousand people are waiting to see you, Caudillo!"

"What do they want?"

"They came to say goodbye."

"Where are they going?"

After his unexpected defeat by Harry Truman, Thomas Dewey was asked for his reaction. He said he felt like the man who woke up in his coffin and wondered, "If I'm alive, what are those lilies doing on my chest? And if I'm dead, why do I have to go to the bathroom?"

Facing an actual death, the comedian often makes light of it.

On his deathbed, Oscar Wilde told a visitor, "I'm dying beyond my means."

Richard Pryor, whose father died during intercourse, said, "He came and went at the same moment."[21]

On the drive back from Chico's funeral, Groucho shared some of his favorite death jokes with his family. One was about a dying man, who raised his head from the pillow and said, "What's that delicious smell?"

His wife eased him back gently. "Shhh, Sam—that's for after."[22]

Henny Youngman told his audience, "I'm so old, when I order a three-minute egg, they make me pay up front."[23]

When W. C. Fields was asked what he wanted put on his tombstone, he reportedly said, "All in all, I'd rather be in Philadelphia."[24]

For their televised reunion, Monty Python brought along an urn with what they said were the ashes of Graham Chapman. He had died, but they wanted him with them for the occasion. In the course of the program, they "accidentally" overturned the urn, walked all over the ashes, swept them under the carpet, and finally disposed of them with a vacuum cleaner.

Since jokes make no claim on reality, they can deal with material that would be too distressing on stage or screen. In the waning years of imperial Vienna, even the death of a child was not taboo.

Rudy and Franz shared a mistress, who became pregnant and gave birth to twins. There was no way of establishing their paternity, and so the two friends agreed each would support one of the children.

A short while later, Rudy called on the woman, who told him one of the twins had died. Joining Franz for dinner that evening, he looked deeply dejected.

"What's wrong?" Franz asked.

"I'm heartbroken," Rudy said.

"What happened?"

"My child has died."

We noted that laughter is a common response to the frightening. When dementia became a common affliction of the elderly, it produced a series of failed memory jokes.

Charlie and Buster are perpetually threatened with physical annihilation, but on the screen death is too immediate and looks too real to be funny.

When the villain in *The Gold Rush* murders two lawmen and falls into an abyss, Chaplin films their deaths head-on, documentary style. But when Charlie shoots a bear, he fires from a window at the off-screen bear, and we know he has killed it because he starts setting the table. Showing us the dead bear would have spoiled the fun, but bridging the gap between firing the gun and getting ready to eat it makes us laugh. We are relieved that the grim fact has been avoided, and enjoy the shorthand of the connection.

> In *The Navigator*, Buster Keaton climbs onto the deck of an ocean liner in a water-filled diving suit. When he can't get the helmet off and is threatened with drowning, he takes a knife, slices across the middle of the diving suit, and reaches into what looks like his own abdomen to empty out the water with cupped hands.

> In *Boudu Saved from Drowning*, we see a disheveled tramp loping along the Seine embankment. The film cuts to a second-floor study, where a maid is watching him through a telescope from a window. The master of the house enters the room, takes the telescope from her, and uses it to ogle women on the street. While the maid scolds him playfully for being unfaithful to her, he picks up the tramp through the telescope, and watches him commit suicide by suddenly leaping into the river.

The distanced, nondramatic, by-the-way rendering of death brings to mind the well-known Pieter Breughel painting, in which the small figure of Icarus falls out of the sky in one corner, while elsewhere in the landscape rural life continues undisturbed.

In our own disconnected lives even an actual death can become laughable.

> Some years ago our phone rang. When I picked up, a man's voice I didn't recognize asked me to sit down. I told him I was sitting, and the caller said he had been asked by the family of "Sandy" to inform her friends that she had died. I knew no one by that name, had never heard my wife mention her, and had no idea who he was talking about. As he went on to report her last illness and described the way her loving family had gathered around, I interjected a few sympathetic phrases—taking a chance that she had children and that they were doing all right. Meanwhile, I was ransacking my memory for a Sandy in our life, but came up with no one.
>
> When my wife came home, she remembered that years before, in a professional context, we had met someone named Sandy, who might have noted our name and number in her address book.
>
> At his execution, Julius Streicher, a notorious Nazi who had built his career on baiting and degrading Jews, was so divorced from his own feelings that he could indulge in gallows humor literally. He had been condemned to death at the Nuremberg trials, and as he ascended the scaffold, his last words to the hangman were "Purimfest, 1945"—a sardonic reference to the Book of Esther, in which a highly placed and savage enemy of the Jews is executed by hanging.

Though physical comedy and animated cartoons thrive on threats of annihilation, illness and disability are not often a source of laughter unless they are faked or—like a toothache or broken leg—inconvenient but not life-threatening. Among the disabled, however, disabilities are a frequent subject of humor. We noted that in the paraplegic ward Bob Hope's "Don't get up!" was greeted with laughter.

Those who face and traffic in death day after day often make light of it. So a fighter pilot will say of a downed enemy, "I spoiled his day," and a U.S. military spokesperson was quoted as saying, "The slaughter was retail, not wholesale."

Teenagers in the middle class are unprepared for violence, disfigurement, or death, and some cope by laughing.

> The fourteen-year-old daughter of a friend lit a book of matches, tossed it into the air, and asked me what it was. Of course, I had no idea.
> "The *Challenger* disaster."

Though a grim form of humor evolved among longtime prisoners in the concentration camps, only a single joke appears to have come down to us.

> An SS officer, who was about to shoot a Jew, said to him, "I'll spare you if you can tell me which of my eyes is made of glass." The Jew looked at the SS man's face, and said, "Your right eye."
> Surprised, the German asked, "How did you know?"
> The Jew said, "I thought I saw a trace of feeling in it."[25]

D

Freud says that both hostile and sexual jokes give us far greater pleasure than innocent ones because they make "the satisfaction of an instinctual drive possible."[26]

We can readily see that aggression finds expression in jokes and comedy, but the satisfaction of our sexual drive in obscene jokes seems doubtful.

In Freud's view, smutty humor gives us direct access to a naked woman—specifically to the sexual parts that civilization hides.[27] He suggests that though jokes disguise it in subtle, often elaborate wordplay—allowing men and women at higher levels of society to enjoy the forbidden as a game—they have their origin in a repressed primary urge: "The pleasure in gazing on [the] sexual revealed in its nakedness is the original motive" of the dirty joke.[28]

In intimate situations, the sight of our sexual organs can be arousing, but invoking them in the public setting of a joke or comic performance is unlikely to have an erotic effect.[29] It won't satisfy our instinctual needs even in metaphoric form. Indeed, it has the antierotic effect of making us laugh.

The words in an aggressive joke substitute for physical blows, but they *can* hurt and may well satisfy or relieve hostile feelings. But it's hard to see how jokes can meet or relieve our sexual needs. Their effect is so nonsensory, they hardly substitute for physical contact and release. We are more likely to find an outlet for our sexuality in pornography, movies, photography, painting, and literature.

By and large, the pleasure men get from telling dirty jokes doesn't seem primarily sexual. The "mood of cheerful humor" they engender would appear to derive as much from bonding, with shared laughter giving expression to a sense of community. We are back in childhood, sharing a secret, being naughty together, making the forbidden less shameful. Moreover, as Freud makes clear, sloughing off the restrictions of society is itself a source of pleasure.[30]

Many sexual jokes are, in fact, not actually about sex. Like most stories, they are told to connect the teller to the listener, with the sexual component as a way of holding interest.

> Two elderly men pass a voluptuous young woman on the street.
>
> "Remember how thrilled we once were to see a girl looking like that!?"
>
> "I do. But I don't remember why."

> After his marriage, a yeshiva boy asked the rabbi if he was now free to dance with his wife. The rabbi looked at him gravely and shook his head:

"No. It is unseemly."

"But we can have sex anytime we please, on the days permitted."

"Absolutely," the rabbi said.

"In the missionary position?"

The rabbi nodded.

"With my wife on top, or from behind?"

"Every position is allowed."

"Oral sex? Cunnilingus?"

"Even that."

"We can have sex standing up?"

The rabbi shook his head. "*That* should be avoided. It might lead to dancing."[31]

Often, sex comes up only at the end, in an unexpected turn—the surprise that makes us laugh.

A little girl was spending the night at her grandmother's house. When she hopped into bed, her grandmother said, "You didn't say your prayers!"

"I don't know any."

"None?"

"Just the one Mommy and Daddy say every night."

"Let's say that one."

The little girl kneeled at her bed, folded her hands, and said, "Oh God, I'm coming—Jesus wait for me!"

Since sex in most societies is encrusted with restrictions, just mentioning the biological components is apt to get a laugh.

When Mark Twain heard that Standard Oil of Indiana had been fined over $29 million for violating federal rebate laws, he was reminded of what the bride said after her wedding night: "I expected it, but didn't suppose it would be so big."[32]

A female comedian told her club audience, "I'm Catholic. When I was home for Christmas, my mother and I were unpacking and she found my diaphragm. I had to tell her it was a bathing cap for my cat."[33]

When another comedian said to her audience, "The diaphragm is a pain in the ass," someone at the back of the room yelled, "You are putting it in the wrong place!"[34]

A young woman learned about 69 from her lover but kept calling it 96.

In *Modern Times*, when Charlie can't keep up with the assembly line, he spins out of the factory with his hands twitching uncontrollably. A stout woman marches along the sidewalk toward him with two black buttons prominently displayed on her ample bosom. We note both their sexual connotation *and* see them the way Charlie does—as two knobs that need tightening.

He can't help acting on his conditioned response, advances toward her with his hands twitching, and puts her to flight.

The gag conforms perfectly to the technique of Freud's sexual jokes. It allows us to indulge our interest in sex and leaves us free to laugh without feeling guilty.

Given his central concern with sex, there are surprisingly few sexual jokes among Freud's examples of tendentious humor, and even those are often charged with hostility. He calls smut "the equivalent of an attempted seduction" but observes that "anyone who laughs at [smutty] talk . . . is laughing like a spectator at an act of sexual aggression."[35]

We might attribute this to the instinctively aggressive sexuality of men, but it seems more likely to have its origin in male resentment of women, who have, traditionally, served the all-important role of inhibiting the freedom of men for the sake of family and community.

As Richard Feynman says, "Women teach their sons how to treat the next generation of women well."[36] They transform inborn male aggression into protective and tender relationships by bonding men in marriage—an institution that, along with the benefits it provides, can turn into a minefield of tensions, resentments, and fears. Since giving them open expression would damage the fabric of family life, they are often expressed indirectly, in humor and jokes.

> An interviewer asked a man who made the important decisions in his family. The man said that his wife decided how many children they have, what house they live in, what car they drive, and where they spend their vacation—but that *he* decided whether the United States should go to war.

Some jokes that voice male fear and resentment of women are brutal.

> Mort Sahl said, "A woman's place is in the stove."[37]

> "How is Mrs. Schwartz?"
> "Fine. I just wish I'd strangled her five years ago. I'd be out of jail by now."[38]

Many are crude:

> "What's the best thing about getting a blow job from your wife?"
> "Six minutes of silence."[39]

The jokes about men told by women tend to be subtler.

> After the widows of men who died at the World Trade Center were each awarded $5 million, Joan Rivers wondered whether, given the choice, she wouldn't take the check.

It has been said that men are the jokers and women the laughers. Until recently, even jokes about the relationship between them—at least those told in public—appear to have originated among men.

"What's a man's definition of the perfect lover?"
"A nymphomaniac who owns a bar."
"And a woman's?"
"A man who makes love to you for five hours, then turns into a pizza."

The first has women catering to men's uncomplicated wishes, the second is inspired by their persistent fear of being swallowed by women psychologically and disappearing as individuals.

Myron Cohen told his nightclub audience that on a recent plane trip he sat next to a woman who wore a ring with a huge diamond. He couldn't resist telling her, "That's a beautiful stone!"
"Thank you. It's famous. It even has a name."
"You mean, like the Hope Diamond? What's it called?"
"The Clopman Diamond. But it comes with a curse."
"If you don't mind telling me—what's the curse?"
"Mr. Clopman."[40]

At screenings of *Annie Hall* I was surprised that both male and female students laughed freely when Alvy tells Annie, "My Grammy never gave gifts. . . . She was too busy being raped by Cossacks." I had assumed it would offend both women and Jews.

I have never been brave enough to tell them another Jewish grandmother joke:

During a pogrom, Cossacks stormed into the house and raped the mother and her teenage daughter. When they turned on the grandmother, the two women fell to their knees and

Both sex and food are critical to survival, but food meets a more basic need. In the films of Chaplin, whose childhood was blighted by severe physical deprivation, the lack of food drives much of the comedy.

A Russian joke from the time of severe shortages leaves no doubt about the priorities:

> When Alexei came home and found his wife naked in bed with a man, he went into a rage, yelling, "Are you crazy?! They're selling sugar at the grocery!"

Once food is abundant, it ceases to be a subject of humor and sex becomes a dominant motif.

No doubt our sexuality was a source of laughter long before the Greek theater, but our own time and society are inundated with sexual jokes and narratives.

Carl Jung said, critically, that for Freud sex became a god, and in our society it often seems to have taken on a sacramental function. In a time of frayed connections, it promises—like religious ritual—to connect us not just to each other but to our innermost selves and to the very forces that govern life. In the arms of another we hope briefly to find our place.

Claude Lévi-Strauss recounts the laughter of couples around the campfires of South American Indians at night. Though we, too, may laugh playfully in bed, sex is serious and intense for many of us.

We noted that seeing someone intensely engaged in an activity can be a source of laughter. But there have been few attempts to make the sex act funny on the screen. Two naked bodies are vulnerable and engage our own sense of vulnerability.[41]

We are, today, caught in a contradiction. For even as sex can hold out the promise of replacing the connections that religious institutions no longer provide, it has become so widely available in hookups and "screw dates" that require no relationship or commitment, it is often reduced to nothing more than a purely biological encounter. Perhaps even pornography—a multibillion-dollar industry catering largely to men—is a sadly misplaced and inadequate attempt to connect.

Given our high expectations and, conversely, the way some try to meet their physical needs without making a human connection, it isn't surprising that *to fuck* and *get fucked* and *screw* and *get screwed* have come to connote exploitation, cheating, and abuse.

Sexual jokes have long given expression to our disillusionment.

> In its heyday as a resort for honeymooners, Niagara Falls was known as the bride's second big disappointment.

> Rodney Dangerfield said, "I got no sex life. My dog watches me in the bedroom to learn how to beg. He also taught my wife how to roll over and play dead."[42]

Hoping sex will meet our existential or metaphysical needs is likely to lead to disappointment, and assigning it an all-important role in our lives charges it with stress and anxiety, both when it is available and when it's not.

In a familiar pattern, many sexual jokes serve to reduce its power and distance us by turning it into a laughing matter.

> An old man showed up at the sperm bank and told the staff that a woman wanted to have his baby. They were dubious but when he persisted, they gave him a test tube and sent him to the bathroom with a stack of *Playboy* magazines. He stayed for a long time, and they could hear him grunting with effort. Finally he emerged and handed the nurse the test tube.
>
> She held it up, and said, "It's empty!"
>
> "Yes," he said. "I tried with my left hand, with my right, and then with both—I couldn't get the cap off."

Many jokes give voice to the persistent male fear of sexual inadequacy.

> After intercourse, Mia Farrow tells Woody Allen, "That was fast—it probably helped I had the hiccups."[43]

Because our relationship to sex is fraught with complexity, contradictions, and fear, some jokes use a sexual situation to build up our anticipation and a faint sense of discomfort, only to have it take an innocent turn.

A man ran into a friend who was riding a brand-new woman's bicycle.

"Why didn't you get the male model?"

"You won't believe me, but I was sitting in the park when a beautiful woman stopped by on her bike. She sat down next to me and we started kissing. She got so excited, she opened up her fur coat, and under it she was completely naked. Then she told me I could have anything I wanted. So I took the bicycle."

His friend shook his head. "You should have taken the fur coat!"

A middle-aged man called a brothel and asked the madam whether she had a woman who was six feet tall and weighed under a hundred pounds. The madam said that in all her years she had never seen anyone like that. But she told him to leave his phone number.

A few months later, she called and said she had found a woman with his specifications. He made an appointment, and when he showed up, the madam was startled to see him with a little girl, whom he introduced as his daughter.

Accustomed to everything, the madam took them to the woman's room, but couldn't resist listening at the door. She heard the man ask the woman to take off her clothes and told his daughter to pay careful attention. There was a rustling of clothes, and then he said, "See—that's how you'll look if you don't eat your soup!"

Dr. Seuss said he always wanted to draw a nude, but could never get the knees right.

A middle-aged Jewish man suffered from a painful form of ulcers, and was told that his only hope of relief was mother's milk. His worried wife hired a woman who had just finished nursing her child, and since the man was small, the woman put him on her lap.

He started to nurse, and when she became aroused, she asked him, "Is there anything else I can do for you, Mr. Goldberg?"

Mr. Goldberg nodded. "You have for me, maybe, a cookie?"

We are back in the innocent days of childhood before sex enriched, constrained, and complicated our lives.

A joke can charm us with its innocence even when it refers to sex physically.

A newly appointed priest, calling on one of his parishioners, asked her how many children she had.

"Ten, Father. Five pairs of twins."

"You always have twins?"

"No, Father. Sometimes we have nothing."[44]

CHAPTER FOUR

Disconnected

A

We continually separate one thing from another—the permitted from the forbidden, you from me, and me from myself. Without this ceaseless process of discrimination no relationship or community could survive.

We are ourselves the main source of the disconnections, for consciousness must, in some measure, separate us from the object it is aware of—fragmenting our experience of the world and ourselves.

Early on, the family that shelters us begins gentling us into exile, initiating us into the balancing act of being neither wholly connected nor altogether separate that living with others requires.

Though our ties to family, lovers, friends, and community come close to recreating the sense of being whole and part of a whole, we cannot—for more than a moment—safely return to the state of unconscious fusion in which the creature and the infant live.

Just as a flaming sword keeps Adam and Eve from reentering Eden, we are blocked from returning to the paradise of early childhood—a state of wholeness of which we cannot even become aware until it is lost.[1]

As we mature, the process of socialization *dephysicalizes* our biological links to others and ourselves. In all but intimate relationships, the

more distant senses of sight and hearing replace those that depend on
contact or proximity. As Freud says, gazing replaces touching.[2]

Since relationships and community depend on inhibiting or delay-
ing action, we learn early on to give verbal expression to physical impulses, and since even words can provoke a physical response, we try
to leave unspoken those words that give voice to aggression.

Though we remain grounded in matter, *alternate connections*—like
family and love—come to substitute for the original state of oneness.
They bridge the essential gap that must open up between us and others, and compensate for the self-divisions on which relationships and
community depend.

Human existence could be described as a *web* of alternate connections. Apart from vital but elementary functions, little about us has
remained purely physical.[3]

Language in its many forms—words, numbers, images, and musical
sounds—helps us not only perceive and understand the world and
ourselves but discover and generate new connections.

To *exist* means "to stand out." If we did not experience our separation from others painfully, we would not be driven to make relationships or join into communities. The very forces that isolate us generate the need for new structures and configurations.

Maintaining, finding, or making connections is central to our well-
being and at the core of our activities. Connections may be as significant as a scientific discovery or as slight as finding that the traveler in
the next seat went to the same high school. They join together shards
of our fragmented reality and help us find our place in it.

What Aristotle says about art—that it gives us pleasure by allowing
us to recognize—is as true of the deep satisfaction and pleasure that
connections and reconnections give us in life.

B

The smile of the infant, like his cry, begins as an involuntary physical
symptom. But before long he discovers that his smile elicits a smile

from others and links them to him. In time, he becomes aware that their smiles are also a sign of recognition: they prove he exists.

Thus, from the start, the smile is rooted in our bipolar reality: it tells us both that we belong *and* that we are separate.

Often, when someone smiles at us, our own smile is as reflexive as the infant's.

Mimicry is intrinsic to our biology and—without being fully aware of it—we tend to respond to others in kind. Imitation helps us both to fit in and to defend ourselves. So we parry, reflexively and with a parallel move, the movement, action, and often the feelings of the person facing us. Surely this is why we get trapped in a comical mirror dance when we try to avoid someone on the sidewalk.

We smile for many reasons, but most seem rooted in connections.[4] We smile when we see someone we know, understand something, find a missing link, or solve a puzzle. We smile when we emerge from uncertainty and find ourselves back on safe, familiar ground. Smiling at others confirms a relationship and signals that we are like them—that they have nothing to fear from us. When women took to smiling at me on the street, I knew I had grown old and harmless.

A smile is an opening. If someone doesn't return our smile, we may feel rejected and switch off the smile that made us vulnerable.

Laughter, too, is more often a way of expressing likeness and approval than a response to something funny. When we hear people talk in the next room or on television, they tend to laugh frequently even when the conversation isn't amusing. We don't question their response but take it for granted; if we were in the room, we would likely be laughing as well. They laugh because they have established or want to establish a likeness, a temporary community. Their laughter is relaxed and free of tension. Unlike our response to the comic, it does not need to overcome obstacles or resistance, and resolves no contradictions.

By beginning with a joke, the public speaker gathers his audience into a community, makes them comfortable with him and each other, and more receptive to what he is saying.

When we laugh without apparent cause, others will ask us to share the joke. They feel excluded and want to be in on it.

We noted that laughter is infectious. Most of us suffer giggling fits in childhood and youth. The word or situation that elicits them is seldom commensurate with the effect it produces. An uncontrollable inner process not only keeps regenerating and reinfecting us but induces the same reaction in others. As long as one person is laughing, no one in the group is safe, and only exhaustion will put a stop to it.

Navajo belief has it that a child isn't fully human until the first time it laughs.

Until we are truly separate, we have neither the capacity nor the need to laugh. There was no laughter in Eden. As Baudelaire says:

> In the earthly paradise . . . in which it seemed to man that all
> created things were good, joy did not find its dwelling in laughter
> . . . Laughter and tears . . . are both equally the children of woe.[5]

Laughter and consciousness surely evolved together. For laughter is at once a shocked response to the disconnect, and briefly makes whole what consciousness has sundered.

C

Like laughter, art makes or remakes connections, heals divisions between and within us, and gives us a sense of being whole or part of a whole.

People choose the music or movie that makes them feel connected.

The pictures we hang on our walls tend to confirm us; they mirror our perceptions or wishes. Few people choose to live with a painting that disturbs them.

New music often sounds dissonant, and audiences resist it; we don't go to concerts to be disconcerted. When jazz musicians play the theme or "hook," we break into spontaneous applause. It serves as a familiar and reassuring base for the barely recognizable variations that follow.

Surely an unfamiliar melody has a stronger effect the second time we hear it because it harkens back to an earlier moment. The pleasure of *re*hearing it runs deep, for our identity is predicated on our continuity or connection in time—a continuity that is, today, often in grave doubt.

Like a joke, art serves as a medium of exchange. Playing our favorite music for someone is an offering or opening and makes us vulnerable, especially when we are young. If the other person doesn't respond, it can feel like an unreturned smile—a rejection.

"Do you like Brahms?"
"Not really."

Myths and stories are elaborate riddles that begin with a disconnect, separation, or problem, and take us to its resolution—usually a wedding or the grave, where all are rejoined to the whole.

We come to stories, as we do to the comic, seeking the very thing we avoid in life: a disconnect or problem. Like the gap in the joke, the disconnect engages and activates us, and since we are safe, the more deeply we are engaged *and* disconcerted, the greater our pleasure once the fragments are joined or rejoined.

We noted that though stories take us on a journey with surprises that may be distressing, they have a known and guaranteed end. Their structure isn't simply a formula that satisfies the wishes of the audience but reflects a basic reality. For life both ends—as it does for the central figure in tragedies—yet is continually regenerated, as it is in comedies, where the focus is rarely on an individual.

Stories engage us in a process of tension and release that builds gradually to a climax, whereas jokes and riddles are short, engage us briefly, and merely make us wonder how they will resolve.

Once we have heard a joke, hearing it again gives us little pleasure. We do, however, enjoy telling it to others, for making them laugh connects us to them.

When someone tells a familiar joke, we seem compelled to announce that we know it. Since we cannot join the community of those who haven't heard it and are about to laugh, we may be trying to connect with the person who is telling it. We don't want to be left out.

Freud points out that "writers have long been fond of defining wit as the knack of discovering similarities between dissimilars."[6]

The further apart the elements in a joke or story appear to be, the greater our pleasure in seeing them linked.

> It was said of an actor in the part of Claudius that he played
> the king as though someone else were about to play the ace.

Bergson notes that "in every wit there is something of a poet." A poem, like wit, often links words we don't think belong together until the rhyme proves that they do. But rhyming "June" and "moon"—like the joke with a predictable punch line—affords us no challenge, surprise, or fun.

In puns, the link between dissimilars depends on similar sounds, often with no regard for meaning.[7] We groan even though we are laughing, for instead of making a surprising but meaningful connection, most puns return us to early childhood, when words were meaningless playthings. We laugh but feel a bit stupid.

Not all punlike humor is devoid of sense or interest.

> When the pope threatened to excommunicate all Italians who voted Communist, a friend said that it was the first time a bull had been waved at a red flag.

A punlike similarity may be unintended.

> My foreign-born mother insisted the word is *carage*. Every time we corrected her, she would say, "But our *car* is in it!"

> During World War II, a group of men in the uniform of the Free Polish Air Force walked up to the cashier of a London bookstore with copies of a book titled *Polish Up Your English*.

Discovering similars in dissimilars can motivate the scientist no less than the artist. In 1905, the year of his three foundational papers, Albert Einstein said, "It is a glorious feeling to discover unity in a set of phenomena that seem at first to be completely separate."[8]

Like a scientist working outside the accepted paradigm, artists who venture into the unknown are trying to bridge what most of us have yet to perceive as a break in continuity. Their work often disturbs us; it seems disjointed and meaningless.

Hemingway was told that his first stories weren't stories, while readers at a later time had no trouble recognizing the connections. They reflected a new reality—their own.

D

When the shaman draws a circle around himself, he creates a separate realm in which the supernatural and dangerous can become real, while the participants remain safe.

The frame around the work of art—literal in painting and implicit in the edge of the movie screen—marks a clear dividing line between what happens within it and our own reality. We can believe what we see or hear without running the risk of being overwhelmed by it. The event is invoked but isn't happening in *our* space.

When he wrote *The Gold Rush*, Chaplin drew directly on the documented experience of the Donner party; its members ate their shoes and their dead. But when Charlie faces starvation and is threatened with being eaten by animals or by his crazed companion, we are safely distanced and laugh. There is a gap or disconnect between his reality and ours.

If a waiter carrying a large tray with food is seized by a sneezing fit and barely manages to keep the contaminated dishes from spilling, we laugh until we realize he is bringing our dinner.

> I once heard a woman in a fight with her daughter quote the joke, "Insanity is inherited—you get it from your children."

Her daughter was not amused. As Mel Brooks observes, "Tragedy is when I cut my finger. Comedy is if you fall into an open sewer and die."

Chaplin says, "Life is a tragedy when seen in close-up, but a comedy in long-shot."[9] For the most part, Charlie is seen full figure, in medium or medium-long shots. But there is nothing funny about the close-up that ends *City Lights*.[10]

The figures in the work of Mack Sennett are filmed from a distance that makes them look like fleas, whereas a tragic figure like King Lear looks small on stage but is brought close by his words. Our ears don't distance him, and his words pour right into us.

TV comedy is traditionally shot from front-row center, as though it were happening on stage. The play space is not penetrated, and the camera doesn't engage us kinetically or viscerally, as in most dramatic films.

Chaplin works almost exclusively with a fixed frame, and his figures move *across* the screen—in a plain parallel to ours—far more often than toward or away from us. There is just one dolly shot in *The Gold Rush*: Charlie and Big Jim are sailing home and stroll on deck in their millionaire's finery. The camera maintains its quasi-objective distance by pulling back as they move forward.

The passage of time, too, can distance us. Abraham Lincoln's assassination is remote enough to be the subject of humor—"Other than that, Mrs. Lincoln, how did you like the play?"—but a joke asking Jackie Kennedy how she liked Dallas would make us wince.

Corpses look too much *like* us to be funny, but skeletons can make us laugh, especially if—instead of lying prone and lifeless—they are upright and moving. An early Disney short has them dancing to music by Camille Saint-Saens, disassembling and reassembling themselves and turning their bones into musical instruments.

> I once asked students to bring in their favorite jokes, and they came to class with an air of happy anticipation, eager to share them. When not a single joke got a laugh, a pained silence fell on the room. The following year, I decided to bring in my own favorites, and again no one found them funny. But when I told classes in later years what had happened, everyone laughed.

As Steve Allen says, comedy is "tragedy plus time."

E

Bergson says, "Laughter has no greater foe than emotion" and calls the comic "a momentary anesthesia of the heart."[11] When the clown weeps a bucketfull of tears, another clown bathes his feet in them.

Feelings, both in the physical and psychological sense, bring us close. By connecting us to others and ourselves, they eliminate the distance that allows us to laugh.

Alice Roosevelt Longworth lost her mother at birth, was something of a stranger in the home of her stepmother, and had been distanced from her feelings and sensations by her upper-class heritage. When she had a double mastectomy late in life, she said she was "the only topless octogenarian in Washington."

Unlike tragic figures, who engage us in their intense experiences, comedians short-circuit deep feelings and close attachments.

In *It's a Gift*, W. C. Fields tells his eight-year-old son, "I hate you." We know he means it, but he speaks in a flat, matter-of-fact voice that denies the feelings his words convey.

In *City Lights*, Chaplin spins a comic skein out of rejections that would be painful to watch if Charlie actually experienced them on screen. We laugh when the blind girl falls in love with him by mistaking him for a classy gentleman, and when the drunk millionaire calls him his best friend yet rejects him when he is sober. But once the blind girl gains her sight and sees Charlie for what he is, we are suddenly brought face to face with the pain that Chaplin has short-circuited throughout.

Directing his Hollywood comedies, George Cukor would tell his actresses, "Faster, ladies, faster!"

The speed at which the comic happens allows no room for feeling. We are too busy keeping up.

Significantly, Chaplin slows down the action to render emotion. In *The Immigrant*, when Charlie sees that the girl is in mourning for her mother, he pauses briefly to show his sympathy before resuming the breakneck pace.

In physical comedy, the action is uninterrupted and the figures never stop moving. Buster Keaton may appear to be passive but is, in fact, continually active or reactive.

In farce—the word comes from *facrio*, "to stuff"—there are no pauses or empty moments that might allow feelings to seep in.

We seem to be more open to feelings in a passive state. It is hard to act *and* feel at the same instant. Passivity is apt to leave us receptive and vulnerable, and sensory experiences tend to be most intense when we are passive.

The devil and his demons are often depicted as laughing derisively. They are instinct figures that live in the bowels of the earth and deride us as God's creations. But God in the Bible laughs just once, at evildoers.[12] As Mark Twain says, "There is no humor in heaven." The Judeo-Christian God cares about us, and what we are and do matters to Him. We may be tragic like Saul and Absalom, but we are never ridiculous.

In contemporary usage, *intense* is the opposite of *cool* and suggests discomfort. Intensity involves us so deeply with ourselves that we are apt to lose touch with what is happening in and to others; it isolates us.

Intensity is the opposite of irony. It makes the individual and his experience significant. The passion of Romeo and Juliet could not survive comic treatment. We would be too remote, and the feelings their tragedy indulges at length would strike us as absurd and very likely boring.

If, however, the comic figure did not care intensely about himself and his affairs, our own detachment would be meaningless. Don Quixote is as monomaniacal as Captain Ahab, and we take pleasure in the discrepancy between his perceptions and ours. One could think of it as comic irony.

Two people having sex are deeply engaged with each other and themselves, but if we saw them from a distance they might well appear comical. We would recognize ourselves in them and might even be touched, but most likely we would smile. Couples in pornographic movies are never filmed in long shot.

We smile, as well, at the intense absorption of children in whatever they are doing. Freud suggests that we compare how *we* would do it and smile at the difference.[13] But we may, instead, be amused or bemused because we sense that our own endeavors are often as intense and excessive.

F

Freud says, "The release of distressing affects is the strongest obstacle to the workings of comedy."[14] But as we noted, without the *threat* of distress we won't laugh. Tendentious jokes and most comic situations make us potentially uncomfortable. We are emotionally disengaged, but the figures often put us in conflict with ourselves, and their situation is apt to put us under stress.

Mary Todd Lincoln is as dead as the murdered president and can't be hurt by a heartless joke. It is *we* who are troubled and can't help laughing, though we may feel we shouldn't. Our sympathy for the bereaved widow and our deep respect for Lincoln are undermined. The joke simultaneously invokes a potentially painful, empathetic response in us *and* short-circuits it. Pulled in two directions at once, we laugh against our better judgment.

The emotional disconnect is like the gap in many jokes: it undermines an assumption—in this case, our self-perception. We respond to the shock of seeing ourselves as uncivilized, uncaring creatures with the laughter that releases us from stress.

> In a Second City skit, the doctor tells a young couple he
> has found a lump in the woman's breast. There is a troubled
> pause. Then the young man says, "But you're a dentist!"

A dire medical situation is transformed into a sexual one, and we laugh even though the young couple is, ostensibly, made to suffer twice.

The comic also distances us from situations, real or fictive, to which others have responded with exaggerated sentiment.

Oscar Wilde said that anyone who doesn't laugh at the death of Little Nell must have a heart of stone.

Our teenage children referred to *The Sound of Music* as *The Sound of Mucus*.

Though feeling is the foe of comedy, *good* feelings enhance our pleasure.

In most comedies, they don't prevail until the end, but musicals with their songs and dances are harmonized from the beginning. In *Singin' in the Rain*, the dilemmas facing the figures need not be taken seriously by them or us; there is no tension and no need for relief. Instead, we laugh with delight at the physical skill and grace of Gene Kelly and Donald O'Connor, and don't worry about the insignificant problems of their characters.

Though feelings undermine laughter, they can enrich the comic.[15] Shakespeare endows some of the figures in his comedies with greater reality by allowing them to feel, though neither their love nor hate for each other runs deep.[16]

Even in jokes and anecdotes feelings need not stop us from laughing:

> A village priest in France told the story of the Easter Passion with so much feeling that many members of his congregation were weeping. When he saw how deeply his words affected them, he said, "My dear children, remember it happened a long time ago, and perhaps it isn't altogether true."

Chaplin's feature films are clearly autobiographical and more open to feeling than the work of most comedians. In *The Kid*—a film he began shooting two days after his newborn son had died—the Kid is brutally torn from his father and is about to be placed in an orphanage, as Chaplin himself had been. Charlie's grief isn't subverted or short-circuited but given open expression, and there is nothing funny about it. Significantly, his grief turns into ferocious anger—the only occasion in his work when Chaplin makes no attempt to hide the pain and rage he must have felt as a child but couldn't afford to show.

In the shorts, Charlie is energetic, aggressive, and often self-propelled, but the features draw directly on Chaplin's early life and render him as a figure without will or direction. He drifts or stumbles into situations not of his own making, and though he struggles bravely and often ingeniously, the outcome is largely determined by chance or fate. In the shorts, he must fight for his physical survival, while the features threaten him with emotional devastation. The threat is, of course, subverted in both.

If we were either wholly identified with Charlie's experience or altogether safe from it, we wouldn't be subject to the tension that is released in our laughter. We are engaged in a contradictory process that has us alternately separate and connected, frightened and delighted, troubled and entertained, pinioned and released.[17]

One might guess that the alternation reflects the ceaseless but largely unconscious process of connecting and separating we go through day after day—and indeed, hour by hour—as we connect with and separate from each other. For as we noted, we are obliged to be both *part of* and *apart from* the whole.

If we were totally open to what is happening around us, we would implode, and if we were totally insulated we would shrivel up and perish in our shell.

G

Quentin Tarantino's *Pulp Fiction* hovers on the tenuous line that separates the horrifying from the comical. The continuous killings and injuries are filmed realistically, and the world of drug users and dealers is sufficiently unfamiliar to seem credible to us. Yet what happens to the figures arouses no painful sensations or feelings in them or us. The violence and death have a kinetic, sensory immediacy, but, as in cartoons, leave us emotionally untouched.

Much of the time, however, we are not altogether sure of our own reactions. When Vincent Vega plunges a large needle with adrenalin straight into Mia Wallace's heart, we are viscerally and even empathetically engaged, albeit for just a moment. We know how he feels: if she dies of the overdose, he, too, is as good as dead. His dilemma is palpable, but we are laughing—both to relieve tension and because both of them survive. Even the reaction of a bystander—"That was fucking trippy!"—is at once horrific and funny.

Pulp Fiction frequently has us in a state of shock and keeps us tense throughout. As in physical comedy and horror movies, the pressure is released at the end of each episode, usually after an explosion of violence—only to be ratcheted up again in the next scene. Our quasi-sensory participation makes the situations and experiences seem real, while our laughter lets us shake off the visceral response that the violence has induced. Like Alfred Hitchcock, Tarantino consistently distances injury and death with macabre humor: we are not expected to feel anything. He goes considerably further than *Bonnie and Clyde* and *M.A.S.H.*—earlier films that allow us to laugh in the face of injury, mutilation, and death.

A tone of cool detachment is established in the first scene, with Vega and Jules Winnfield driving to an execution while discussing what Burger King calls their hamburgers in Paris. Even when a central figure is briefly tense or frightened, he quickly regains his detachment. The moment after Vega shoots a teenage boy in the head, he and Winnfield become preoccupied with the mess they have made in the borrowed car. We are diverted from the shock of seeing the boy dead and allowed to laugh with relief—just as wondering about Mrs. Lincoln's reaction to the play distracts us from thinking about her dead husband.

In *M.A.S.H.*, the figures are emotionally disconnected for understandable reasons. Battlefield surgeons cannot save lives and limbs unless they disengage from their feelings. The disconnect is justified and puts us on their side. In *Pulp Fiction*, however, that isn't how we respond to anyone but Butch Coolidge. He is the only figure who believes in loyalty, love, and common decency. Except for a few moments of tenderness he shares with his girlfriend, no one cares about anyone else.

The episodic structure of the narrative contributes to our disengagement. Most of the figures appear in several episodes, but the fragmentation of their stories stops us from becoming involved with anyone for long. Though *The Gold Rush*, *Bonnie and Clyde*, and *M.A.S.H.* are also structured episodically, we follow the central figures and become sufficiently engaged to identify with them.

Since the time sequence of *Pulp Fiction* is inverted, characters die in one episode and return to life in another. Vega is shot dead by Coolidge, but the narrative undoes his death and lets him reappear. Conversely, the death of Bonnie and Clyde is irrevocable.

Like most comedies, *Pulp Fiction* has a happy—or quasi-happy—ending. In the last scene, Winnfield, who saw himself as God's own instrument of vengeance, retires from professional killing and lets two people he would have shot without hesitation earlier walk away unharmed.

When Tarantino talks about his work, he claims to be wholly focused on playing with genre variations. But in *Pulp Fiction*—perhaps by happenstance—he struck a vein that reflects the reality of our experience, rather than merely invoking our knowledge of other movies. He uses the conventions and familiar elements of thrillers and film noir to render the often absurd, apparently disconnected events that constitute contemporary experience.

Much of what happens in the film makes no sense. Several killings are entirely accidental. A toaster pops and Vega gets shot; Vega's gun goes off when the car hits a bump, and a boy in the back seat dies. Survival, like death, is subject to chance. A teenager who hid in the bathroom while his roommates were executed emerges suddenly and fires a point-blank barrage at Winnfield, but misses with every shot. The situations are determined and resolved by luck. The figures have no control over them.

We laugh in recognition. For though we are obliged to believe our will is effective and that we are responsible for what we do, we know—even if we cannot admit it openly—that we have little if any control over events that often determine our lives. Much of the time, what happens to and around us makes no more sense than the action in *Pulp Fiction*.

We laugh, as well, because we recognize the discrepancy between what we are *supposed* to feel about violence and death and our total lack of feelings. Once the visceral impact of the surprises has worn off, the action has no emotional effect on us despite its realistic rendering. It's all mere spectacle.

In contemporary life, what we see and hear extends far beyond the severely limited reach of our empathy. We are continually made aware of human situations that would, if we were involved, arouse powerful emotions in us. Our lack of response to the gruesome events in the film accurately reflects the emotional overload that leaves us feeling helpless and inadequate about most conditions and events in the world today.

Pulp Fiction allows us to recognize and laugh at our *inability* to respond. Day after day, we are made aware of human suffering and cruelty almost at the instant they occur, yet see them rendered in images that have scarcely more impact on us than a video game. Our feelings cannot extend beyond a narrowly limited realm without shutting down. Joseph Stalin's remark that a single death is a tragedy while a million is a statistic testifies, brutally, to the limits of our capacity for identification.

We may well laugh at *Pulp Fiction* because it relieves us of the "obligation" to feel what we cannot feel. We connect with the disconnection.

CHAPTER FIVE

Bergson and High Comedy

A

While Freud is focused on the inception of the joke in the psyche of the individual, Henri Bergson's essay "Laughter" (1900) is largely concerned with the effect of the comic on the community.

For him, laughter "must have a *social* signification."[1] "It is [its] business . . . to repress any separatist tendency . . . [and] readapt the individual to the whole."[2] It serves as a corrective that frees us of obsessions, rigidity, automatism, and inelasticity and allows us to become full-fledged members of the community.

> Any individual is comic who automatically goes his own way without troubling himself about getting in touch with the rest of his fellow-beings. It is the part of laughter to reprove his absent-mindedness and wake him out of his dream.[3]

However, figures like Don Quixote, Malvolio, and M. Jourdain *don't* wake out of their dreams. They remain prisoners of their own rigid, obsessed ways from beginning to end—loners out of touch with others and their situation.

Bergson's study isn't concerned with the outsiders *on stage* who make us laugh but with deviant tendencies in the audience.

As he sees it, the principal source of laughter in both life and fiction is scapegoating, which he calls by the more kindly "ragging." The comic figure is the object of a "plot"—by the author and those onstage who speak for the community—to free him of the qualities that have made him an outsider.

In daily life, scapegoating often takes the form of teasing—drawing attention to a quality or habit that makes a person different, irritating, or offensive. Since others are usually present and laughing, it functions like shaming. The German *Auslachen* makes the process clear: the targeted person is "laughed out," or excluded by laughter.[4]

Scapegoating allows us at once to project onto others qualities we don't want to acknowledge in ourselves *and* to unify the group. By focusing on someone who is different, we exile our own fear of difference, and by laughing about him we become alike.

Every group or community uses the threat of isolation to conform the outsider or newcomer. Like children, who mercilessly tease those who are physically or psychologically different, a group of adults can be primitive in its treatment of anyone who deviates from their norm.

For many of us, moments of being excluded are among the most painful memories of childhood. In English schools, shaming took the semiofficial form of shunning, or "being sent to Coventry." No one would speak to you or acknowledge your existence—a schoolboy version of solitary confinement, the most feared punishment in our prisons, where it is known to drive inmates insane.

We need so deeply to feel connected that scapegoating is highly effective. But it is apt to scar permanently those who don't succeed in conforming to the norm.

Most of us take our membership in the group or community for granted from childhood on, and don't venture far from it unless we are actively urged on by others.

When a comedian, magician, or hypnotist invites a member of the audience on stage, he or she becomes vulnerable. Yet they rarely refuse even if they are reluctant, for they are under pressure not just from the performer but from the audience. As they come on stage, they usually laugh in embarrassment, aware they have been separated from the safe anonymity of the group and are likely to become the laughingstock.

Bergson recognizes no difference between high and low comedy, with which he, like Freud, may not have been familiar,[5] though it was standard fare in Paris music halls and circuses.

While his emphasis on scapegoating as the source of laughter is valid for high comedy, it isn't the major component of most comic situations and jokes. His observations report a *phase* of the process we go through when we laugh at the clown. As long as we think we are different and superior, we are scapegoating him. But once our laughter signals that we are like him, we *integrate* the deviant in ourselves and become one with the community of others, who are acknowledging their own deviancy and are laughing along with us.

Bergson's focus on the social neglects the psychological. It assumes that the deviant in us needs to be "corrected" rather than given its rightful place—a place no community or individual can deny without severely limiting itself.[6]

B

Low comedy celebrates the very figure Bergson's comedy exiles. The out-of-touch loner who is ridiculed in Molière is its *hero*. We side happily with the skunk at the garden party, the violator of good manners and civilized behavior—with Charlie and Punch.

We like the Marx Brothers and W. C. Fields *for* their reprehensible, aggressive, and nasty qualities. In their refusal to be likable they resemble the villains of melodrama, who aren't the least bit interested in joining the community. Punch respects no authority, order, or rank, cudgels the police and the judge, and treats the devil and his own grandmother the same way—disrespectfully. He is a raging infant who acts out his primitive impulses and delights in the insults and injuries he inflicts.

Low comedy is asocial or antisocial and ridicules the norm. The comic hero doesn't give a damn about others or the community. He is the antithesis of the loner heroes in melodrama and Westerns, who save the community from destructive outsiders. He speaks for an unspoken part of ourselves—no doubt the reason that he, like the villain, is far more interesting to us than the all-too-familiar hero we may be trying to emulate in daily life.

Although at the end of *The Gold Rush*, Charlie is a millionaire, he remains no less an outsider than at the beginning, when he was alone, lost, and penniless. Chaplin makes a community of the audience by making himself a figure of fun, and joining it in the only way he can— as an inspired and highly skilled deviant. He never really belongs.[7]

Buster, too, is not truly at home unless he is alone on a runaway locomotive or adrift on an ocean liner. Fate may put a woman aboard, but he never connects with her and treats her as one of many objects he must juggle in order to survive.

In fairy tales and melodrama, there is usually a pair of outsiders— the hero/heroine and the villain. The hero or heroine has been exiled by circumstance or by the villain, whereas the villain is self-confirmed in his difference, uses it, and often takes pride and pleasure in it. The story doesn't explore the circumstances in his past that exiled him, but his limp or hunchback suggests he did not *choose* to be an outsider. In the end, he is punished and the hero or heroine joins the community, though usually—like Chaplin in *The Gold Rush*—in an exalted position, sustaining their difference. The poor, abused girl in the fairy tale becomes a queen.

Charlie and Buster are the central figures in their stories, and we see what happens from their point of view. Chaplin says that the audience must always know what Charlie is feeling—just as we always know what is happening to Hamlet and King Lear.[8]

But Charlie and Buster are exceptions. For unlike tragedy, neither high nor low comedy subscribes to the importance of the individual, and single figures rarely dominate. Prospero comes close, but he isn't funny, and Don Quixote is a melancholy character who rarely makes us laugh.

Though this is consistent with Bergson's emphasis on the social or communal aspect of the comic, it leads him to the surprising conclusion that the comic is not like art.

> Art always aims at what is *individual*. What the artist fixes on his canvas is something he has seen at a certain spot, on a certain day, at a certain hour, with a coloring that will never be seen again.[9]

He says that because "every comic character is a *type*"[10] and, as a type, has widely shared characteristics and reduces us to them, the comic figure isn't unique.[11]

He fails to recognize that although Falstaff and Charlie contain elements of the typical, they are highly individualized and no less differentiated than King Lear and Captain Ahab. Like all memorable fictive figures, they are at once representative of many and distinctly themselves. The most persuasive of them could be said to stand for all of us, even as they remain unique.

We know that even in traditions in which conventionalized stock figures appear and reappear, great comedians endowed them with their own distinctive marks. Descriptions of commedia dell'arte focus on performers who gave the familiar types singular and surprising qualities. The great clown often emerged into the limelight by making an anonymous everyman like Charlie into a unique figure. Like all of us, he is *and* isn't like everyone else.

In high comedy, the dominance of a single excessive or obsessive trait—Malvolio's or Don Quixote's—obliterates all other qualities, and reduces the individual to type. The figure is simplified, uncontradictory, and loses the complexity and shadings of the people we know well. At least in theory, the focus on a single characteristic allows us to recognize our own deviant qualities—like greed or deceit—in pure form, whereas most of the time they are comfortably obscured by our mixed motives and feelings.

Moreover, the speed at which comic figures move, and the distance from which we observe them, might well make them look alike, and so they must be easily identified if we are to understand the action. We often recognize the comedian by a single, exaggerated physical feature—Jimmy Durante's nose; John Cleese's tall, thin figure; Groucho's mustache and walk. In this sense, they resemble caricatures. We recognize Franklin Delano Roosevelt by his grin and cigarette holder.

C

Bergson's focus on the social function of the comic suggests a failure to understand the role of the individual in the community.

We noted that society must insist on our separate existence, for we, as individuals, play a critical part in keeping potentially destructive drives under control. As a result, the individual remains "deviant" to the core—a bundle of conflicts and contradictions we must repress or ignore. We may even say it is our deviancy that makes us individuals.

Communities are, moreover, deeply indebted to those who openly display their contradictions and differences—who won't or can't adapt and refuse to compromise. They often become leaders, pioneers, scientists, artists, or performers. Indeed, many of them derive their energy from trying to rejoin the community from which they have been exiled, usually at an early age.

Almost invariably, the new first appears in an individual. The comedies on which Bergson draws were the work of highly individuated authors who were surely, at least in part, motivated by an urgent need to connect with others. Unlike low comedy, with its often loose, episodic form, the structure of high comedy—particularly in France—is "tight," and tight forms are unlikely to result from the work of a group.

Even the material in improvisational comedy—going back to commedia dell'arte and continuing in our own day—originates in an individual, and is then elaborated and perfected by the group.[12]

In World War II, printed signs appeared in army latrines with the legend, "Please don't throw your cigarette butts into the urinals!" GIs added the hand-written observation: "It makes them soggy and hard to light."

During the build-up of troops before D-Day, English women, who had never before seen an African, asked who the black soldiers were. GIs told them they were "night fighters."

Surely jokes, like folks songs, originate in an anonymous individual, and are then purged of inessentials by those who pass them on, like stones polished by the sea.

D

High comedy is focused, as Bergson says, on the exterior—on behavior, manner, and gesture.[13] Like its civilized and educated audience, it keeps the body and its biology at one remove, rarely invokes our physical senses or experiences, and ignores—in their raw form—the conflict and tension between body and mind, or biology and civilization, that elicit our laughter in low comedy.

High comedy has no use for the instinctual, anarchic, and antisocial; ignores the inner realm; and doesn't invoke the primitive and potentially destructive stuff in us—very likely because the audience has learned to express aggression and sexuality in words rather than action.

In high comedy, no dark forces are at work in or around us. Caliban is powerless and subservient to Prospero from the start. His inclinations are wicked and primitive but, unlike the witches and evil stepmothers in fairy tales, he cannot act on them. We worry about Snow White, but not about Miranda.

Whereas in low comedy, as in animated cartoons, the figures teeter on the edge of extinction, the situations in high comedy are seldom existential. No one's survival is at stake. The central conflict is between the group and the individual, with the group sure to win. Malvolio stands no chance with Olivia, and becomes a clueless victim of Maria and Sir Toby, who represent the community.

Instead of having us laugh at physical aggression and sex, high comedy, as Bergson says about the comic in general, "appeals to the intelligence pure and simple." As in all stories, situations are the building blocks of the narrative, but the essential action is verbal. Most of the time we are laughing at the skilled, witty use of language. The body is seldom engaged, and our connection to the figures is far less immediate than in low comedy.

Surely women have always played a marginal role in physical comedy because using their bodies as objects of aggression violates a taboo that would stop us from laughing. Lucille Ball subjects her body to physical insults, most of them self-inflicted, but doesn't allow it to become an object of male aggression, nor does she use it suggestively.

Since *verbal* aggression and suggestiveness, however, are permitted women and indeed expected of them, they play a major part in high comedy. Millenia of civilization and the division of labor based on biological differences have honed their skill with words. In battles of wit they are the equals of men, and often their superiors. There are no female clowns in Shakespeare, but many witty women.

E

Neither high nor low comedy allows a significant ranking of importance or interest. They share a reductive, democratic perspective. High comedy subsumes the individual in the group, and low comedy tends to bring everyone down to the lowest common denominator—the biological drives that make us alike.

But they treat the audience very differently. Whereas low comedy reduces us to the level of those onstage, Bergson's high comedy allows us to feel superior to the comic figure.

We don't identify with Malvolio, and though we may recognize a distant link to Don Quixote, we don't see ourselves actually tilting at windmills. Even when we are the intended *target* of high comedy, it doesn't cut to the bone—at least not ours. Conceivably, though we side with those who scapegoat M. Jourdain for his pretensions, the action is meant to purge us of our own. But our participation is indirect, comfortable, and relaxed. We remain above the fray, laugh *at* him, and don't suddenly burst out laughing about ourselves.

The deviant figure in high comedy—like the villain in tragedy, fairy tales, and melodrama—remains at a safe remove. He is compelled and helpless, but since we are presumably free, we respond with a smile instead of the involuntary, convulsive laughter elicited by the clown.

High comedy is populated by fools and knaves, who take advantage of each other, or try. Often, there is a schemer onstage—a wily servant, who represents the community and brings down the knave or villain. He stands between us and his victims, and since we are usually in on his scheme, we become passive coconspirators and members of the community in good standing. He takes on the devious task of exposing the deviant figure, and leaves us with clean hands.

Bergson describes the comic person as blind or unconscious, while everyone else onstage can see him clearly.[14] But in low comedy *all* of the figures are blind. We in the audience are not as unknowing as they, yet rarely stand in the ironic relationship to them that high comedy fosters. Since Chaplin and Keaton not only *played* Charlie and Buster but rendered them out of their own core experience, they are far more closely identified with them than Shakespeare and Molière were with Malvolio and M. Jourdain.[15]

Almost no one in low comedy stands above the action, but in high comedy there is often a superior, detached, even wise figure. Prospero and Feste see everyone and everything clearly, as do some of the servants who assist in or originate the schemes; they observe the foibles of their social betters with a reductive, critical eye. Our own detachment often allows us to see the action from the vantage point of Puck—"What fools these mortals be."

Bergson says, "Laughter . . . being intended to humiliate . . . must make a painful impression on the person against whom it is directed . . . [and] would fail . . . if it bore the stamp of sympathy or kindness."[16]

High comedy is indeed ruthless with the deviant figures onstage, but it lets the spectator off easy. In life, scapegoating is derisive and cruel, but watching it in the theater leaves the audience unscathed. We don't participate in the action directly, and are rarely made fearful or even tense.

Much of the humor in the works of William Congreve, Richard Brinsley Sheridan, Oscar Wilde, and George Bernard Shaw is without sharp edges. Tendentious jokes that might make us squirm in life lose their bite when directed at an onstage figure. Like wit that targets humanity at large, they don't trouble us personally. "'Tis better to have loved and lost than never to have lost at all" aims at and distresses no one in particular.

The settings in high comedies are social and governed by familiar rules and laws. The action rarely veers out of control, as it does in farce, and fate or chance seldom plays a determining role until the resolution. The known world is disturbed at the outset, but our values and belief system are never undermined, and we are rarely burdened with anything we don't want to know. Shakespeare explores human darkness in his tragedies, but skirts the disturbing and truly surprising in all but his late comedies.

With the audience exposed to little risk, the situations in high comedy need not be carefully framed as untrue or absurd, and can stay much closer to the familiar and everyday than in low comedy. Significantly, Bergson describes comedy as "the study of actual life."[17]

Though movies are far more realistic than stage comedy, few moments in Chaplin and Keaton could be said to resemble "actual life."

F

High comedy is largely focused on our pretensions, deceptions, and self-deceptions, not the darker secrets we keep from ourselves. Often, the unfolding of a scheme or intrigue drives the plot, and one or several characters may be masked or in disguise.

This is consistent with Bergson's view that comedy stresses adaptability. A primary subject is the pretend face, or mask, that we show others.

Unlike the figures in low comedy, the middle and upper classes don't face a threat to their survival and can focus on personal and social relationships. Since they are spared poverty, hunger, violence, and imminent death, they are free to make adaptation, or fitting in, a central concern.

In daily life, adapting and deception are closely linked. Tangential encounters between us and others depend largely on harmless untruths and camouflage. Like courtesy and white lies, they spare us conflict and discomfort.

In the small, homogeneous communities of the past, deception and lies were largely pointless. Everyone knew everything of significance about everyone else *and* their parents and grandparents.

Today, however, communities depend largely on the "inauthentic" to function. Many relationships that were once secured by tradition and social or economic obligations have become personal, uncertain, and vulnerable. They depend on courtesy and consideration that often camouflage what we actually know, feel, and think.

For most of us, the way we treat others is not, of course, a disguise or mask but a genuine modification of who we are, or rather were in childhood. Social life is predicated on turning our first nature into the good behavior—or second nature—that comes to most of us as effortlessly as breathing. As we noted, what begins as a mask becomes the face.

We not only adapt to society and others but try to manipulate them—most often, we like to think, for their benefit as well as our own. But while we remain at least marginally aware of the benign or malign deceptions we practice on others, the subtlest, most successful manipulations are those we practice on ourselves. These, too, become second nature to us, for without them we might not retain enough self-regard and confidence to survive.

Once we are fully socialized adults, most of us cease to experience the difference between what we "really" are and what we "pretend" to be. But adolescents, who haven't yet fully submitted to the demands of the community, can experience a stark discrepancy between acceptable public behavior and their own inner reality, and are uncomfortably aware of being educated, manipulated, or forced to conform to what society requires them to be. While some rebel or drop out, most respond to what they perceive as the contradictions and inauthenticities of the adult world with skeptical or derisive humor. Eventually, of course, most submit to the force majeure of the community and put on the imaginary clothes worn by the emperor and by the great majority who have left the realm of the authentic—childhood.

Low comedy, like the poor who were its largest audience, is not concerned with pretensions, deceptions, or masks, for among the poor there is no privacy, no space to hide, no doors to keep out others. Their lives are lived in public, often on the street.

Since they own little or nothing, no one is scheming to take advantage of them, and their experience from childhood on has made them mistrustful and skeptical of anyone who tries to tell, or sell, them anything.

They need all their energy just to stay in place, and since the passage of time in their lives is not commonly marked by ambition or clear direction, low comedies tend to be plotless. Their structure is episodic and rarely builds on an intrigue in which a central figure, like Volpone, schemes to achieve his ends.

Whereas in high comedy the violation of good manners is a notable transgression, low comedy thrives on the rude and crude. It has no room for polite formalities.

G

The difference between high and low comedy would seem economic and social in origin.

The higher we move up the socioeconomic ladder, the further we separate not just from those "below" but from our peers, with whom we may be competing economically and who, like us, have developed specialized skills.

Since the audience for high comedy was composed of educated, differentiated, and in this sense "deviant" individuals—people with private lives, privileges, and educations that set them apart—high comedy stresses connecting. It integrates the isolated comic figure *and* the equally disconnected spectator into a community.

Those attending low comedy, however, were far more like each other. They were effectively *overconnected*, and since they could survive only by obeying laws that kept them in place and often exploited them, their comic heroes were misfits who thrived on violating the social order.

In high comedy—performed for an audience of individuals who deemed themselves free and self-determined—deviations from the norm are scapegoated, while low comedy gave people with severely restricted lives a chance to vent anarchic, antisocial impulses.[18]

Since the poor don't see themselves as existing separately from the group, their comic figures are loners, while high comedy ridicules and punishes anyone who sets himself apart. Falstaff is an exception. He lives at an interface between high and low—both belongs *and* doesn't.

Audiences tend to identify subjectively with comic figures who openly display the very qualities they have suppressed in themselves. But though the figures serve a compensatory function, at the surface— where the performer connects most immediately with the spectator— entertainment accurately reflects the *surface* lives of the audience: low comedy is physical, and high comedy is verbal.

Since the audience for them has largely disappeared, both forms of comedy have—in their pure state—become museum pieces with a half-life in universities and occasional revivals.[19] Vestiges of high comedy survive on Broadway and in the screwball comedies of the 1930s that were, for the most part, written by New York playwrights.

Over the past century, movies and television have largely taken over the role of the theater, and since the cost of production obliges them to play to the largest possible number, comedy, too, has been broadened or leveled into a volume business.[20]

Moreover, historical forces and democratic institutions have evened out some of the differences between the privileged and the poor. In theory, no one in our society is confined to—or assured of—a fixed, permanent place, and most of us subscribe to values that see us as equals.

As a result, movie comedies that were once either physical and low-brow or verbal and sophisticated have become a mix of high and low elements. But though they may contain physical and sometimes visceral humor, the aggression and sexuality in them are seldom disruptive, and our laughter is rarely derived from violence, danger, injury, or death. The audience no longer expects to face existential issues but wants, instead, to be distracted from them.

With the exception of stand-up, comic entertainments today are almost invariably genial and often sentimental. Though they subscribe to Bergson's "laughter has no greater foe than emotion," love is seldom treated skeptically, and romantic feelings triumph.

In life, scapegoating remains as common as ever, but ragging on the screen is rare. Even an unpleasant, classically deviant figure like the central character in *The Devil Wears Prada* is treated kindly. After abusing everyone in the film, she is allowed to develop feelings not only for others but for herself.

Perhaps we all need so badly to feel included that excluding any-one—even a fictive figure—makes us uncomfortable enough to spoil the fun. In television and movies today, "likeability" or "relatability" is essential to the success of both characters and performers. However badly they behave, we expect them to redeem themselves and emerge as essentially decent and trustworthy—the kind of people we want to be and have as neighbors.

H

Soren Kierkegaard says, "Wherever there is life there is contradiction, and wherever there is contradiction the comical is present."[21]

Bergson contributes to our understanding of the comic, but since he is unaware of the contradictions that are as basic to laughter as they are to human existence, his perspective lacks complexity.

In his view, we laugh at repetition because it is mechanical, but fails to note that in our laughter we ourselves become repetitious and therefore "mechanical." In many instances, moreover, repetition is reassuring, and we laugh because what is repeated is—or becomes—familiar and makes us feel at home.

Whereas in life we can never be altogether sure what will happen next, even—or especially—within the family, the substitute families in television sitcoms are predictably the same week after week. There is nothing truly surprising or undependable about them. They delight us *because* they repeat, just like the bedtime story or song we asked for night after night in childhood.

Bergson says, "The attitudes, gestures and movements of the human body are laughable in exact proportion as that body reminds us of a mere machine."[22]

This may be true of high comedy, which isn't rooted in biological life, but he extends it to the comic in general. Though he claims that we need not think of his formula that "rigidity is the comic and laughter is its corrective" as a definition of the comic, in his essay it becomes just that.[23]

When Carol Burnett as a dimwitted secretary carries out every request her boss makes by crossing the office at an excruciatingly slow pace, we don't just laugh because she is predictable or machinelike, but because her way of walking gives expression to the resentment and repressed aggression that anyone who has ever worked for others recognizes and enjoys. She is a white-collar version of Stepin Fetchit.

Bergson opposes the machinelike to the living, but fails to note that biological life, too, is repetitious and mechanical. Our instincts repeat,[24] and so do all functions controlled by the autonomous nervous system. If our heartbeat were not "mechanical," we would have to spend every moment, day and night, making sure that it keeps beating.

He calls rigidity "an encrustation on the living," but doesn't recognize that society and civilization, too, are "encrustations." Without rigidity and repetition no society could sustain itself. We expect our community to be dependable or predictable, and are in turn obliged to become predictable and "mechanical" ourselves. Our socialization consists of acquiring good habits—"*the frequent repetition of the same acts.*" Our clothes, too, were until recently known as *habits*, and we dress our naked or natural bodies just as our learned behavior "dresses" our original, or naked, actions and reactions.

Bergson points to vanity as a rich source of the comic, but fails to add that it inheres in almost everything we feel, think, and do. Though a comic figure blinded by vanity is an extreme and highly visible case, we all delude ourselves about our own importance—a necessary illusion that is fostered by the community. Most of us survive by remaining in a collective fool's paradise, just as entire communities sustain themselves by believing they are significant and unique.

I

Bergson says, "We laugh every time a person gives us the impression of being a thing."[25] Since Keaton is often a "thing," he would appear to meet Bergson's criteria. But when he is in a crisis, Buster is also adaptive and brilliantly resourceful. Key figures in low comedy are often both rigid *and* elastic—as we ourselves need to be to survive.

Bergson's essay was published in 1900, before movies were widely seen, and one wonders what he would have made of Keaton and Chaplin, though he would, of course, have seen clowns like them had he visited the music halls and circuses of Paris.

Groucho, Chico, and Harpo could be called "mechanical," since they misbehave as we expect them to. But we never know what they will actually do or say. Unlike machines, they are continually surprising, and it is people like Margaret Dumont's characters—representing *society*—who are rigid and predictable. Significantly, this reverses Bergson's perspective, in which the comic individual is rigid while the community is elastic.

In *M.A.S.H.*, the community is made up of men and women who have adapted to the horrific task society has assigned them. They spend their free time in drinking, horseplay, and promiscuity, violating civilized behavior in order to carry out—and survive—their work, while the two figures who observe the rules are scapegoated and exiled. Bergson's central premise is reversed: Those who represent society at large are mechanical and on the side of "death," while a band of irreverent nonconformists is able to save both the lives of others and their own sanity.

Bergson barely mentions contradictions. He clearly doesn't believe them to be at the core of our situation, or a primary source of tension in both life and art.[26] But to be human is to be suspended between opposites that cannot be permanently reconciled. All we, or society acting on our behalf, can do is try to remain in balance by oscillating between them. Unlike Bergson, our religious and social institutions don't ignore the conflict between biology and civilization, though they can only *appear* to resolve the multiple paradoxes that derive from it.

The source of contradictions would seem to be the individual—particularly the loner—but he is merely the place at which they become explicit. Making them visible—or, in low comedy, visceral—could be called the "function" of the many comic and tragic figures who find themselves outside the sheltering rules and laws of the community and subject to raw contradictory pressures.

Both contradictions and the stress they induce are made tangible in double-bind situations. Agamemnon faces two alternatives, both of them bad: he must sacrifice his daughter, or the Greek fleet won't sail. Though the dilemma in his story is presented as a choice, a double bind can also be imposed by the narrative structure. In *City Lights*, Charlie helps the blind girl see but by doing so makes their relationship impossible.

In tragedy, the irreconcilable conflict between opposites is briefly suspended when the death of the central figure releases him and the audience. Comedy ends with a similar moment of relief when the action comes to a stop and we are made whole by our laughter. We note, however, that the solutions are temporary, and in jokes and riddles often nonsensical.

A contradictory, highly differentiated individual like Charlie has no place in Bergson's comic realm. In his view, a conflicted figure is a deviant, whose problems would disappear if he were absorbed into the community. Indeed, most high comedies keep irreconcilable paradoxes off stage through the social system that contains and governs the action—much as our own institutions spare us from having to deal with them in daily life.

Watching high comedy and its contemporary variants is pleasant and reassuring, but the pleasure seldom runs deep. For though we try to avoid paradoxes and double-bind situations in life, we actually enjoy facing them in art.

The more conflicted and tense they make us, the greater our pleasure. Easily resolved conflicts offer us but shallow relief.[27]

J

Bergson says:

> A man, running along the street, stumbles and falls; the passersby
> burst out laughing. . . . They laugh because his sitting down is
> involuntary. . . . Perhaps there was a stone on the road.[28]

In low comedy, there is *always* a stone on the road. Bergson continues:

> [The man] should have altered his pace or avoided the obstacle.
> Instead . . . through a lack of elasticity and a kind of physical ob-
> stinacy, *as a result, in fact, of rigidity or of momentum,* the muscles
> continued to perform the same movement when the circum-
> stances of the case call for something else.[29]

He *should* have recognized his situation and adapted to reality? So
should King Lear, Madame Bovary, and Mother Courage. But they
can't. Their situation, their nature, their past, and the preclusive structure of narrative will not let them. If they *could,* they surely would—
though, if they could, there would *be* no story.

Bergson's constricted view of the comic as a corrective[30] may reflect
the strong tendency of many philosophers to be prescriptive.[31] They
mean to show us how to live and structure our communities and relationships, rather than merely observing and analyzing them.

The prescriptive is predicated on the assumption that we are free
and can choose to be different from the way we are. Significantly,
Bergson opposes what he calls "free activity" to the "mechanical" that
he identifies as the source of the comic.[32]

But it is the premise of comedy, as of all narrative, that the figures
have no freedom or choice. Since we know from the start what will
befall them, they can have no greater control over their fate than Oedipus does—though it is an essential part of their fate to *think* they do.

Bergson believes that when we laugh at a comic figure *we* are free,
though he or she is not. But as Girard observes, the moment we begin
to laugh, we lose control over our reactions and cease to be free ourselves. We should, however, note that high comedy, with its appeal to
the intelligence, leaves us more detached and—in this sense—marginally freer than low comedy.

Bergson says, "There are innumerable comedies in which one of the characters thinks he is speaking and acting freely, and consequently retains all the essentials of life, whereas . . . he appears as a mere toy in the hands of another, who is playing with him."[33] But rather than illuminating relationships *within* a comedy, this describes the relationship of the preclusive narrative to *all* who are caught up in it. They think they are acting freely, while we see them as mere "toys" or victims of the plot.

Bergson defines *inelasticity* as a tendency to adapt "ourselves to a past and therefore imaginary situation when we ought to be shaping our conduct in accordance with the reality which is present"—a view many in our society share.[34]

Again, the use of *ought* is significant. Aeschylus, Shakespeare, Flaubert, Dostoevsky—and indeed every traditional storyteller—would deem the word irrelevant to the figures in their stories. As *storytellers*, they might even be obliged to conclude that human freedom is a necessary illusion, and that the present is as little subject to our will as the past. This is, of course, the view of Freud, who saw our generic and personal past as ever-present, and believed we can do little more than camouflage or repress it.

Needs, obsessions, and passions drive the central figures in both comic and tragic stories. We, who stand apart and watch, are freer than they—if only with respect to *their* stories. But we may sense that our own lives are no less bound and determined. It isn't something we can afford to believe consciously, but our helpless laughter reveals that—with a part ourselves—we do.[35]

For Bergson, freedom is "one of the essentials of life."[36] Most of us agree. But stories tell us otherwise, and so we put them out of mind as mere fictions. In current usage, that makes them untrue.

Yet stories were once deemed deeply relevant, and we continue to believe those that reinforce the assumptions of our community. The problem today is that while popular fictions *seem* to confirm our core belief—that we are in charge of our fate both individually and as a species—they actually tell us the opposite. Like all stories, they undermine the freedom that Western communities deem essential.

The idea of freedom is inculcated in us at an early age and at such a deep level, we find it nearly impossible to free ourselves from it. It is intrinsic to our existence as individuals, who are assumed to be separate from—or free of—others. Indeed, there are situations when we are expected to stand apart from communal institutions and laws and let our own perceptions and individual conscience guide our actions.

A conscious belief in our freedom could be said to define us as human beings. It is an obligation imposed on us by society as we emerge from childhood, and builds on our growing mastery over our bodies. Clearly toilet training is a critical step in our development and socialization, because it proves to us that we are in control and free to make choices.

But just when and where our vaunted freedom begins—at what point we become responsible and are obliged to counter the pressure of others, the values of the community, and, indeed, the commands of our country—is shrouded in uncertainty and has been a central concern of all religious and legal systems.

Bergson's insight into the comic may well be limited by his faith in human freedom and an unwillingness to consider that in comedy, as in all stories, we willingly face the possibility that we are neither free nor in control of our lives.

When a woman asked Bertrand Russell whether he believed in free will, he said, "Madame, I have no choice."[37]

In *The Gold Rush*, the plot and Charlie's fate are determined by blizzards, bears, and hunger. He survives because fortune is on his side. The immense energy that powers him and keeps him going is not his own but biological—a manifestation of the survival instinct inherent in all life.

Though Chaplin was the world's most admired comedian and well aware of his genius, he never forgot that, from childhood on, his life resembled a fairy tale, and that—but for forces and circumstances beyond his control and gifts not of his own making—he would have suffered the fate of countless children who were wiped out by poverty and abandonment in nineteenth-century London. Though his childhood marked him indelibly, he was able to convert its destructive impact into vital work.

In high comedy, too—despite its social setting—chance often plays a larger role in the origin of events and their outcome than our will or reason. Human foibles and intrigues generate and complicate the action in *Twelfth Night*, but the story has its inception in a storm at sea and a shipwreck.

> E. M. Forster says, "A God is hidden in *Tristram Shandy*. His name is *Muddle* . . . *Muddle* is almost incarnate. . . . [It] is the deity that lurks behind this masterpiece—the army of unalterable muddle, the universe as a hot chestnut."[38]

Muddle, twice italicized by Forster, is an equivalent of the god of chance, whose plan—if he has one—is utterly inaccessible to us. The novelist's own digressions may be seen as an equivalent of the unpredictable, often disconnected—or apparently disconnected—events in the world at large.

Fate in the form of chance or coincidence plays a critical part in most stories, even if it merely brings the figures together, "arranging" for them to be ill or well met. Fictive events, like accidents, often arise from a set of "curious chances" that in stories, as in life, may well constitute fate.

Given the preclusive structure of fiction, we cannot blame the figures for what they do or don't. Like the heroes and heroines in fairy tales, the comic figure is lucky and the tragic figure unlucky. We may legitimately praise or criticize the actors for their performances, but not the characters they play.

In life, too, we can hardly blame those who are unable to make their way out of poverty, illness, or disaster—even if we, in the enlightened West, cannot hold this view of ourselves or our own situation. We learn early on to deem ourselves and others praiseworthy or blameworthy, and so prop up our obligatory illusion of free will. But we can hardly fail to notice that millions on earth deserve neither the good nor the bad that befalls them.

In evolution, life itself emerges out of mutations, or chance events. As a biologist tells us, "Chance *alone* is at the source of every innovation, of all creation in the biosphere. Pure chance, absolutely free but blind, [is] at the very root of the stupendous edifice of evolution."[39]

Though in some earlier societies chance was deemed a deity and even made to decide innocence and guilt, we cannot, today, acknowledge it as a major force in our lives. We entertain the possibility only in fiction.

The Enlightenment persuaded us that we can achieve mastery over our lives, and surely Bergson, with his nineteenth-century confidence in human freedom and control, explicitly rejects surprise as a component of the comic,[40] since it carries the clear suggestion—albeit in playful form—that we cannot know or control the future and aren't in charge.

Significantly, the mechanical and predictable comic figures he cites make us smile but not laugh—until they come up against the surprising. As we noted, it is the *unpredictable*, odd, or peculiar—the unexpected stone in the road, and not the repetitive and mechanical—that makes us laugh out loud.

Even wit—a principal source of laughter in high comedy—depends on an unexpected combination or use of words, while in farce, though the characters are as predictable as the figures making the rounds in the steeple of a medieval church, the clockwork goes crazy and makes a hash of their lives and plans.

Bergson contrasts the rigid and automatic with what he calls "the living." But in *his* thinking, the living does not appear to include biology. He never mentions it, though it is both the motive force in low comedy *and* the source of the very correctives Bergson finds in high comedy.

Innumerable comic plots, both high and low, revolve around *la pré-caution inutile*—a useless attempt to intervene in the natural order of procreation: fathers lock up nubile daughters, old men lust after young women, and rich geezers with young wives try, in vain, to keep them from more suitable lovers.

If, as evolution suggests, biology has found an effective way of preserving and perpetuating our species through the community, then the social structures that "correct" Bergson's deviant figures must be themselves informed and largely determined by biology.

In his limited and limiting view, comedy "accepts social life as a natural environment . . . and in this respect . . . turns its back upon art, which is a breaking away from society and a return to pure nature."[41]

But art is hardly "a return to pure nature." Moreover, the comic seems far closer to the earth and natural life than a great deal of high art.

Comedy as we know it had its beginnings in a festival that invoked and celebrated the fertility of the earth, and in low comedy biological life continues to bubble up, inexhaustible and unstoppable.

It is the instinct-driven comic hero and not his more civilized counterpart who refuses to stay down and returns us to nature.

CHAPTER SIX

Blind and Helpless but Alive

A

In *The Circus*, a pickpocket deposits a stolen wallet and watch in Charlie's pocket for safekeeping. When he tries to retrieve them, a policeman catches him red-handed and arrests him. The officer courteously returns the items to Charlie, who is utterly clueless but accepts them as gifts of an unaccountable fate—only to run into their original owner and to find himself accused of being the thief.

A while later, he is hired as a roustabout by a circus, but is so inept that when he turns up inside the ring, the audience assumes he is one of the clowns. However, they only laugh as long as he doesn't know he is funny. Once he *tries* to make them laugh, he fails utterly.

The clown claims not to know he is different and comical. As Baudelaire says, "The most distinctive mark of the absolute comic is that it should remain unaware of itself."[1]

During a barroom fight in *The Gold Rush*, Charlie's hat is pulled down over his eyes. He thrashes around blindly, hits a pillar, and jars loose a large clock that knocks out his opponent. When he gets the hat off his face and sees the man on the floor, Charlie thinks his blow has felled him and walks away, the proud victor.

123

In *Swing Time*, Fred Astaire dances with three giant shadows of himself, but his back is turned to them and he doesn't notice that they start moving independently of him.

The aerial shows touring rural America during the first decades of the twentieth century often featured a man dressed as a local farmer. He stumbled onto the field, climbed into one of the planes, and took off before anyone could stop him. After a series of death-defying maneuvers that appeared to have the plane spin out of control, he would make a bumpy landing, climb out, and disappear into the crowd.

In a variation of the same act, a circus aerialist dressed as a clown loses his way onto the high-wire, performs a series of hair-raising stunts that threaten him and others with death, and ends up plunging precipitously into the safety net.

An ignorant or naive person is effectively blind.

> In *Black Orpheus*, two boys climb a hill every morning, convinced that unless they strum their guitars, the sun won't come up.[2] When it rises above the horizon while they play, they think they have once again assured the coming of day.

> Asked to name the wife of Noah, a boy in Bible class said it was Joan of Arc.

> Reagan's secretary of the interior described his Coal Mining Commission as a model of diversity: "I have a black, I have a woman, two Jews, and a cripple."

Stupidity is a form of blindness, and many comedians—Laurel and Hardy, Abbott and Costello, and much of the time even Chaplin and Keaton—play stupid. The theme song of the Three Stooges is "Three Blind Mice."[3]

Keaton says, "Audiences love the slow thinker"—no doubt because they recognize themselves. We aren't as dumb as Roseanne Roseannadanna, who can't understand "all the fuss about violins on television," but we know we, too, constantly make mistakes.

We don't, however, recognize ourselves in Feste, the clown in *Twelfth Night*. Wiser and far more self-aware than the rest of us, he makes us smile rather than laugh.

The comic figure, like Oedipus, fails to see his own situation or himself, and we enjoy the discrepancy between his perception and ours. We derive pleasure from comic irony because it allows us to face, in a safe context, what we must deny or ignore in life. We, too, are often blind to our situation and don't see ourselves as laughable.[4]

Though neither the comic nor tragic hero is in charge, we perceive what happens to them very differently. Most clowns originate and appear in their own material. Charlie is played by Chaplin, who wrote and directed his own films; Astaire choreographed the dance in which his shadows take control; Harpo Marx devised his own routines; and John Cleese coauthored the scripts that turn him into an utterly ineffectual Basil Fawlty.

But actors who play tragic figures don't determine their own trajectory, don't write their own lines, and don't usually direct the plays. We take satisfaction and even pleasure in watching Captain Ahab and Antigone go to their doom, but are far freer to enjoy the helplessness of Charlie/Chaplin, whose ultimate control is never in doubt.

When Rudolf Nureyev called him the world's greatest dancer, he was thinking of the command Chaplin has over his body and its every movement. As the producer, moreover, Chaplin controlled every aspect of his work. No executive could stop him from shooting ninety thousand feet of film for a short that runs just three thousand.[5] He used to say take 50 was the most spontaneous, surely because it was the most concise and elegant, yet seemingly the least studied. But few filmmakers owned their own studios, had the cast and crew on their personal payroll, and could call in the morning to cancel work because they didn't feel funny.

Chaplin would show his cast—even Marlon Brando on *A Countess from Hong Kong*—every move, and expected them to mimic him.

His actors were effectively puppets and seem alive largely because he animated them with his own extraordinary energy, inventiveness, and observational gift.

Since Chaplin's own control is always evident, he could place Charlie in situations that have him clearly at the mercy of impersonal forces—going berserk on an assembly line, propelled helplessly by the cocaine he has poured all over his food instead of grated cheese, and victimized by a machine that shovels food into his mouth—yet leave us exhilarated by his skill and mastery.

Conversely, the victimization of tragic figures must be camouflaged—both from them and us—by their confident activity and the conviction that they will master their fate. Though we *know* there is nothing they can do, we keep forgetting it, and lend ourselves to their efforts as though they were free to change the outcome.

B

Loss of control over ourselves and our lives may well inspire our deepest fears. Some 87 percent of the people seeking assisted suicide in Oregon in 2004 gave the loss of autonomy as their reason.

From early childhood on—with toilet training as a marker—we learn to be in charge of our bodies and, inferentially, of our actions and emotions. Painful experiences teach us that losing control over our temper or our bladder isolates us from others.

But once our energy becomes focused on our own ambitions and projects, we forget that the sense of freedom and empowerment that enables us was initiated by the community, which could not survive if we deemed ourselves helpless.

Often enough, when we think we are doing something, larger agencies are doing it through us.

Until recently, "mental problems" suggested that we had lost command over ourselves. They imbued us with a deep sense of shame, and seeing a psychiatrist was deemed a mark of weakness. A highly intelligent woman told me she was greatly relieved when the third physician she consulted for severe headaches diagnosed a brain tumor. The first two had said her problem was psychological.

Though "losing it" terrifies us, we in fact give up control over much of our lives early on, as a matter of course and without being aware of it. We surrender it to habits and all the customs, rules, and regulations we internalize in childhood that turn us into social beings. We leave most major decisions to the structures of the community that is itself made possible by law and habit—just as our creature life functions by virtue of the autonomous nervous system.

But though most of our "decisions" are not actually made by us, we disregard all evidence suggesting that our freedom may be a necessary assumption, rather than a demonstrable fact.

It should come as no surprise that stories—both tragic and comic—focus on the very loss of control we find so threatening. Since "losing it" is a constant threat, watching someone become the victim of larger forces is a source of both tension and relief.

Gravity, as Girard says about the comic, is the crudest of the forces that have us in their grip. We countermand it when we learn to crawl, stand, and walk, and—as adults—take it into account without giving it a thought. But the instant we see a comic figure fall—physically or psychologically—he loses the control on which our freedom is predicated. Though we know the comedian is in command, the threat to us is so immediate and visceral that we burst out laughing with relief when he recovers.

For the duration of their stories, we believe in the autonomy of tragic figures. They resemble us in appearance and behavior even if they are kings and queens, and we endow them with the freedom we assume for ourselves. But comedy appears to be unreal, and so it can turn figures that seem utterly different from us into victims of circumstance without distressing us.

The outcome of Chaplin's feature films is determined by fate or chance, and Keaton remains passive and often immobile until he is compelled into movement—by a driverless motorcycle, an unmoored ocean liner, a hijacked locomotive, or a cataclysmic storm.

Farce—sweeping its denizens into a whirl of frantic motion that seldom deposits them where they mean to go—is but the most extreme version of the basic comic condition.

A loss or lack of control will make us laugh even in life as long as the consequences aren't serious. When a woman's grocery bag breaks open on the bus while she is trying to pay her fare and the apples roll down the aisle, most of us will be tempted to laugh even as we help her pick them up.

> Mrs. Schulberg, the wife of a film industry magnate, called on the head of Paramount Pictures and found him ensconced behind his desk. She drew herself up and said in her grande dame manner, "When a lady enters your office, Mr. Cohen, I would expect you to stand up like a gentleman."
>
> "Madame," he said, "I *am* standing up."

Cohen was barely five-feet-two—no less a victim of his circumstances than Agamemnon.

The comic figure is often unable to stop himself from acting and reacting compulsively. When Laurel and Hardy are seized by a frenzy of destruction, its grip on them is as powerful and unconscious as the impulse to steal that propels the pickpocket in *The Kid*: even while he is asleep his hand travels through Charlie's pockets searching for loose change.

Nothing can dissuade Don Quixote from his quest, and when Charlie Brown's kite gets stuck in a tree, he holds on to the string for eight days. Bergson calls their obsession "a mechanization of life," and believes it to be the key to the comic. But it is as characteristic of the tragic figure. Antigone, Macbeth, and Captain Ahab are no more able to change themselves or their course of action than Falstaff.

But while the failure to adapt dooms Antigone and Ahab, it guarantees the survival of the comic figure, who may be opportunistic at the surface but is immutable at the core—just as we are ourselves.

Since, in life, we survive by shifting and adapting, at first glance both comic and tragic figures seem utterly different from us. But they wouldn't hold our interest if we didn't recognize ourselves in them. For at the deeper levels of habit and instinct we, too, are inelastic—trapped in patterns of unconscious repetitions.

C

What G. K. Chesterton says of Dickens—"He was the character . . . anybody can hurt and nobody can kill"—could be said of many clowns.

Just as we take pleasure in watching the comic figure lose control because the comedian is in charge, we enjoy seeing him exposed to mortal danger, since his survival is assured.

King Lear and Madam Bovary are subject to *time* and must die, but comic figures exist in a realm that is impervious to time and change. Charlie is always Charlie, Mickey Mouse always Mickey, and Punch always Punch. We recognize them as soon as they appear, no matter in what settings or circumstances. They constitute the stuff we deem eternal—life itself—even if, at time's end, it must return to cosmic dust.

Comic figures don't die, and on the few occasions they do their death is undone. English clowns traditionally came on stage crying, "Here we are again!" Harlequin made his miraculous escapes through unseen trapdoors in the walls or floor of the pantomime theater,[6] and in French *feeriques*—stage performances that had their origin in fairy tales and were a source for the magical shorts of Méliès—the figures were beheaded or hacked to pieces only to become whole again, like the creatures in our animated cartoons.

It is thought that Attic Comedy had its origin in a festival celebrating the return of spring and the beginning of the growing season—a fertility rite that invoked "the expulsion of death and the induction of life."[7] Tragic trilogies were followed by a satyr play featuring instinct figures—just as Road Runner and Wile E. Coyote keep enacting variations of their death and resurrection. We engage in a similar ritual on roller coasters, with our screams turning into laughter whenever we come out of a sheer drop.

One of the few things that can be said with certainty about the life force in which the comic is rooted is that it seeks to survive and perpetuate itself. No scientific explanation has yet accounted for it. It remains as inexplicable as the energy that created the universe, and would seem directly linked to it.

D

The tragic figure is highly differentiated while the comedian appears, like most of us, to be made of common stuff. But we noted that the great clown is often more individualized than Oedipus, and—at least on the surface—as different from us as Hamlet, since he acts out what most of us suppress.

We noted, too, that though Punch is aggressive, disrespectful, and vindictive, we identify with him, for he gives us access to energies we need to survive, especially if we are poor or feel inadequate.

In the shorts, Charlie is impervious to feeling, a primitive creature who owes his survival to unconscious anarchic drives. Chaplin's early films are swirls of energy, like the canvases of Van Gogh and Jackson Pollock—driven by the very forces most of us have learned to inhibit. Were we to meet someone who acts them out in life, we would steer clear of him.

The central figure in noncomic fictions can be pure and innocent, like Snow White and Juliet. But in life we can afford their purity—the innocence of the child—only in the safety of home. Indeed, we often owe our survival to the far less pure energies that animate both comic heroes and villains. In noncomic fiction, the innocent usually perish. They end up safe and happy only in melodrama—with its sentimental slant on reality—and in fairy tales, where supernatural powers protect them.

Flight is often the easiest way to survive. To avoid conflict and danger even large animals tend to turn tail unless they are cornered. We, too, are cautious creatures by nature, and though the human male may be instinctively aggressive, risking his life in battle must be drilled into him. Significantly, the comic hero is a coward and lives to fight another day, while the brave hero of tragedy ends up dead.

Day by day, our own escapes are far more likely to be psychological than physical, with evasion and camouflage the most common forms of flight. The situations we find ourselves in resemble those of W. C. Fields in *It's a Gift*, not the physical crises that confront Charlie and Buster.

As a storekeeper in a small town, Fields, as Harold Bissonette, is trapped in the constrictive setting of marriage and family and victimized by women and children. Even a blind and deaf man can terrorize him and wreak havoc on his business.[8] Bissonette survives by withdrawing into a shell of fraud and evasion that keeps everyone and everything at a distance—no doubt a defensive posture Fields himself adopted early in life. The film lays bare the sense of helplessness underlying the aggression and bluster he displays in most of his work. His mumbling speech is largely addressed to himself, for even speaking so others can understand could make him vulnerable. Being understood, moreover, is pointless. There is nothing to be done, nothing worth doing. His slow responses bespeak his fatalism: his view of the world is gloomy, misanthropic, and paranoid. It serves as a counterpoint to the bustling community all around. At the end of the film, he is alone with his dog and his drink on an orange plantation—as safe and content as he will ever be.

In life, Fields was as defensive-aggressive as the characters he plays, and as disconnected. When J. Edgar Hoover—apparently an admirer—called on him, Fields kept addressing him as Herbert. There is no record of Hoover's response.[9]

E

If a fight can't be evaded, the comic figure is bound by no principles. With his survival at stake, or merely to gain an advantage, he will use anything and everything within reach. Unlike Oedipus or Captain Ahab, who are forced into a single-minded pursuit and governed by an internal or external code, Charlie and Punch are instinctive opportunists, who go wherever the way opens up. They are the very opposites of the figures in Bergson's high comedy, who never leave their rut. The comedian—like the Joker in a deck of cards—has no assigned place or fixed identity, and will assume any role that serves his purpose.

> When Cary Grant interviewed a Hollywood agent who was hoping to represent him, he asked the man whether he was Jewish. The agent hesitated for a moment, then said, "Not necessarily."[10]

Chaplin says, "We must laugh in the face of our helplessness against the forces of nature or go insane."[11]

We noted that when a situation is grim or hopeless, a joke can serve as a psychological escape.

> A nineteenth-century anecdote tells of a Jew who was challenged to a duel and honor bound to accept. Certain he would die, he told his opponent, "If I'm late, start without me."[12]

> In the 1930s, German Jews said that the pessimists among them went into exile, the optimists into concentration camps.[13]

> When he toured below the Mason-Dixon Line, Fats Waller said he went down by Greyhound and came back by bloodhound.

> Jimmy Durante once forgot his lines in front of a live TV audience. Unfazed, he turned to his fellow performer, John Wayne, and said, "Who's got the next line—me or you?"

Years ago I made the mistake of asking our three-year-old to carry a five-pound jar of honey into the house. He tried to put it on the dining room table, but dropped and broke it. When I came in with the rest of the groceries, he was standing in a lake of honey with his thumb in his mouth. He knew I was upset, and looked up at me with a worried face. Then he said, "Funny honey."

As James Cagney said, "If they're laughing, they can't get mad at you."

The comedian's skill is central to his performance and is far more obviously on display than the craft of the tragic actor. His evident mastery—physical in low comedy and verbal in high—makes us laugh with pleasure. Like the control of the great athlete, it appears to empower the spectator, and countermands our own fear of stumbling, fumbling, and failing.

Until recently, most comedians made their first appearance in front of a live audience who, through their immediate reactions, helped to shape the performance. In music halls and vaudeville theaters, the audience was knowledgeable and discriminating. Like today's spectators at hockey games, bullfights, and rock concerts, they knew the tradition in which the performers worked, could appreciate the subtlest variations of a familiar routine, and had no patience with inferior material. Their instantaneous and vocal response helped shape the work of Chaplin, Keaton, Laurel, Fields, and the Marx Brothers.

Today, only stand-up comedians learn their craft in the pressure cooker of live performances.

The speed intrinsic to the comic is central in most displays of skill and control—whether on the violin or in a series of tongue twisters. Art Tatum's breakneck runs on the piano make us laugh with the same amazed delight as Keaton's rapid execution of maneuvers we can't perform at any speed.[14]

A quick response is the key to winning many games, just as it can determine victory or survival on the battlefield. Though we are far more often in psychological than physical danger, here, too, speed matters. Freud notes that a quick-witted response to a verbal attack is apt to make witnesses laugh with pleasure.

> Lady Astor told Churchill, who was known for his antifeminist positions, "If I were your wife, Mr. Churchill, I'd put poison in your coffee." Churchill shot back, "And if you were my wife, I'd drink it."

> President Calvin Coolidge and Mrs. Coolidge were visiting a poultry farm, but touring different parts. When Mrs. Coolidge asked her guide how often the rooster performed his duty, she was told several times a day. "Tell that to Mr. Coolidge," she instructed an aide. The message was delivered, and the president promptly inquired whether the rooster performed with just one hen.
> "No," he was told, "Each time with a different hen."
> "Tell that to Mrs. Coolidge."[15]

Focused as they are on externals, many comedians are expert mimics.

Like stage magic, mimicry delights us with its approximation of the real. But whereas the magician hides his craft, mimicry lets us see both the person mimed and the mimic himself. We laugh both at the obvious discrepancy between them and at the skill and economy of the performer.

In *The Gold Rush*, Chaplin transforms his face and two dinner rolls into a ballerina. We see nothing more than his face and hands and marvel at the likeness he is able to conjure up without tricking us. Conversely, the illusion in magic seems perfect, but we never forget we are being deceived.

> Marlon Brando says his exceptional mimetic gift was honed by emotional insecurity: "When you are a child who is

unwanted or unwelcome . . . you look for an identity that will be acceptable. . . . You make a habit of studying people, finding out the way they talk, the answers . . . they give and their points of view; then, in a form of self-defense, you reflect what's on their faces and how they act."[16]

The economy of means used by the comedian or athlete is evidence of his skill. Chaplin gets maximal use out of each situation and object. Like Keaton, he would elaborate an idea through improvisation and not relinquish it until he had exhausted every comic possibility it offered.

Among the poor, little is discarded until it falls apart. Raised in poverty and playing to spectators who had few resources, Chaplin's aesthetic is one of scarcity—the very opposite of the Marx Brothers, who waste or trash everything they get their hands on.

My grandparents were poor and lived in a basement. On Mondays, my grandmother would buy a live chicken and let it roam through their two rooms. Night after night, my mother could hear its beak pecking on the floor as it fed on the plentiful cockroaches. Then, on Sunday, it was killed and served for dinner, and on Monday my grandmother brought home a new chicken.

After working his way out of poverty, my grandfather wanted a chauffeur-driven car. He acquired a taxi and driver instead, so they could take him where he wanted to go and collect fares until he needed them again.

Like fear and necessity, poverty is a rich source of invention.

> At a men's clothing store in an immigrant quarter, the sales clerk pretended to be deaf. When a customer asked about the cost of an item, he would call to his boss at the back of the store, "How much is the beautiful navy blue suit?"
>
> His boss shouted back, "Forty dollars," and the "deaf" clerk would tell the customer, "Twenty."
>
> Many men plunked down their money and quickly left the store, delighted with their bargains.[17]

Like all pressure, the risk of exposure may produce an inventive and unexpected response.

> The Gaon of Vilna, a renowned Jewish scholar, traveled far and wide with his coachman, Yossele. Wherever they went, the Gaon was welcomed and celebrated while his coachman had to wait outside. One winter night he heard his coachman mutter, "I wish I were the Gaon of Vilna and *he* were the coachman!"
>
> To reconcile Yossele to his station, the Gaon changed clothes with him. When they came to the next town, Yossele went into the rabbi's house in his master's finery, while the Gaon stayed out in the cold, waiting for the inevitable disaster.
>
> Inside the festive room, the learned men of the community wined and dined Yossele. Then they escorted him to the synagogue, and asked him to explain a passage in the Talmud that had long puzzled them.
>
> "That?!" said Yossele, greatly surprised. "Even my coachman knows the answer!" He called in the Gaon, who played along and explained the passage to the astonished assembly.[18]

Watching someone outwit others in comedy or life is apt to make us laugh.

> When the Postal Service announced it would henceforth return all mail without the correct postage to the sender, our daughter addressed letters without stamps to herself, and put down the names of her friends as senders. The post office delivered every one without charge.

> Carol Burnett, whose parents were alcoholics, lived with her grandmother on the ground floor of an apartment building. The old lady worked, so Carol spent a great deal of time by herself or playing with a small boy, who waited for her in the lobby until she came home from school.

One afternoon, she entered the building and walked right past her friend as though she didn't know him. She went quickly to her apartment, changed clothes, climbed out the window, and walked right back into the building—this time recognizing and greeting him as she did every day.

When he told her that someone who looked exactly like her had come in a moment earlier, Carol got very excited and said it must be her twin sister, Karen, who was expected for a visit.

During the next two days she had great fun being alternately Carol and Karen and making him think he was seeing twins.[19]

Lonely or unhappy children are apt to develop imaginative and inventive faculties that allow them to escape their situation.

As a student, Bertolt Brecht was in danger of failing a class that would have put him back an entire school year. Teachers in Germany marked errors in red ink, with points subtracted on the margin to arrive at a grade. When the teacher, who disliked Brecht, returned his final exam, it was covered with red marks: Brecht had failed.

Faced with repeating the year in a school he hated, Brecht used red ink to add marks where he had made no errors, and subtracted additional points in the margin. He then went to see the teacher, placed the paper in front of him, and—no doubt humbly—wondered what was wrong with the answers he had himself queered. A pattern of wrongful markings emerged, and the teacher—whose dislike of Brecht was well known—became frightened of the consequences and changed his grade to a pass. It didn't occur to him to add up the subtracted points in the margin, or he would have discovered Brecht's ruse.

F

The Latin *joculare* means both "to joke" and "to juggle," and traditional clowns were often jugglers. Early in life, Chaplin wanted to be a "comedy juggler," and both he and Keaton juggle objects—some as large as the house on the edge of the abyss or the locomotive in *The General*—objects that in turn juggle *them*.

Before turning to comedy, W. C. Fields was a world-renowned juggler, who—according to a contemporary account—had "a trick of juggling twenty-five cigar boxes on end, with a little rubber ball on top. First the ball was dropped and caught in his other hand; then each box followed in succession, the top one falling with machine-like precision without disturbing the boxes beneath it."[20]

Off stage, Fields sometimes ate his meals with a beer bottle balanced on top of his head,[21] perhaps to practice holding his head motionless, and he "often played tennis with a racket in one hand and a martini glass in the other," no doubt to distract his opponent.[22] Once he unnerved Humphrey Bogart, who was ahead in a game of table tennis, by catching the ball in his mouth.[23]

Unless they are sick, animals don't often stumble or fall; they rarely leave their familiar terrain and take few chances. But we—who exist at some remove from our instincts and physical reality and keep extending or overextending ourselves—live with the constant threat of losing our balance.

The loss of our physical or psychological equilibrium is alarming, and since the situations in stories address our fears, we get pleasure from seeing fictive figures lose their balance and, in comedy, recover it. Surprises in life, on stage, and in games are apt to throw the players, and we enjoy watching them respond.

The tightrope walker is never more than a step away from disaster and stands in for all of us. Since we watch safely from below, we want his risk to be as immediate and real as possible. No one would come to see him perform on a rope two feet off the ground, though the skill required is no different. Nor do we want to see his balance easily achieved, but derive pleasure and satisfaction from seeing him teeter—in danger of injury or death—before righting himself.

The graver the risk, the greater our tension, sense of participation, and relief/pleasure when the performer survives. W. C. Fields deliberately fumbled the objects he juggled before keeping them in the air successfully. No deception was involved; his control was in doubt every time, and the risk of failure was real. Niccolò Paganini deliberately broke several strings on his violin one after the other, yet continued playing unfazed and without dropping a note. Harry Houdini asked spectators to hold their breath while he was submerged in a tank of water, manacled and in a straitjacket. Members of the audience who took up the challenge had to catch their breath repeatedly, while he stayed under water until his death by drowning seemed certain.

Quiz show audiences, who invariably want contestants to risk their winnings instead of taking them home, may be acting out a less primitive form of the impulse that prompts some people to yell "Jump!" at a would-be suicide.

We are mesmerized by performers who court uncertainty and risk. Watching John Belushi, we sense that he himself didn't know what he would do next, just as the paintings of Van Gogh derive immediacy and force from an energy loosed on the canvas that seems barely under the artist's control.

The endangered performer is usually a soloist—a loner like the hero of old stories, who must fight the monster or villain by himself. He can lean on no one, just as *we* are expected to maintain our self-control and balance without help.

Fittingly, the actor's name appears above Shakespeare's and the pianist's above Ludwig van Beethoven's, for they are at risk of public failure, while the playwright and composer are safe in their graves.

Artists who don't work in front of a live audience are under less immediate pressure. The filmmaker can reshoot scenes and the painter destroy failed pictures. But the stand-up comedian is engaged in a high-wire act. When his jokes misfire, he "dies." Moreover, his "death"—unlike Hamlet's or Lear's—won't leave us comfortably distanced. Like the actor who flubs his lines during a live performance, his failure distresses us and may, indeed, so enrage a club audience that they heap insults on him.[24]

Most of us try to stay in our comfort zone, where we appear to have a measure of control, and in the company of people we understand and trust. Whenever possible, we avoid uncertainty, ambiguity, and surprises.

Some, however—with performers prominently among them—are exiled by birth or circumstance. Since family relationships, where most of us find security, acceptance, and a sense of belonging, are closed off to them, they try to win public approval through exceptional achievements, and keep risking failure in hope of validation. But even when they succeed, the affirmation is likely to be temporary. Their self-doubt and anxiety are but briefly allayed, and soon drives them back onto the high-wire.

A highly accomplished juggler says, "A juggler is not a secure person. The juggler, by definition, *should* be . . . insecure."[25]

When I was twenty-one, an old Irishman operated the elevator in the film building where I worked, and since I was sent on errands all day, I spent a good deal of time in his company.

One morning, after a famous entertainer and his entourage got off the car, Gary turned to me and said, "Who needs it?!"

Who indeed?!

That was sixty years ago, but I have never forgotten Gary or his question. For the best of reasons, he couldn't fathom why some are driven to excessive efforts that require an exaggerated sense of their own importance.

I know now that they don't choose their fate. But sometimes their experience allows them to speak for all who, like them, live marginalized, disenfranchised lives—be it for economic, social, or inner reasons.

CHAPTER SEVEN

Childhood

A

Charlie is frail and small, often the smallest figure on the screen. Like a child, he has trouble walking and keeps falling down or tripping over his own feet. His clothes don't fit, and his trousers are too large. He is forever trying to make friends with those who are bigger and stronger, and will jump into another man's lap to ingratiate himself, to stop him from hitting, or to express gratitude.

In *The Pawnshop*, he and his fellow clerk pounce on each other as soon as the storekeeper leaves and go into an elaborate charade of working the instant he returns. When Edna surprises them in the midst of battle, Charlie flings himself on the floor and goes into a crying act to arouse her maternal sympathy.

He is infinitely changeable and thrives on every kind of contradiction. He shifts effortlessly from stupidity to ingenuity, scraps like a street urchin one moment and displays exaggerated drawing room manners the next, waddles like a toddler, yet has a dancer's control over his body.

In his films, inanimate objects have a life of their own, as they do in fairy tales and animated cartoons. *One A.M.* is an extended encounter between Charlie and the world of things, climaxed by his battle with a Murphy bed. But objects are not just enemies; time and again they save his skin: a lampshade over his head turns him into a piece of furniture and fools the policemen who are chasing him. Things have unexpected uses and are rich in opportunities for play.

As we grow up, most of us lose touch with the pristine experience of what things *feel* like. We surrender our proximate senses—the concrete, tactile relationship to our surroundings we have in child-hood—and depend increasingly on the abstracted, aphysical reporting of our eyes and ears.

But not Chaplin, particularly in the shorts. When Keaton in *The Navigator* is trapped underwater, the effect is graphic, but the water in the World War I dugout of *Shoulder Arms* is sensory and wet. Charlie lies down on his submerged cot, fluffs out his soggy pillow, rests his cheek on it, and covers himself with a sopping blanket.

It is often said that Charlie represents the common man. But Chaplin's gifts and skills mark him as altogether uncommon, and it is his access to childhood that endows his work with universality and permanence.

Stan Laurel had understudied Chaplin on the English music hall stage, where both of them spoke and sang in adult routines. But once he teamed him up with Oliver Hardy, Laurel, like many silent screen comedians, became a child.[1]

Harpo Marx can't speak and has the attention span of an infant. When he hides his head under a rug, he assumes that since he can't see, he can't be seen. He identifies with animals and doesn't just talk to a frog but understands what the frog is saying. Close to his instincts and without impulse control, he chases after every nubile woman, though he wouldn't know what to do if he caught up with her. Like an infant, he is delighted with himself, and like an infant he is harmless.

In *It's a Gift*, W. C. Fields plays a husband and father but is effec-tively the child in the family. He treats his son as a sibling, and when his wife instructs him to share a sandwich with the boy, he carefully folds the meat onto *his* half of the bread and hands his son the other. In search of a picnic area, he drives across a manicured lawn, hits the statue of a large nude, and smashes it to bits. When his wife screams hysterically, "You've hit the Venus de Milo!" he mutters, "She ran right in front of my car."

In *A Dog's Life*, Charlie is starved and penniless. He steals a bun from a cart when the vendor isn't looking—then gets into a competitive game with the man that ceases to have any connection with hunger or money. It ends only when Charlie has eaten every bun in the pile without getting caught.

In *Duck Soup*, Groucho knows from the start that his reflection in the broken mirror is one of his brothers, but delights in playing his part in the game until he can catch him out.

Comedians who depend on access to their childhood often find themselves trapped in it.

Though in comments about his work Chaplin never calls the Tramp a child, he was well aware that if Charlie was to remain Charlie, he couldn't grow up.[2] A man can change and remain a man, but the child becomes an adult. He knew that if he spoke he would become conscious and lose access to the wide range of his multiple, often contradictory, qualities. It would mean not only abandoning the physical, largely unconscious realm of childhood but also his own highly refined and universally understood comic style.

In *City Lights*, when some of the characters speak, they make a bleating sound, as if Charlie were becoming aware of speech though he could not understand or use it. As he makes his way through a series of comic rejections, he remains unchanged and unconscious, with nothing to prepare us for the last scene when, from one moment to the next, Charlie ceases to be the Little Tramp and becomes a conscious, suffering man. In a startling shift, the blithe unawareness that has protected him is breached. But almost as soon as we realize we are watching a very different Charlie, who—for the first time—sees himself as others do, the story is over and the screen goes dark.

The end of *City Lights* suggests that there is no return to the Tramp, but *Modern Times* brings him back one last time. A few authority figures in the film speak intelligibly—like grown-ups in the world of a child—and at the end we actually hear Charlie's voice. But he sings rather than talks, and in a language he has concocted himself. Then Charlie disappears forever. The broad-based, inclusive, and contradictory child splinters into quasi-adult figures with their distinct and limited identities.

B

For some time after we are born, we are totally helpless. When we are in pain, in need, or fearful, all we can do is cry. But since we are barely conscious, we don't register our helplessness, and in later years what we experienced is shrouded in the amnesia of early childhood.

We noted that the family gradually instills the conviction in us that our will is effective and free. But Chaplin, during the most vulnerable years of his life, had no family to shelter him and must have experienced his helplessness viscerally. His father was an alcoholic who moved in with another woman, and his mother, who tried to support her children by singing on stage, was never well. When she was taken to an insane asylum, the authorities placed Chaplin and his half-brother Sidney in an orphanage where children were flogged. After a brief family reunion, Hanna Chaplin was again taken to the asylum, Sidney went to sea, and Charles—terrified of being returned to the orphanage—lived on the street and supported himself with jobs he often lost the day he was hired. When he was twelve, he found work in a traveling theater company that became a kind of home.

If his childhood resembles the dark ordeal at the outset of many fairy tales, his worldwide success evokes their miraculous endings. But Chaplin never forgot how utterly beholden his life had been to circumstances beyond his control. Moreover, his gifts were so exceptional that, like many artists of genius, he knew they were gifts as much as accomplishments. Though he controlled every aspect of his work, he consistently cast himself as a figure at the mercy of impersonal forces.

He often derived his plots from melodrama—itself rooted in folk and fairy tales, where the action is rarely determined by human will and effort. In *The Gold Rush*, a storm blows Charlie and Big Jim to their fateful meeting in the cabin; a bear threatens to kill them but instead saves them from starvation; another storm blows them to the edge of an abyss where, after nearly falling to their death, they discover Jim's lost gold mine; and a final coincidence reunites Charlie, now a millionaire, with Georgia and allows her to prove she cares about him.

As Chaplin says, "Fate—it is always fate—played its little joke."[3]

At the end of *Balloonatics*, Buster Keaton and his girl are drifting blissfully downstream in a canoe, unaware they are headed for a deadly cataract. We see them drift toward it, but at the very instant we expect them to plunge to their death, the camera pulls back to reveal that the canoe is tethered to a balloon that carries them over the edge of the falls without a bump. They continue their airborne voyage safely— innocent of the disaster they have escaped. As in *The Gold Rush*, a highly accomplished clown has bent his gifts and skill to make himself appear a lucky fool.

Though Chaplin used his own control to make us lose ours in laughter, he was himself clearly compelled by the situations in his films. They keep repeating, and while we delight in the comic surprises he springs, they allowed him to reenact the frightening shocks of his early life. As he told his second wife, Lita Grey, "I don't get pleasure from my work. I get relief."[4]

Baudelaire says, "Genius is no more than childhood recaptured at will."[5] But *at will* suggests a degree of freedom that Chaplin's life and work don't bear out. Rather, like Freud's joke teller, he is someone who can't stop himself.[6] He was nakedly exposed to unpredictable and overwhelming experiences in childhood, and could never forget them. Unable to shake a deep sense and fear of helplessness, he kept reliving and exorcising it in his work.

Other artists are no freer. Joan Miró says, "It is difficult for me to talk about my painting, since it is always born in a state of hallucination, brought on by some shock or other—whether objective or subjective—for which I am not the least responsible."

Auguste Rodin reported that, on a visit to his studio, the actress Eleonora Duse told him she would rather have been a milliner. Speaking from experience, Rodin added, "As if she had a choice."

Artie Shaw said that when he almost cut off his finger chopping firewood, his first thought was, "I'll never have to play the clarinet again."[7]

A sense of helplessness could be said to inform every narrative, even when the action of the figures seems to countermand its preclusive structure. The storyteller, by *telling* the story, proves—as Chaplin does in making his films—that he is not just a passive victim. But he can never free himself of an underlying sense that we are not in charge.

Since that is the burden of all stories—and a common source of religious feeling—it is a sense or awareness that may have been with us from the dawn of consciousness.

In our own day, human control over events seems ever more tenuous.

When the Yiddish writer H. Leivick was a schoolboy in Poland during the 1930s, his teacher told the story of the sacrifice of Isaac. It upset the boy so deeply that he burst into tears. The teacher tried to reassure him by pointing out that God had sent an angel to intervene, but the boy was not consoled: "What would have happened if the angel had come too late?"[8]

Leivick himself escaped the Holocaust, but for millions the angel never came. They suffered and died in camps that became an analog of both human evil and utter helplessness. After they were opened, many in the West found it difficult to maintain their Judeo-Christian faith in a caring God or divine justice.

Those who survived the Holocaust often owed their lives to the courage of comrades or to their own exceptional constitutions. But many were spared by pure chance. A quirk of fate saved hundreds of thousands in Hungary, when the fascist dictator Miklós Horthy became convinced that an allied bombing raid, designed to achieve purely military objectives, was intended as retribution for his extermination of three hundred thousand Jews. He was so disturbed that he ordered the deportations stopped.

We have substituted human agency for our faith in an all-powerful divinity, but it is hard to believe that we are in charge of much in our lives.

From the evidence all around us, and despite our faith in freedom, it is hard to avoid the conclusion that we do not *deserve* what befalls us—neither the good nor the bad.

The leak in our confidence and our uncertain agency have always been the predicate of stories, both of the tragic and the comical.

C

Chaplin told an interviewer, "It's very hard to respond to affection. I can respond to antagonism. But love and affection . . ."[9]

Most people, even in our large, fragmented communities, feel basically connected to life and to others—a connection that is self-understood and largely unquestioned. But in many artists and comedians this fundamental biological link—our taproot—is damaged. They grow up without faith or trust in others, and often feel they haven't the right to exist.

A young singer who lived with W. C. Fields during the last decade of his life has left a description of him.

> [He] harbored a deep distrust of any member of the human race, and when I first moved in with him, that included me. He would purposely leave sums of money in conspicuous places around the house, thinking it might tempt me. Once I saw a pile of money on a coffee table. Counting it, I noted there was $365. Feeling impish, I added five dollars of my own money, but he made no mention of the increase.[10]

On another occasion, he asked her to bring $50,000 in cash from the bank to see if she would run off with it.[11]

Her account of his death gives us a glimpse of his heartbreaking, fiercely defended inner desert.

> On Christmas Day, shortly before noon, he said to me, "Grab everything and run. The vultures are coming. . . ." "Goddamn," he repeated, and his eyes opened wider than I'd ever seen them. His voice was the rustling and crackling of dry leaves. "Goddamn the whole friggin' world and everyone in it but you, Carlotta." Those were his last words. He was shaken by a violent stomach hemorrhage. Moments later he was dead, at the age of sixty-eight.[12]

Mistrustful of intimate relationships, the comedian and artist depends far more than the rest of us on alternate connections. His work and its effect on an audience become his way of belonging.

Janis Joplin said to an interviewer that no man could give her what thousands of her fans did, and when a young man told Dorothy Parker how much he liked her poems, she said, "Will you marry me?"[13]

Comedians can be haunted by their insecurities. Chaplin told Lita Grey, "Almost everything frightens me."

We have all heard and used the words *heart attack* many times, but only a comedian, Mel Brooks, would think of saying, "I hope my heart won't attack me." It's funny, but its source is clearly fear.

Fred Astaire's accomplishments and success didn't resolve the deep-seated anxiety that made him rehearse his routines for weeks before starting a movie. Like most who depend on public approval, he was terrified of public failure and its physical manifestation. Stand-up comedians know it as "flop sweat." Fields says about his time as a juggler:

> Though I was only a kid, I had sense enough to know that I must work my mind and not just my hands. If I hadn't realized that, I'd be on the shelf today. People would be saying, "Bill Fields? Oh yes! He used to be a juggler."

Despite his success and wealth, an ingrained insecurity prompted him to add a comedy routine to his juggling act, and drove him from vaudeville to the movies and radio. Like Chaplin and Groucho, he hoarded money and food. Groucho was so stingy that his wife and son took to stealing change from his trouser pockets, and he was known to serve a single chicken to six dinner guests.

Fields, after sleeping poorly for years, became so anxious and restless at night that he often tumbled out of bed, and during the last years of his life took to sleeping in a gigantic antique cradle.[14] The sound of rain had a calming effect on him and, during his stay at a rehab center, the woman who shared his life would spray water from a garden hose on the tin roof of their bungalow to help him fall asleep.[15]

He left her a small monthly sum in his will.

The outsider artist/comedian serves the community by remaining open to the very fears we try to ignore. But even as he succeeds in channeling them and giving them a recognizable, manageable shape, he may not feel in command of them, and when he does, it's not for long.

We expect him to stay on top of the wave in his work, like a surfer, but he himself is often at risk. Many artists live in danger of being overwhelmed by fear, and seldom feel safe from failure and exile.

As Paul Cézanne says, "With every brushstroke I risk my life."

D

From fear and mistrust to rage is a short step.

Many comedians are imperfectly socialized. The artist we applaud for voicing a forbidden truth can't always convert his anger and destructive energy to creative use. The raw forces that engender his work may seep into his life, and living in close proximity to a monster—the one inside him—can turn him into one.[16]

Groucho was abusive to women both on the screen and off. He took delight not just in beating his first wife on the tennis court but in humiliating her. To disconcert and infuriate her, he'd sing:

"Just hit the ball to Mother,
And you won't have to hit another."[17]

Passing through customs on the way home from Europe, he asked her in a loud whisper, "What did you do with the opium? D'you still have it in your girdle?" She had to submit to a skin search.[18] "On a visit to his daughter's school, he surveyed the young women and said, 'It's hard to believe that in ten years most of you girls will be collecting alimony.'" The headmistress wasn't amused and asked his humiliated daughter to escort him home.[19] During a visit to Parliament with his family, he "stood up in the visitor's gallery . . . and at the top of his voice started singing, 'When Irish Eyes Are Smiling.'" They were thrown out and asked never to return.[20]

Groucho had a low opinion of his brothers as entertainers. He thought Chico was "a fair dialectician and a lousy pianist, and . . . felt that Harpo was a great pantomimist and very accomplished at the art of making funny faces—if one cared for that type of comedy, which he didn't."[21] He said, "The only sure way to test a gag was to try it out on Zeppo. If he liked it, we threw it out."[22]

Harpo found a more benign expression for his aggression in practical jokes. On an official 1933 tour of the Soviet Union—the first by an American artist—he told party officials in Leningrad that he was a distant cousin of Karl Marx.

The source of most humor in fear, rage, and pain is well understood. Unlike most of us, comedians laugh when it hurts.

> To make good vaudeville, you take the most tragic situation possible, a situation to make a mortician shudder, and try to bring out its burlesque side. . . . All comics are sad: They always think "sad" first.[23]

Fields says, "I never saw anything funny that wasn't terrible. If it causes pain, it's funny; if it doesn't, it isn't. I try to pretend that it isn't painful."[24] He called the African American entertainer Bert Williams, whom he greatly admired, "The funniest man I ever saw, and the saddest man I ever knew."

Even comic strips can derive laughter from pain. Charles Schulz believed that "you can't create humor out of happiness." "All the loves in [*Peanuts*] are unrequited; all the baseball games are lost; all the test scores are D-minuses; the Great Pumpkin never comes."[25]

By converting pain into humor, comedians not only distance themselves from it but make a temporary connection with others that substitutes for the close relationships they can't trust. Of course the money comedy earns provides added consolation. Woody Allen says that when he wants to be funny he hits his occipital bone: "I do it for the money."

Like pain and helplessness, rejection can itself become a source of humor. Rodney Dangerfield claimed his mother didn't breastfeed him because she liked him as a friend.[26]

As George Bernard Shaw says, if you have a skeleton in your closet, you may as well make it dance.

A childhood sense of isolation and difference can leave the artist or comedian seeking a state of perfect harmony not just in his work—where he might actually achieve it—but in life.

Fields once told a friend, "That was the part that got next to me—all was going fine, but I didn't have anything, somehow. I was on a train rushing toward a good place, but I couldn't seem to get there."[27]

Alberto Giacometti said sometimes he couldn't sleep because the relationship between his shoes and the bed was incorrect.

For good reason, Louis-Ferdinand Céline calls the dream of perfection—of undivided wholeness—a kind of death. It can destroy relationships in life, since they are bound to be imperfect.

Perfect harmony, or oneness, is possible only in art, infancy, ritual, and death.

E

A cat doesn't doubt its own existence, but human beings can and do. Consciousness weakens our creature connection to life and ourselves—our nature-granted right to be.

When we first become aware, we derive our existence as separate beings from the response of others. D. W. Winnicott says that the infant first senses he exists when he sees himself reflected in the mirror of his mother's face. Perhaps this primary experience initiates our lifelong dependence on being recognized and confirmed by others.[28]

The community uses our need for recognition to turn us into good citizens. Starting in early childhood, we are given to understand that proof, or approval, of our existence and worth is conditional on our behavior. In response, most of us adapt to what others need and expect of us.[29]

Paradoxically, we are expected to be freestanding yet observant of communal standards and rules—separate yet dependent.[30] The double bind may make us intensely uncomfortable if we become aware of it.

We used to derive our existence and identity from being connected to a place and acknowledged by a stable, seemingly static community. As the phrase has it, we knew and kept our place.

But once we started moving, and today many move frequently, the places we live in and the people we live among can no longer be counted on to substantiate our existence.

In his travels through nineteenth-century America, Alexis de Tocqueville was surprised by our pervasive anxiety, and could see no reason for it. But it may be the price we pay for our democratic ethos and our vaunted freedom.[31]

The constant changes we are neither free to choose nor reject burden many of us not just economically but psychologically. With no one and nothing fixed in place, we must continually adapt to new situations and new people, and find it increasingly difficult to maintain an identity, at least in the traditional sense. In evolving a new, fluid, situational sense of self, we are understandably insecure, and may indeed remain permanently anxious.[32]

Most of us try to stay connected and strive for approval. But a frail sense of self and a ravenous need for confirmation drive some into isolation, where their existence can be neither undermined *nor* affirmed.[33]

My own tenuous hold is brought home to me whenever someone steps on my toes. If he apologizes, my faint physical discomfort doesn't bother me. But if he fails to acknowledge it, I become angry. Though my reaction is absurd, I feel he has undermined my existence.

More than most people, my wife needed the acknowledgment of others to feel she had a place in life. When I asked her why she disliked a city we had visited in Eastern Europe, she said, "No one on the street smiled at me—not even the children." Late in life, she told me, "Anyone who smiles at me is my friend." When recalling her childhood, she sometimes mentioned a clubhouse her father had built for her. One day I asked her who was in her club. She had to think for a moment before she said, "Anyone who wanted to be."

F

Starting at the age of three, Buster Keaton was featured in the vaudeville act of his parents. His mother, Myra, had sewn a handle into the back of his jacket, and his father tossed him around the stage, shooting him through the air like a "ballistic missile." On one occasion he allegedly fired him into an unruly audience.

As significant as the physical and psychological impact of their stage act on the boy were the increasingly tense off-stage relationships. As Joe Keaton aged and could no longer dominate the act or his family physically, he became a heavy drinker—fiercely competitive with his son and violently abusive of both his wife and Buster.

On the screen, Keaton is a small, spare figure often seen in long shots and dwarfed by empty landscapes. Though he is at the center of the action, he seems less a presence than an absence. Like Charlie, he must fight for his survival, but while Charlie reacts to everything and we never doubt his existence, Buster underreacts and doesn't seem altogether real.

Known as the Great Stone Face, Keaton moves only when he must and shows no emotion, even if his expression is stoic rather than blank—a mask to hide his feelings. His father had kept him from smiling on stage, and while he smiled freely in life, he couldn't get himself to smile on camera. Perhaps performing took him back to childhood experiences that had undermined his self-determination, even as they charged him with the energy and need to perform.

Keaton is never showy and pays us no attention, whereas Chaplin, at least in the shorts, often looks at the camera and plays directly to us. He draws attention to himself and his performance, courts the audience, and on occasion even takes a bow.

Everything about Charlie, from his clothes to his walk, is different and peculiar, but we would hardly notice Keaton in a crowd; only his hat is distinctive. Whereas Chaplin's gags are intricate, elaborate, and milked of every comic possibility, Keaton's stunts are executed and completed rapidly. His scenes are sketchy and never, like Chaplin's, dense or intense.

Chaplin sometimes referred to Charlie as a dreamer, but it is Keaton who moves through his stories like a somnambulist, dissociated and oblivious until his survival is at stake. Unlike Charlie, he makes little effort to connect with others. He is stiff, far less physical, and never visceral or tactile. His films are visual, almost linear in their imagery, with the figures seldom hitting or even touching each other.

Buster has no ego, and his identity is often in doubt. A dream in *Sherlock, Jr.* transforms a hapless movie projectionist into the Great Detective, who, in turn, morphs into several other roles. In *The Play House*, multiple Keatons appear both onstage and in the audience, as do twin girls. He is engaged to one of them, though he is never sure to whom; before the wedding he marks his bride with an X. At one point in the film, Buster plays a monkey, who—in turn—is dressed as and trained to mimic a man.

Uncertainty about himself and the world may be the one thing Keaton feels sure of. He builds not just his films but sometimes the physical settings on it. The walls in *The Play House* and the buildings during the storm in *Steamboat Bill, Jr.* keep collapsing or vanishing.

Though it is tempting to attribute complex appearance/reality games to him, after a childhood spent on stage and backstage what *we* call "appearance" may well have been utterly real to him. The theater was the stage on which the painfully real drama of his family life was enacted.

His sketchy figure embodies the very doubt that other comedians hide and countermand in their work. Like many artists, he was—as an *adult*—fated to live with the uncertain, permeable boundaries of childhood. Whatever was happening around him flowed into him, and he in turn flowed out into the world. His life and work exemplify the uncertain identity of the actor, writer, and painter. They allow him to become another, to lend himself utterly to a feeling, situation, or landscape—an uncertainty, absence, or "negative capability" that is a critical element of the creative process—an absence that, paradoxically, enables him to generate proof of his existence.

Though Chaplin identified with Charlie, the creator and his creation remain distinctly apart. But Keaton's work collapses the distance between Buster and Keaton.[34] He was himself painfully close to the sketchy figure he plays. His wives often had to make sure he was properly dressed, and he had little understanding of authority, power, or money. While Chaplin retained full control over his own productions, industry power brokers easily outmaneuvered Keaton.

Unlike many artists, Keaton was genuinely concerned with the well-being of others when he was aware of them. A colleague who said he was too good for this world surely meant that he was trusting and innocent like a child.

Though Chaplin and Keaton were both outsiders, they responded very differently to their threatened existence. While Keaton was without a clearly defined identity or ego, Chaplin asserted both his genius and his own needs, and was largely indifferent to others. He played Hitler in *The Great Dictator*, a twentieth-century Bluebeard in *Monsieur Verdoux*, and thought about playing Napoleon.

Fortunately, artists can prove their existence and live out their darkest fantasies on paper, canvas, or the screen rather than, like murderers and dictators, in life.

We noted that, in their urgent need to please, some artists—once they discover what the audience wants to see and believe—cater to communal assumptions. Others, like Chaplin and Keaton, render their own troubled, troubling experience as outsiders, and are first recognized and applauded by those—most often the poor—who are not vested in communal assumptions and values.

Chaplin and Keaton were immediately popular, but the existential doubts and fears of others are so distressed and singular that their work is recognized by just a few, often after they are dead.

G

In *The Gold Rush*, when Charlie clings to the icy cabin floor, we are viscerally and kinetically engaged, but we know he is not in danger. Despite moments in his films when he seems at risk—on the high-wire in *The Circus* and on the swaying ladder in *The Pawnshop*—we don't worry about his physical survival.

Keaton, however, continually risked injury and death. Like Harold Lloyd's "thrill pictures," his films combine stunts and gags. But while Lloyd played it safe—filming shots that appear to have him balanced precariously on high-rise structures from deceptive camera angles—Keaton actually *performed* his life-threatening acrobatics. He refused to hire a stunt man, and we can enjoy watching him largely because the film itself is evidence he survived.

As his collaborator Clyde Bruckman says, "No one ever doubled for Buster. He rides the handlebars of the driverless motorcycle in *Sherlock, Jr.*, flies through the air on a tree in *Steamboat Bill, Jr.*, goes over the waterfall in *Our Hospitality*."

In *Sherlock, Jr.*, he jumps off the roof of a freight car by grabbing a water feed that washes him down onto the track. It was done in a single forty-second take, and the fall broke several vertebrae in Keaton's neck. While shooting the climactic end of *Our Hospitality*, he barely saved himself from drowning in the rapids. The outcome of his stunts was so unpredictable that he instructed his crew never to stop shooting until he himself yelled, "Cut!"

Keaton has left a description of his most dangerous stunt, when the front of a house in *Steamboat Bill, Jr.* comes down on him "like a giant fly swatter."

First I had them build the framework of [the] building and made sure that the hinges were . . . solid. It was a building with a very tall V-shaped roof, so that we could make [the] window exceptionally high. . . . Then [we laid the] framework down on the ground and [built] the window around me. . . . The top missed my head by two inches, and the bottom of my heels by two inches. We [marked out the] ground . . . and [drove in] big nails where my heels [were] going to be. Then [we] put that house back up . . . [and] put up our wind machines with the big Liberty motors. We had six of them and they . . . could lift a truck right off the road. Now we had to make sure that we were getting our foreground and background wind effect, but that no current ever hit the front of that building when it started to fall, because if the wind warps her she's not going to fall where we want her, and I'm standing right out in front. But it's a one-take scene and we got it that way. You don't do those things twice.

In the film, the moment comes and goes so quickly that unless we know what was at stake, we are apt to miss it. Though he risked his life, Keaton makes nothing of it on the screen, whereas Chaplin, in the climactic scene of *The Gold Rush*, puts us through a prolonged quasi-physical identification with Charlie, though he himself was perfectly safe.

We may wonder why Keaton placed himself in grave danger in film after film. His audiences would surely have accepted a stunt substitute, for they were well aware that the medium is itself built on artifice, with twenty-four still frames creating an illusion of movement.

Girard and others assume that the threat in the comic is at once "overwhelming and nil." But the threat in Keaton's work is hardly nil—not for the performer. Perhaps Girard would question whether the stunts are comic. But Keaton remains a comedian even though he is often also an acrobat.

We noted, moreover, that gags and thrills have much in common. Both make us tense, and since the clown, like the acrobat, often surprises us with his hairbreadth escapes, both allow us to release tension in laughter.

Keaton not only insisted on doing the stunts but on *convincing us* he did. Like Fred Astaire, he shot the most difficult scenes in single takes that covered the action from beginning to end, so the audience could see that no editing or "movie magic" was involved. Prior to a complicated stunt in *The Three Ages*, he said, "We get it in one shot, or we throw out the gag." When they succeeded, seventy-six takes later, he said, "Now they'll know it was real."[35]

Though the audience would surely have settled for less, he had to prove to himself that he could *actually* do what he might have only *appeared* to be doing.

Despite their fanciful narratives, Keaton's films were utterly real to him. He said about *The General*, which makes Buster the Confederate hero of events that the historical record reports very differently:[36] "I took that page of history and stuck to it in all details. I staged it exactly the way it happened."[37] No doubt he believed it, at least during the production. Indeed, what happened in front of the camera may have had greater reality for him than everything else in his life.

Perhaps Keaton felt compelled to place himself in actual danger in film after film in order to relive the fears of his childhood, and in reliving them, to prove he survived and existed.

No one but he needed the proof. Yet we, too, may harbor suppressed doubts about our identity and existence—doubts readily embodied in the very fear Keaton confronts and overcomes: our fear of nonbeing—of death.

His stunts are similar to those of Houdini—who had himself locked in a bronze coffin, manacled and submerged in a water tank, suspended in a straitjacket from a tall building, shackled and tossed into a hole in the ice that covered the Detroit River, and buried under six feet of earth with only a piece of cloth over his face.

Like Keaton, Houdini actualized situations that were familiar to his audience from melodrama. Immobilized, apparently helpless, and facing certain doom, he escaped by dint of his will and skill—though on several occasions he barely made it out of the death traps he had himself designed.

What Bernard Meyer says of him—that his acts were "the active repetition, under his own guidance and control, of a frightening experience to which he had originally been subjected as a passive and helpless onlooker"—would seem true of Keaton as well.[38]

CHAPTER EIGHT

Making It Real

A

Young children seem biologically impelled to play, build, or make things. It exercises their hands and minds, allows them to accomplish things, and gives expression to inchoate impulses and feelings.

But once they are old enough, most turn to activities involving others; they prefer playing with friends. Only those who have exceptional gifts or find connecting with others difficult will go on playing or making things by themselves.

To those of us who are truly disconnected, other people aren't altogether real, and since we derive our reality from others, if *they* are not real, neither are we.

That way lies madness, and so making the world real is, for some, a matter of life and death.

The artist works to invest reality *with* reality. Only if he or she can believe the object they are making—whether it is an abstraction or a photograph—will they become real themselves.[1]

William Carlos Williams says, "Everything depends on this red wheelbarrow." Rilke spoke of making things out of fear, and T. S. Eliot says, "These fragments have I shored against my ruin."

When Keaton says about a stunt, "Now they'll know it's real," he is also saying, "Now *I* know *I'm* real."

Though initially the object—a painting, poem, or performance—may be intended to attract attention or serve as a connector, its validity *as* an object becomes primary.[2] When artists are asked to compromise their take on reality to make it more accessible or acceptable to an audience, many refuse, for compromising the integrity of the object would undermine their own hard-won reality or identity.[3]

The object may replace the mirror of the mother's face.[4]

Rilke said that throughout his life he had searched for words he could believe.

The scientist, too, is searching for a foundation he can build on, and many in the physical and social sciences have found a dependable base and faith in matter and its evolution.

Though most in the West believe in scientific truth, for many its rock-bottom faith in matter is too reductive and doesn't meet the complex, contradictory needs of our existence. We may be materialists but add whatever we need to get through the day, even if it contradicts the hard truth of science.

B

Goethe said when a feeling threatened to overwhelm him, he fled into a metaphor.

Artists use their work not only to prove they exist but also to contain powerful impulses and feelings that threaten to spill or flood out.

Projecting their experiences and feelings into an object keeps them from erupting and rupturing their relationships to others. The artwork or metaphor allows them to render and exorcise what is happening to them, especially when it is painful or frightening. Objectifying it grants them a measure of detachment that can seem like freedom.

The dispersal of their experience onto the page, canvas, stage, or screen may not be altogether unlike the dissociation seen in victims of abuse who flee into multiple personalities. By projecting the violence, confusion, and fear they suffered onto a series of split-off selves—like the figures in a story—their "I" is spared suffering. They are both them and not them, just as Shakespeare is *and* isn't Lear and Macbeth.

Kafka often laughed when he read his stories to friends. The process of objectifying his painful experiences and feelings allowed him to find them funny. They were no longer his.

The artist's gift/curse comes with a tendency to refer everything to himself, to take everything personally. He makes up for his sense of being no one by seeing—and, whenever possible, placing—himself at the center.

Because early on his center or identity was under siege, it is more heavily fortified than most. If his gifts and his isolation did not push him into observing and rendering the world around him and the reality of other people, he might well become an empty fortress and shrivel up within it.

His situation is contradictory. His isolation prompts him to reach out and connect with others, but opening himself to them and their reactions makes him vulnerable and may, in turn, push him into withdrawing.

When Henry James suggests that an artist is someone on whom nothing is lost, he is clearly thinking of himself. Yet he is largely blind to all but the rich and privileged—the "immemorially protected"—and even they are rendered from a limited perspective.

Though the experience of the artist forces him to confront aspects of reality the rest of us ignore, he may fail to register matters of urgent concern to his contemporaries.

Kafka's journals for the years 1914–1918 make almost no mention of the war raging in Europe.

We noted that by the time we are adult, most of us have withdrawn into gated communities of one kind or another, and make but brief forays into the uncertainties beyond.

Though we are not islands, most of us live on one.

Artists, too—if they are successful—tend to withdraw into safe, unchallenging zones. Some, however, must continue to live out their lives within uncertain and permeable boundaries. They remain as vulnerable and defenseless as they were in childhood.

When a friend asked Thelonious Monk, "What's happening?" he said, "Everything, all the time." He had no way of separating himself from the chaos that seemed to surround him. The gated communities or structures that protect most of us offered him no shelter.

Marcel Proust was so permeable that he could experience people, events, and even his own reactions only at a distance, indirectly and retrospectively—in the shelter of his cork-lined bedroom and the quasi-fictive recreation of his life. His experience threatened to overwhelm him until he had withdrawn from physical contact with the world and could safely face and recover what had happened to him—the lost years of his own life.

The spectator, like the artist, can use the artwork to free himself of forbidden impulses and fearful experiences.

Since we must keep them largely hidden or repressed and can't be sure when and how they will surface, they remain shapeless and keep us under tension, even if we are barely aware of them.

But when our most powerful feelings—fear, rage, lust, jealousy, and the need for vengeance—are given concrete, recognizable shape in a story or painting, we are given safe access to the forbidden and repressed. The artwork, like the joke, can free us of tension and anxiety.

In order to use the aesthetic object as a container, we must believe in it, at least for the duration. If the figures in a story don't seem credible and we fail to recognize their situation, we can't identify with them and won't endow them with our own fears and wishes.

We don't need to insist—as Chaplin himself does—that Charlie must wear a sack around his foot throughout *The Gold Rush* because he has no money for new boots, nor would we mind if a stunt man had substituted for Keaton. But unless we are transported into the reality of the story, our physical distance and safety become irrelevant. We feel disconnected and bored.

In the early days of movies, spectators are said to have fled the theater when a train came rushing toward them on the screen, just as the unfamiliar physical realism of Renaissance painting may, on occasion, have prompted viewers to probe a canvas with their fingers, convinced that little people were fixed to it.

Though we may doubt that spectators ever forgot they were looking at a two-dimensional image, we do want to believe what we are seeing. As we noted, we go to the movies to have *our* experience, and for that to happen, events on the screen must become real to us, even though—*or rather, because*—we know they are not.

Our relationship to an artwork is reciprocal. It confirms our experience and our experience, in turn, confirms the work of art.

The rendered scene on the canvas, page, or screen exists outside us, but something within us begins to vibrate, as it does when we listen to music.

Since we don't doubt our own reactions—whether we are laughing, crying, or frightened—once a scene elicits a response from us, it becomes credible. What happens to us authenticates the events; *we* make them real by lending ourselves to the figures caught up in them.

C

Because we know the story isn't true, we want it to be persuasive; since its effect on us is largely psychological, we want it to seem as physical as possible; and since we are not in danger, we want our balance and equanimity to be put at risk.

In a graphic medium like painting or film, when the human body is engaged in a tense, potentially dangerous situation, our own bodies respond and become quasi-physically engaged, even though we perceive it through the abstracting senses of sight and sound. But if our *proximate* senses were involved, sharing the visceral or tactile experience of another would be experienced as invasive and prompt us to withdraw.

In *The Adventurer*, Charlie and Edna are eating ice cream on a second-story balcony. When he piles a whole scoop onto his spoon, it slips off into his pants, leaving him visibly uncomfortable even as he tries to appear poised. He continues chatting with Edna, while shaking the ice cream down his trouser leg onto the iron slats of the balcony floor, from where he surreptitiously kicks it to the balcony below. There it lands on the bare back of a dowager, who jumps up screaming as the ice cream slides all the way into her dress. A heavyset man tries to retrieve it by reaching down her back, but she slaps him away in outrage and sinks back onto her chair—only to land on the ice cream that has slid down to her bottom and prompts her to jump up screaming again.

As we follow the passage of the ice cream through Charlie's clothes and onto the dowager's skin, our own sense of touch is engaged. Not unlike music, the ice cream has slipped into our senses without becoming a fully conscious experience.

Low comedy reaches down to a biological core that is so unchanging and universal, it might be called objectively true. Since physical humor works through the senses, it enables the audience to share an experience regardless of personal and cultural differences, just as an injury to the body—at one time in painting and in photographic images today—has an immediate, quasi-sensory effect on us.

Life is *rephysicalized* in an *aphysical* medium. Touching appears to have replaced seeing.[5]

M.A.S.H. begins with helicopters ferrying wounded and dead bodies from the battlefield to a front-line hospital, where we are confronted with bloody but totally credible scenes as surgeons try to save gravely injured and dying men in an operating tent. The scenes have a visceral impact that makes us tense but also allows us to understand and, indeed, enjoy the off-duty shenanigans of the doctors and nurses, who find relief from gore and death in alcohol, sex, and pranks.

Our own reactions mimic theirs. Horrified by the carnage, we, too, seek and find relief in laughter. Significantly, once the film moves from the wounded and dying to the golf course and football field of

Rest and Relaxation, all tension leaches out. The movie decompresses and turns into a standard service farce.[6]

No doubt *Lysistrata* is the most frequently performed Greek comedy because we continue to be intimately familiar with the way women can deny sex to men in all but its most primitive form. Their power is exercised psychologically but trumps the physical superiority of men, whose biology can turn them into beggars.

We perceive films through our eyes and ears, but the medium is predicated on movement and could be said to engage us biologically. Anything that moves draws our involuntary attention by signaling change, danger, or an opportunity: we may be eaten or see something to eat.

Just as a cat's eyes follow movement, we instinctively observe and follow movement on the screen.

Speech put an end to purely physical screen comedies. But although words pass through the mind before reaching the senses, they, too, can elicit a quasi-physical response.

Woody Allen spoke of a boy in his analysis group who was "a Southern bigot and a bed wetter. . . . He used to go to his Klan meetings in rubber sheets." In an interview, Allen said that his idea of a big thrill would be "jumping naked into a vat of cold Roosevelt dimes." Woody naked and immersed in thousands of cool, silvery coins with the face of FDR on them invokes a surreal but tactile experience.

Comedy is often topical, and humor that targets a well-known person or situation will reach a large audience. Topical humor, moreover, is usually harmless and seldom injures anyone present. But since the surfaces of our lives, unlike our bodies and instincts, are in constant flux, topical humor dates rapidly. What makes us laugh today becomes irrelevant and often inaccessible tomorrow.[7]

Unless we are familiar with the attitudes and speech of the British upper class, we won't laugh when an aristocratic twit in *Blackadder*, about to lead his men over the top in World War I, calls out to them, "Last one in Berlin is a rotten egg!"

Some Jewish jokes are incomprehensible to non-Jews, and many are more effective if we are familiar with Jewish experiences and attitudes.

> Mrs. Goldstein was on the beach with her grandson, when a huge wave swept in out of nowhere and washed him out to sea. In despair, Grandma fell to her knees pleading, "Dear God, please bring back my only grandchild!"
>
> A moment later, another huge wave swept the boy back onto the beach. Weeping with relief, the old lady embraced him, then looked up at the sky and said, "He had a hat!"[8]

D

Since art is itself an abstraction, it strives to be as concrete as possible and has little use for symbols.

Photographs, as Ernst Gombrich points out, would have had no meaning in the Middle Ages, since they don't render the spiritual core of existence. The halo that marks the saint is a physical emanation of the spirit that was, we may assume, as real and present to the medieval painter as the body and matter are to us.

Some years ago, a group of Navajo students were given movie cameras and asked to film their experience and perceptions of life. The only film they completed tried to render the presence of the Great Spirit by photographing tumbleweed blown every which way in the wind.

We noted that the camera is an instrument with built-in assumptions; there is no way it could render a central element of Navajo experience. The students were reduced to indicating the spirit with an analog, instead of making it happen to our senses. We *understand* the symbol of wind and tumbleweed, but it doesn't become a concrete experience for us.

This is not to suggest that symbols today are necessarily abstractions to those who believe in them. For many, the flag is a great deal more than a piece of colored cloth, and they deem damaging it a desecration. To believers, the Torah isn't a scroll with an ancient, handwritten text but the living word of God that must be buried in sacred ground when it becomes too frail to use. For the devout, the Eucharist is a far more intense physical experience than the artwork can offer. Wafer and wine are transubstantiated into the body and blood of Christ and ingested by the communicant.

It was an artist, Flannery O'Connor, who said that if the Eucharist is a mere symbol, then the hell with it.

E

Chaplin says, "The thing that puts a person in an embarrassing predicament must always be perfectly familiar to an audience."[9]

The "predicament" is an equivalent of the situation that forms the basic building blocks of stories. It limits or traps the figures in comedy, tragedy, melodrama, soap opera, and horror movies. It frames them, puts them under physical or psychological pressure, and allows us to put ourselves in their place. For we know, without being fully aware of it, that we, too, are situated or framed—though seldom as graphically as a fictive figure.

Henri Matisse told his students, "Assume the pose of the model." We, too, assume the pose of the "model" or figure when we watch someone who is caught in a situation—just as we wince when we see someone slice into his finger.

To engage us, a predicament need not be as immediate as Charlie's in *The Gold Rush* when he clings to a doorknob over an abyss.

> Milton Berle's television show was so popular that the moment there was a commercial break the water level in the reservoirs of Detroit dropped because his viewers were rushing to the bathroom and flushing their toilets.

Though remote from us in time and space, the dilemma of thousands of people holding it in so as to miss nothing Berle might say, then rushing in a herd to relieve themselves, is engaging and funny.

A Diane Arbus photograph, "A Jewish Giant at Home with his Parents in the Bronx," shows the family boxed into a small room, with the gigantic son not only towering over his parents but forced to bend his neck to fit under the ceiling.

We are likely to lend ourselves to a fictive situation that gets us to work along with it—involving us in the same processes of discovery as everyday life, guessing at what happens next, often prompting us to draw the wrong conclusions, and frequently leaving us surprised.

F

Mimicry is an accurate surface rendering that can make the absurd and unreal seem real to us.

Mel Brooks gives *The 2000 Year Old Man* credibility by capturing the speech and attitudes of an elderly Jewish man many of us recognize.

> *Reiner:* "You were present at the crucifixion—"
>
> *Brooks:* "Oh boy!"
>
> *Reiner:* "You knew Jesus?"
>
> *Brooks:* "Yeah. Thin lad, wore sandals, long hair, walked around with eleven other guys. Always came into the store, never bought anything. Always asked for water."

The image of Jesus is both familiar and unexpected. We recognize his physical appearance, though we may wonder about the "eleven other guys" instead of twelve. The picture of him is reduced from a long tradition of religious imagery to the down-home perspective of a Jewish shopkeeper, who remembers that Jesus always asked for water, no doubt because it was free.

In Monty Python's *The Life of Brian*, we listen to the Sermon on the Mount—reported by the Gospel in close-up, with every word perfectly clear—from the edge of a vast crowd, where we, too, would likely have stood:

> "What did he say?"
> "Blessed are the cheesemakers."

The touch of commonplace reality—a large, outdoor gathering could hardly have heard what Jesus was saying unless he had a microphone or bullhorn—turns us into his contemporaries and makes a sacred occasion funny.

G

In discussions of art, what we now call *reality* used to be called *truth*—a concept that has fallen into disrepute. We have, however, learned that reality is no less subjective. Once we get beyond basic sensory information, everyone's reality is different even if, for the sake of comity, we and our institutions suppress the differences in daily life.[10]

Monty Python, King Lear, Citizen Kane, and *Annie Hall* are utterly dissimilar, yet all equally true or real.

Clearly, the element that makes an artwork persuasive is not verisimilitude. What we respond to even in a realistic work is not factual information.

Fiction *uses* facts but has never been about them. None of the stories about kings tells us how to run a country. Harry Truman observed scornfully that Lear couldn't even run his own family.

However faithfully fiction may render facts, they are subordinate. They become transparent like a stage scrim to give us access to the inner realm of the figures—and, more significantly, to ourselves.

The hidden is made visible, as it is in life when someone commits a crime or makes a telling joke.

We call the content of a story or painting its *subject,* but it might be called its *object* instead. The ambiguity implicit in *subject* seems to suggest that external events, scenes, and objects are not the primary concern of art.

H

In daily life, we are governed by whatever our community declares to be the truth or reality. Differences in individual experience and perspective are deemphasized and conformed to it almost automatically. Even intimate relationships are largely determined by it.

We are nonetheless aware that our own experience of the world and ourselves doesn't always coincide with the expected or prescribed form.

But while some—artists among them—live with experiences and impulses that threaten the social order and their own place in it, the mismatch for most of us is slight. It involves no critical issues and causes us little discomfort.

On the contrary, the difference between us and others—the specificity of our experience—textures our lives and becomes a precious marker of our existence as individuals without undermining our connection to others. As we noted, our individuality—provided it is limited to inessentials—is important to the community, since it appears to prove that we are separate and therefore free and responsible for our actions.

I

The central figures in fiction are almost always loners and different from others—dragon slayers or murderers, heirs to the throne like Hamlet, or misfits like Kafka's human cockroach.

We identify with them because we, too, are different and alone, though we may pretend otherwise. They allow us to acknowledge our differences while remaining part of the whole—to have our own, often intense experience without feeling alienated.

The fundamental reality of narrative, as of all art, is the reality of individual experience—the artist's as objectified in his work and our own in response to it.

Persuasive stories are true to the reality or shock of the experience that generated them, and render it in a form that doesn't compromise it, even as they make it accessible to us. The manner or style of the presentation is irrelevant as long as the experience, whether it be a king's or a beggar's, becomes ours as well.

If the experience is real to us, any way or style of rendering seems valid. *The Gold Rush* remains true to Charlie's poverty by having him wear a sack around his foot throughout the film, but when Big Jim becomes a victim of hunger hallucinations, Charlie turns into a huge, utterly unrealistic chicken. His moth-eaten costume isn't the least bit lifelike, but it enhances the impact of the situation by rendering both Jim's delusional state *and* Charlie's sense of being helplessly trapped inside it. In a radical break from the quasi-reality that the film has established, Charlie as an unpersuasive chicken renders the *subjective* reality of both men.

J

Music, poetry, and painting can privilege subjective reality and disregard social and economic circumstances. But stories are centered on relationships and are seldom free of the objective factors that limit all of us. Though Gregor Samsa finds himself imprisoned in the unlikely carapace of a cockroach, he can't escape the constrictions of family life.

Stories are of the world and must accommodate the impersonal forces that govern us. Even fairy tales are set in a familiar context of poverty and wealth and framed by the values of home and community. Despite the appearance and intervention of fairies and witches, the figures are subject to the limits that hunger, fear, love, hate, jealousy, injury, and death impose on all of us.

Relationships change with historical circumstances, but their biological and even some of their social functions have changed little. We continue to recognize the family obligations and conflicts in the Old Testament and in Greek myths—even those of the gods on Olympus.

K

Film is a two-dimensional projection, but since the camera and microphone capture the world as we today experience it, it seems more persuasive than other forms of storytelling. It effectively renders the materialist and realist perspective that has governed much of our thinking since the Renaissance.

We noted that people in the Middle Ages would not have known what to make of photographic images, but we—who say when something is significant that it *matters*—are persuaded by them. Indeed, they seem so real to us that we guard against being manipulated by a photograph, whereas a painting no longer poses a threat; it can't deceive us.

Despite their fidelity to the surfaces of reality, screen stories do not render the welter of information entering our eyes and ears. They, too, depend on a blueprint, or preexisting form, that we recognize consciously or unconsciously; it separates the significant from the insignificant, and conforms what we see and hear to what we *already* know.

Believing is, indeed, seeing. Even vérité documentaries are built on assumptions, just as scientific experiments are predicated on theory. Like most questions, they imply a limited range of answers.

L

Some forms in art and life are ancient and have been tested against the experience of generations, who have worn or washed away everything inessential. Some forms—like the pyramids—are so primary or fundamental that we seem to perceive them without having to process them through the mind. Their shape and weight speak their meaning without requiring our conscious understanding.

Perhaps this is true of the preclusive structure of narrative as well, since it hasn't changed from the epic of Gilgamesh to the movies at the multiplex. It derives from an awareness that we may not be in charge of our lives and from the limitations that biology imposes on us.

When Walter Benjamin says that stories are sanctioned by death, he may mean that they limit the autonomy of the individual at the center of the narrative. Our awareness of death and the flow of time that carries us toward it hold together the incidents of the plot and the experiences of the figures, much as death—however indirectly—informs and, indeed, structures our lives, even if we put it out of mind.

Conceivably, evolution has deposited geometric forms like the pyramids in our brain genetically, so that we are born with them as we are with the foundations of language. But it seems more likely that we recognize the structure of narrative because, from childhood on, we have heard countless stories, and—once we were old enough to realize that all living things must die and that our will and freedom are limited—found their forbidding form confirmed by experience.

Unlike the laws of physics, the structure of narrative is derived from human existence. But since it is true for all of us, it could—in this limited sense—be called objectively true. It may well remain true and relevant until we discover a way of living forever.

What a physicist says about the physical realm—that "the shape of any object represents the balance of two opposing forces"—would seem to be true of art objects also.

The pyramids stand as an interface between the human and the eternal, just as medieval cathedrals are monuments to the glory of God but were thrust into the sky by us. Though the precluded plot of narrative tells us we are not in charge, *we* are the ones who tell it, and though stories, like the fairy tales we asked for in childhood, hover on the edge of the unknown and terrifying, they allay our fears with a known ending. It makes no difference whether the end is happy or sad as long as it is certain.

The walls of our structures at once limit us and make us feel safe.

M

Most of us don't question the fundamental structures of our community, or the aesthetic forms that have evolved from our shared encounters with the human condition. They are doubted only by those whose trust in relationships and communal values was undermined. As outsiders largely driven by fear, they must try to ascertain and reprove repeatedly what the rest of us have no trouble believing and passing on.

Doubt and anxiety compel some artists, philosophers, and scientists to search under the surface for hidden flaws and dangers that most of us are glad to leave undiscovered. Paul Dirac said that fear drove his inquiries into the fundamentals of quantum physics.[11]

Artists who live outside the structures that reconcile contradictions for the rest of us may find themselves nakedly exposed to them. Like the aesthetic forms they use or evolve, they are *themselves* an interface between opposing forces—buffeted between creation and destruction, arrogance and humility, passivity and aggression, connection and withdrawal.

An early and indelible experience of helplessness often drives them to seek control not only over their work but through it, over others. They strive to *make* us laugh or cry, doing to us what was done to them, albeit in a harmless, nonphysical form.

One might say that instead of remaining victims, they victimize us. Keaton casts himself as an unaware, passive figure apparently at the mercy of circumstance—only, as he says, to "double-cross" us. Dickens delighted in terrifying audiences at his public readings with the murder of Nancy: "There was a fixed expression of horror of me, all over the theater, which could not have been surpassed if I had been going to be hanged. . . . It is quite a new sensation to be execrated with that unanimity, and I hope it will remain so." He clearly relished the power his work conferred on him.

We noted that the physical or psychological risk an artist takes can, temporarily, free him of his fears. Moreover, overcoming them in a public arena and astonishing multitudes can produce an addictive high.

Churchill, who throughout his life eagerly and gratuitously exposed himself to mortal danger, says, "There is nothing quite so exhilarating as getting shot at without getting hit." He was a lifelong outsider—a political maverick who, like Benjamin Disraeli, not only wrote fiction but ended up *living* the story.

N

Just as a sense of helplessness drives artists and others to empower themselves, the childhood experience of isolation and alienation may force them to seek or make connections to substitute for those that were severed or failed them. An early and fundamental disconnect prompts them to uncover links that were overlooked by others—to perceive a new and unified whole in what can, to the rest of us, appear to be a meaningless cluster of fragments.

The connections they discover or make not only spare them a life in limbo or despair but may prove useful to the community. For often the structures that failed or excluded them turn out to have grave flaws they noticed long before everyone else.

Though their work may initially appear to be an attack on communal structures and values, it frequently ends up preserving and revitalizing them.

In both science and art, outsiders or misfits fit together the puzzle pieces of our experience—what we call reality—in a new way. Like Charlie and Buster, they serve the community by remaining outside it.

The validity of their discoveries is not always recognized until they themselves are gone, for the news they bring is often distressing or hard to understand. But if they were to simplify or compromise it in order to make it more accessible, they would betray both their work and the tradition that has for centuries sustained both the sciences and the arts.

O

An artwork or performance requires no direct contact, and is often the only relationship an artist will trust.

Most of us are firmly rooted in life and connected to others through family, community, or religious faith. But we, too, use art and entertainment to make or sustain relationships. We go to movies, concerts, museums, and ball games with friends or family, and what we see or hear becomes a relaxed, pleasurable point of contact and communication.

As members of an audience we become part of the community created by a television show or best seller. But though we share our responses with others, we don't expect art or entertainment to meet our existential needs. Unlike many artists and performers, we don't think of them as a lifeline.

We noted that if the artwork is to serve as a container for our repressed impulses and feelings, we must believe in it enough to lend ourselves to it. But we don't require it to have an independent reality and certainly don't want to be subjected to the distressed experience that generated the work. Brief exposure to it in a separate, clearly defined arena is quite enough. Most of us, moreover, draw no clear line between art and entertainment: we expect both to give us pleasure and nothing more.

Connecting with the spectator can be critically important to the artist, but connecting with artists is of little interest to the audience unless they are celebrities. We sense they are best kept at a distance—behind glass or bars, like circus animals. Not long ago, actors who acted out dangerous and forbidden deeds or relationships on stage were housed in accommodations decent people shunned.

P

Until recently, the preclusive structure of narrative confirmed a fundamental aspect of the human condition that people all over the world—in cultures and societies that had little in common—believed to be true.

Today, however, the disparity between what story tells us and what we, in the West, live by has become so wide that the structure of narrative diametrically contradicts what we believe. Traditional stories—the *Iliad*, *King Lear*, *Moby Dick*, and *The Great Gatsby*—countermand our faith in individual freedom and the effectiveness of our will. Though, deep down, we, too, may sense that the preclusive plot remains a valid reflection of human reality, we don't want to be reminded of it. Perhaps our confidence is too shaky.

As long as necessity ruled us, we had little leisure and the stories we told and believed were central to our existence. But once we had *surplus* time we were free—or obliged—to fill our leisure with distracting entertainments.

At one time, myths and fairy tales constituted popular narrative *despite* their forbidding burden. But today the spare energy of our culture flows largely into stories, music, and images that don't openly challenge our assumptions or the way we live. Confronting the uncertainties and unresolved contradictions that inform traditional story is not how we choose to wile away leisure hours that might well terrify us with their emptiness.

Even now, however, the arts and, more significantly, entertainment help us survive, even if all they do—or *appear* to do—is distract us.

Q

Early in life, we learn that the easiest way to be accepted is to conform.

Children who are neglected or worse often try harder to please than others. If they fail, they turn contrary, withdraw into isolation, or deny their own needs entirely and live in rigid conformity with what is expected of them.

While the childhood experiences of the entertainer are apt to resemble an artist's, his particular gift often permits him to make an easy connection with his audience. Noel Coward called it "a talent to amuse."

Since public approval may come to him early and link him to others without friction, he doesn't require his work or performance to prove his existence. His focus, instead, is on the connection it allows him to make with the audience. For an artist, however, whose conflicted experience and personality deny him easy access to others, the connections *within* the work are primary.

The entertainer is likely to be focused on the experience of the audience, and the artist on his own. Since his life is exposed to contradictions and doubt, his experience seems alien to most of us and, as we noted, prevents him from making it easily accessible or "relatable."

The entertainer runs the opposite risk. Though the energy driving his work is likely to spring from a disconnect, his easy connection with the audience can get him addicted to popularity. Once the wishes and reactions of the audience become his paramount concern, he is apt to "write the audience"[12] instead of the story or song. His craving for approval is the major source of his energy, and may prompt him to turn whatever was new in his experience and work into a formula for continued success.

A student on the varsity football team told me that one Saturday in the stadium he looked up at the cheering fans and realized he was "appearing in their movie." After great success in high school and college, he had come face to face with his urgent need to please, and realized he no longer needed the drug of public approval. Instead of being in *their* movie, he needed to be in his own, and resigned from the team.

R

The high cost of producing movies makes pleasing a large audience the central concern of the industry.

Early in his career, James Cameron, a director of successful screen spectacles, analyzed the elements shared by the ten most profitable American movies, and he made sure to work them into his own productions. Though the settings of his films are remote from *our* experience, he has been well aware that we need to believe what we are watching, at least for the duration: "I do a lot of things in the pursuit of creating a patina of reality in what is basically a fantasy."[13]

By acknowledging that his stories reflect our wishes and not our existence, and by reducing reality to its "patina," he escapes the dilemma of the storyteller in contemporary society.

We noted that in traditional narrative the outcome is determined by nonhuman forces—fate, chance, or the gods. By drawing our attention to surfaces—the spectacle of *Titanic* and the 3D effects in *Avatar*—and by marshaling the complex technology they require, Cameron takes over the determining role himself. We are focused on *his* surprises and manipulations, not on those visited on his figures by forces beyond their—or the storyteller's—control.

Whereas traditional stories commanded the storyteller, today popular storytellers command the story. Significantly, the publicity for both *Titanic* and *Avatar* emphasized their artifice and the enormous effort and expenditures that went into the simulation of events that occur either in the safe past or in an imaginary future. Our sense of human control and agency is enhanced, not undermined.[14]

Both movies conform to the basic assumptions and wishes of the audience and are clearly Cameron's own. "There is no fate but what you make," he told an interviewer.[15] He has no use for the fundamental uncertainty invoked by traditional narrative, and what happens in his films occurs in accord with well-known and reassuring genre conventions.

Titanic skillfully adopts the format of disaster movies that begin, as their name indicates, with an event "from the stars." Although the collision with the iceberg that dooms the ship constitutes an Act of God, the story centers on the impassioned romance between a boy in steerage and a girl in first class, who assert their own freedom by refusing to be kept apart by differences in their social and economic status.

The disaster is skillfully used to give the romance a bittersweet ending—the boy dies and the girl lives to a ripe old age but never forgets him. The movie, unlike most American screen romances, doesn't ask us to believe that love conquers all, but it is the disaster and *not* insuperable class differences that puts a stop to it.

The boy's death preserves the "patina" of fact—most steerage passengers drowned—yet allows the audience to believe that, but for the iceberg, the young couple would have lived happily ever after. The romance that lifts *Titanic* above run-of-the-mill disaster movies subscribes to the myth of a classless meritocracy so dear to us. Their love is allowed to retain its high sheen, and is never made to pass the test of reductive socioeconomic reality or of time.

Having your cake and eating it, too, is an earmark of popular stories, and may, indeed, be a seductive component in a great deal of art. But our pipe dream of an undivided, noncontradictory existence is seldom as blatantly indulged and exploited as in *Avatar*.

The film adopts—and simplifies for melodramatic purpose—the liberal eco-friendly perspective of today's educated middle class. The U.S. Marines and their capitalist sponsors stand for all that's macho, hate-filled, exploitative, and destructive of the earth and its creatures. Their innocent victims are inhabitants of an Eden in space and live in tribal communities invested with the respect for the Great Spirit, nature philosophy, and rituals of movie Indians that are but one of the genre ingredients Cameron stirs into his stew.

Like most science fiction, the film is free to disregard the complexity of human consciousness and the often ambiguous knowledge and skills it has evolved. It reduces our contradictory situation to the reassuring good and evil of video games. The audience can at once enjoy the violence of the evildoers *and* sit in righteous judgment over them.

While the same thing could be said of *Macbeth* and *Crime and Punishment*, neither sanitizes violence of its horror. Dostoevsky doesn't spare us a description of the axe blade, matted with the bloody hair of the old women Raskolnikov has slaughtered. Since, like Macbeth, he is a murderer for whom we have a measure of empathy, the story doesn't leave us comfortably free to project our own destructive impulses onto another.

All popular stories are manipulative, but few go about it as unashamedly as *Avatar*. It allows us to maintain a flattering image of ourselves, encourages us with an easy spirituality, and sends us out of the theater with a possibility or promise of eternal life.

Biology decrees that we are born innocent suckers. But while a great deal of art and entertainment draws us in with a promise of childhood wholeness, one wonders why adults today would want their milk quite as watered down and artificially sweetened.

S

Entertainment is generally honorable and makes no claim on reality. But sentimental fictions tend to be realist in style and expect us to believe them. Since the reality they conjure up caters to our wishes and feelings, the audience is glad to collaborate.

In life, we pay a steep price for letting wishful thinking dominate our decisions, and learn to mistrust feelings not borne out by physical fact. Words unsubstantiated by action are cheap, and we are expected to put our money where our mouth is. Few women will long believe a man loves them just because he *says* he does.

Sentimental stories and movies, however, don't bother to prove or earn the feelings they claim. Like most art, they serve an inner reality that is necessarily shortchanged in daily life. But unlike traditional stories, they indulge our positive feelings without substantiating or undermining them with physical, social, and economic fact. Though the heroes and heroines are sorely tested, they are free of the inner conflicts, ambiguities, and contradictions that—at least occasionally—trouble most of us.

Since everything in sentimental movies is of a piece, consonance is easily achieved. Not only the music but the weather speaks to the inner state of the figures. A storm rages when they are in turmoil, and at movie funerals even the sky is apt to weep.

Conversely, the only rainstorm in Chaplin's films occurs at the end of *The Immigrant* when Charlie and Edna are about to be married—traditionally a sunny occasion.

As long as our relationships were determined by economic, social, and religious structures, there was no need to stress sentiment. Feelings as we think of them today did not gain ascendance in life and art until relations between us and others ceased to be firmly grounded in communal and economic realities. Even marrying for love, a common motif in nineteenth-century fiction, only became important after more substantial connections attenuated.

The focus on romantic love—singular feelings for a singular person—in popular stories, entertainments, and songs may be a reaction to the ever more doubtful existence of the individual. Our identity and difference are ostensibly confirmed by the special and intense feelings we have for *one* other, who responds with equally intense and special feelings for *us*.

While the comic gives us access to the repressed and forbidden and undermines assumptions we have about ourselves, sentimental stories meet socially sanctioned wishes and show us as we want to be.

In low comedy and tragedy we identify with Groucho and King Lear, whom we would avoid in person. But sentimental stories allow us to identify with an admirable hero or heroine, and use a villain— someone utterly unlike us—to scapegoat the impulses and faults we don't want to acknowledge in ourselves.

Aristotle and Freud are no doubt right to say we come to art for pleasure. But our pleasure in tragedy, low comedy, and even in fairy tales is complex.

The Gold Rush, like the story of Oedipus, is determined by outside forces, and keeps confronting us with our limits. Though we laugh and may feel consoled or empowered by Chaplin's genius, the film could also leave us wondering—like the Jewish boy who was told the story of Isaac—what if the rope that kept the cabin from sliding into the abyss had slipped from the rock a moment sooner? Chance or a whim of fate makes Charlie a millionaire instead of wiping him out. Like the myth of Oedipus, the film leaves us with questions we can't answer.

They are *not* questions we often ask—and when we do, we don't want the answer that the story gives us.

Though comedies are, on the surface, less real than other fictions, they tend to be closer to a hidden existential truth. With our laughter camouflaging *why* we laugh, comedians are under less pressure than other storytellers to falsify their experience. Chaplin's work may have found wide acceptance and a long life even though—or because—it has its source in fear, deprivation, and a profound sense of uncertainty.

T

Low and high comedy are free of deep feelings and not given to sentimentality. But once the middle class emerged, so did a sentimental form of comedy.

The figures in it are caught in situations that hold no real danger and have problems with known or easy solutions. Instinct-driven characters are rare, and we are seldom made fearful or even tense. We noted that though incest is invoked in *Back to the Future*, the relationship between the time-traveling son and his future mother never makes us uncomfortable.

The narrative of *Tootsie* isn't subject to coincidence or chance. It runs along a predictable track, and—unlike *The Gold Rush* or traditional farce where no one is in control—the plot is clearly manipulated by the scriptwriter to confirm that we are masters of our fate.

Dustin Hoffman as Michael Dorsey can't find work as an actor until he disguises himself as a middle-aged woman and becomes a runaway success on television. The flaw in his character—his insensitivity to the feelings of women—is corrected with little effort or pain. Unlike Charlie, who emerges from his adventures in *The Gold Rush* totally unchanged, Dorsey goes through the positive transformation—we can change our lives by changing ourselves—so dear to our thinking and our popular fiction. At the end of the movie, he tells the woman he loves, who thought he was her girlfriend, "I was better with you as a woman than I was with a woman as a man." Her reply—"Will you loan me that little yellow outfit?"—lets us have our cake and eat it. The purported feminist message is undercut by her terminally cute femininity that sends us home knowing that everything is as it was and should be.

American life is seen from a far more grounded perspective in *The Last Detail*. Jack Nicholson as Buddusky is part of a two-man team of military police detailed to transport a hapless grunt from Virginia to a naval brig in New Hampshire. The prisoner is a tall, soft boy of eighteen who has been sentenced to eight years for stealing a few dollars from a charity sponsored by the wife of the base commander. Though at first Nicholson despises the boy as a clueless weakling, he develops a measure of sympathy for him, and tries to show him a good time during his last days of freedom.

The movie never sentimentalizes the men or their situation. Buddusky is an angry misfit, motivated as much by his hatred of the navy and all power structures as by fellow feeling, and the boy ends up betraying his trust and getting his guards into serious trouble by trying to escape.

The lonely, rootless sailors and their adventures are observed kindly but accurately by a movie with a sad core that has us laughing throughout.

CHAPTER NINE

Annie Hall

A

The situations in Woody Allen's films before *Annie Hall* are utterly improbable, and the figures seem less real than those in a joke, perhaps because they appear in a realist medium.

One of the most accomplished, *Take the Money and Run,* is a mockumentary that inverts familiar chronicles of crime. The misadventures of Virgil Starkwell and his utter incompetence as a bank robber make no claim on reality, but they engender flights of the surrealist humor that distinguished Allen's stand-up work. Allen himself is in control off stage, while his cartoon hero, like the figures in his early films, is stupid and out of touch.

The persona he brought to his live performances is altogether different—aware, intelligent, complex, and built on a carefully controlled display of his own insecurities and weaknesses. But in *Annie Hall* he goes further still—exposing the very aspects of himself he kept hidden in stand-up. Whereas in the earlier films Allen does anything for a laugh, in *Annie Hall* he lets us see *why*. He bares the insecurity, vulnerability, hostility, and need for control that are both the source of Alvy Singer's humor and the limitations of his personal life.

In his early work on stage and screen, *he* determines what we hear and see. But in *Annie Hall* he no longer controls how we perceive the world or him. Though he remains our main source of information and we continue to see what happens from Alvy Singer's point of view, we are not confined to it.

Clowns like Chaplin, Keaton, and Allen, who generate their own narrative, don't often render anyone but themselves multidimensionally. In *Annie Hall*, however, the key figure of Annie is so accurately and vividly observed by both Allen and Diane Keaton that she becomes as real as Alvy. His friend Rob is just a convenient sidekick, and the people we encounter or watch, like those at the Central Park Zoo, serve as mere objects for derisive comments that make him feel superior. At first, Annie, too, seems a mere extension of Alvy, but once she begins to assert herself, she affords us an independent perspective. Her substantiated existence and his relationship to her crystallize him into a self-contradictory human being and allow us to see Alvy with his limitations.

Despite his own central and insistent presence, the film maintains a balance between him and Annie—or self and other—much as we try to do in our own relationships.

Allen has said that "ambivalence is the death of comedy."[1] But ambivalence is the core of Alvy Singer. His feelings for Annie reveal his compelling need for contact, as well as his panicked fear of it. Though disconnection has been the mainstay of his personal and professional life, he *wants* to connect, or is driven to it by our shared human condition. Annie herself is so unthreatening that she puts him off guard and draws him out of his protective shell with her beauty, her insecure personality, and sex.

But almost as soon as he develops feelings for her, his fear of contact and commitment asserts itself. He has to camouflage how he feels, and says "I lurve you" instead of "I love you." But he is trapped, and though deeply suspicious of feelings, becomes their helpless subject. When Annie sings at a club and a record producer invites them to a party, he is openly possessive. Never before at a loss for words, he sud-denly finds himself tongue-tied and can think of no better reason for turning down the invitation than "we have this thing." When Annie wonders "What thing?" he can only repeat, "The thing." Stripped of his defenses and nakedly insecure, he is spared further embarrassment by Annie's loyal "Oh, the thing."

Alvy's feelings constitute a crisis by dragging him out of the insula-tion and command position of the successful stand-up comedian. We sense early on that he is stuck in his fortified isolation, unwilling and unable to change—in part, no doubt, because the disconnect that separates him from others is also the source of his success and income. Abandoning his alienated stance would mean surrendering the weap-ons he has forged to ensure his survival: the comedian might cease to be funny.

Shortly before they break up, Alvy likens relationships to a shark that must keep moving forward or die, and calls their relationship a dead shark. But the dead shark is Alvy himself—too fearful to venture outside his fortified walls and unable to lend himself to anything he can't control. As Annie says, he is an island, or behaves like one until he needs sex—a need he might well prefer to meet without having a woman in residence.

Once Annie realizes that they have no future and leaves him, Alvy follows her out to Los Angeles and asks her to marry him. She rejects him, and he turns into an angry little boy, crashing his rented con-vertible into several parked cars. When a motorcycle cop demands his license, Alvy tears it to bits and lands in jail. But though he is clearly hurt, he recovers quickly and—unlike Chaplin at the end of *City Lights*—turns the rejection into a joke.

Allen makes us laugh, but the picture of the comedian that emerges in *Annie Hall* is sad. Alvy is needy, insecure, vulnerable, jealous, ag-gressive, and obsessed with a hypercritical view of life, other people, and himself.[2] The stand-up comedian can't stop talking—not even when he is in bed with a woman. Words are his way of connecting and of hiding and controlling, but in *Annie Hall* they keep giving him away.

Except for the dolts in his early films, Allen's humor has always been based on a high degree of self-awareness, and Alvy, unlike Charlie and Buster, cannot claim to be an innocent. Like all of us, however, he is his own blind spot.

The original title of the film was *Anhedonia*. Apparently Allen thought that Alvy's core problem was his inability to take pleasure in life—something he is quite able to do, albeit in ways that can seem perverse.

In *When the Shooting Stops . . . The Cutting Begins*—a book Allen has disputed—the film editors Ralph Rosenblum and Robert Karen say that *Annie Hall* "wasn't the film he set out to make." According to their account, when they tried putting the story together on the basis of the script, the material didn't make for a coherent movie. They claim *Annie Hall* was restructured in the cutting room, and that Allen shot substantial new material after principal photography was completed—as he had done for *Take the Money and Run*.[3] The script meant to render the private life of a comedian, but the footage evidently failed to focus on Alvy's central problem—the disconnect that undermines his relationship to others.

We noted that Allen's reductive view of himself is far more radical in *Annie Hall* than in stand-up, but we may wonder whether what he revealed in the film as we know it was what he and Marshall Brickman intended when they wrote the script. Perhaps the core of the story—the core of Alvy—was not apparent to Allen until he looked at the original footage. What he then saw may have surprised him—something that happens frequently to documentary filmmakers and to storytellers working outside a familiar narrative structure.

Throughout the completed film we get the sense that Alvy is off base and trying to understand himself—that Allen/Alvy is engaged in a process of self-discovery. If Rosenblum's account is valid, it would seem that Allen briefly lost control over the story and his own image, but *regained* it by letting the evidence in the footage stand and sharpening it with additional scenes.

Without access to the original script we can't be sure how *Anhedonia* became *Annie Hall*. But letting the figure of Alvy emerge from the facts of his fear-ridden relationship to Annie clearly allowed Allen to create a unique work. If the script and original footage had been as devoid of persuasive relationships as his earlier films, and if Annie were rendered as two-dimensionally as the women in them, the disconnect in Alvy could not have emerged as the core issue.

By appearing on screen without the armor of his stand-up persona—or rather, by letting us look under the armor—he becomes not only unpredictable and richly human but brilliantly funny. By observing and reporting himself accurately, Allen taps into a deep vein of humor that most comedians avoid. No one else has instantaneous access to their own innermost fears and weaknesses, yet few are willing to display them as nakedly as Allen in *Annie Hall*.

"Someone is boring me," Dylan Thomas said. "I think it's me."

In stand-up, Allen performed a psychological striptease of a carefully constructed persona that used revealing bits of himself. In *Annie Hall*, however, we believe we are seeing Allen as he is. In Alvy, as in the figures played by Chaplin, Keaton, Groucho, and Fields, we sense an organic connection between the performer and the role, making *Annie Hall* far more of a personal document than his other films. By laying bare his own fears and failings—by acknowledging them more ruthlessly than most clowns do—he created a figure in whom we recognize ourselves. For the alienation that marks everything he says and does has, today, become epidemic. His disconnect connects him to us.

Perhaps the temporary loss of control over the film and his own image that Allen suffered took him back to a time when he was not yet in command of his life. Though it may have, briefly, left him in a state of confusion and even helplessness, once he was able to marshal his comedic gifts, his powers of observation, his psychological acuity, and his willingness to face uncomfortable truths, the very loss of control may have engendered the unique, deeply authentic structure and sparkling surfaces of *Annie Hall*.

Death, Alvy tells Annie, is "a big subject" for him. Given his many jokes about it, so is sex. Both he and Annie expect it to resolve existential issues: She can't relax in bed unless she smokes pot because it gives her a sense of wholeness that the sex act doesn't, and Alvy asks her to stop using it since he needs "the whole thing," and not just her body. Both are looking for more than tenderness, pleasure, and physical release, and both are likely to be disappointed.

Judging by the laughter that Alvy's bedroom encounters elicit, both his quest and its unsatisfactory result are familiar to the audience. Sex may have become a central issue in our lives because it is one of a shrinking number of ways of connecting with others *and* ourselves. One doubts Americans would spend billions of dollars a year on pornography in order to meet, not very satisfactorily, a purely biological need. Perhaps it is, instead, a forlorn substitute for relationships.

Allen's joke that "sex without love is an empty experience, but as empty experiences go, it's one of the best," camouflages a sad reality.

Alvy suffers from an inability to lend himself wholly to the present moment that afflicts many artists. It surely prompted him to call the screenplay *Anhedonia*.

After screwing a red lightbulb into a lamp before joining Annie in bed, he says, "Now we can go about our business here—and we can even develop photographs if we want to." He deflates one of the few happy bedroom encounters the moment it's over—"That was the most fun I've had without laughing"—and says to one of his wives, "Why do you always reduce my primal impulses to psychological disorders, he said as he unhooked her bra"—distancing himself in midsentence to become an observer.

His jokes keep him at a safe remove, and the laughter of others allows him a fleeting connection to them without actual contact. After he and Annie break up, he reaches out to another woman by repeating the lobster incident. When she asks him, nonplussed, whether he is joking, the lack of connection between them is painfully obvious. Laughter was something he and Annie could share.

Like Charles Foster Kane, Alvy is only comfortable when he is in control, particularly with women. He wants them close but just physically—or so he thinks.

Herman Mankiewicz borrowed elements from the life of William Randolf Hearst for the story of Kane, much as Theodore Dreiser and F. Scott Fitzgerald used men with power and wealth to stand in for themselves. But the figure of Kane was modeled largely on an artist—Orson Welles himself.[4] While there may be tycoons who become enraged and destructive when a woman rejects them, Hearst was in a happy relationship with Marion Davies, and instead of trashing her furniture—or, like Alvy, tearing up his driver's license—he might have used rage to fuel his competitive drive. The Robert F. Kennedy motto "Don't get mad, get even!" is surely valid for most businessmen and politicians, whereas Kane's and Alvy's relationships with women are more characteristic of artists.

When they start seeing each other, Annie is as disconnected as Alvy. He seems more confident than she, though his need for control—he chooses what movies they see and tells her what books to read—suggests that he is, in fact, more fearful. Surprisingly, he prompts her to go into analysis, and so starts her on the process that frees her from their foreclosed relationship. At first, she is inarticulate, but before long her thoughts and observations cease to reflect his, and she becomes eloquently herself when she sings.

From an ironic, emotionally safe distance Alvy notes that he is enabling her to leave him: "The incredible thing about it is, I'm paying for her analysis and she's making progress, and I'm getting screwed." But his reasons for freeing her seem ambiguous. He both wants her to exist as an unthreatening extension of himself and at his service, while his fear of intimacy pushes her into standing on her own. He feels he is getting screwed but must know that her growing independence offers him a way *out* of their relationship without making him reject and hurt her.

B

Persuasive fiction renders not only elements of objective reality that particularize the figures and their situation but also those components of their experience that will make what happens to them happen to us.

Our own "reality" is always a mix of what we actually perceive and how we react to it. A story that claims to be purely objective and doesn't include the subjective, either implicitly or explicitly, will not seem real. We believe factual or historical accounts that don't invoke our experience, but we come to story *for* the experience. Objective facts in fiction are meaningful to us largely as a conduit to it.

We noted that in early childhood there is no inner or outer realm; our experience is undivided and entirely subjective. But as we mature and step away from ourselves, we open up a separate inner—or subjective—space. Though most of us tend to focus on the world around us rather than the world within, we try to stay in touch with both.

In Western culture, the gap—or division—between the inner and outer realm is wider than elsewhere. But even in the West, until societies became urban, heterogeneous, and fragmented, the inner lives of most people *within* a community were substantially alike. It was industrialization and the specialization of labor that turned us into highly differentiated individuals, truly alike at the biological level only.

Though most of us learn to segregate the inner realm and its differences, some continue to be swayed by the subjectivity that governs early life. Misfits, sociopaths, and artists often find separating inner from outer realm difficult. They experience their own sensations and feelings intensely, while other people and the world are not altogether real to them. Indeed, the artist's work may be, in part, an effort to *make* them real—to render them in their separate or objective existence. When George Bernard Shaw says a man's interest in the world is merely the overflow of his interest in himself, he is surely speaking for himself.

Tragedies are largely centered on an individual or a small group, and the narrative is conditioned by their experience and point of view. We see Hamlet's story through *his* eyes, even if we are not blind to his limitations, and we noted that *King Lear* is structured by the inner life of Lear—just as *Moby Dick*, *Citizen Kane*, and *Crime and Punishment* are informed by the existential needs of Ahab, Charles Foster Kane, and Raskolnikov.

Comedies, however, are rarely focused on an individual, unified by a single point of view, or structured by the needs of a central figure. The work of Chaplin and Keaton are exceptions, and so is *Annie Hall*—pervaded as it is by the impulses and fears of Alvy Singer. They are so assertive that they keep blurring the line between the real and the imagined. Alvy has a hard time separating his wishes, needs, and anxieties from his perception of the world; objective or quasi-objective scenes are continually invaded by his subjective reality.

In *Annie Hall*, the inner realm that is *implicit* in Chaplin's physical actions and reactions is made explicit and visible. Instead of Charlie's tangible, sensory reality, the film renders Alvy's *psychological* experience. What happens to him is often as unrealistic as one of Buster's or Charlie's dreams, but we recognize it as psychologically true. We are rarely out of touch with him and understand what he says and does as easily and rapidly as we follow Charlie's physical actions and reactions. Though we have likely succeeded in repressing our insecurities and antisocial impulses, we readily recognize his as our own.

The movie shows us both what happens *and* how Alvy sees or remembers it—often simultaneously. But the gap between objective reality and his subjective take on it is always clear. Sometimes we see the situations and other people as he does; often we don't.

Alvy's issues are no less immediate and present to us than Charlie's physical survival. Unlike the secret life of Walter Mitty, his subjectivity is not focused on wish fulfillment, but lays bare his lack of self-esteem and misgivings about human existence. Since many of us suffer the same doubts, we identify with him even if we don't share his compulsive need to spill his views and hang-ups. Moreover, we always understand why he alters or omits facts that the film allows us to observe clearly.

Unlike most movies, *Annie Hall* remains current thirty-five years after it was made. Ceaseless economic and social changes in our society have produced a large pool of people who see themselves as marginal outsiders. It is continually replenished by young people with uncertain identities, who find themselves trapped in an extended period between adolescence and adult life.

Alvy's insecurity and paranoia are so pronounced that he tries to build up his confidence by putting down everyone else. His low self-esteem feeds the assumption—not uncommon among Jews—that all Goyim are dumb except for geniuses, who are invariably outsiders and therefore "Jews" in their experience and perspective.

Though Alvy's is an extreme case, many of us see ourselves not just as different from many others but, in some subtle degree, superior and/or inferior. We may countermand our pernicious tendency to rank everyone and ourselves, but the process is often unconscious and may be intrinsic to our condition—perhaps a response to a deep-seated sense of insecurity, uncertainty, and self-doubt.

C

Annie Hall is governed by Alvy's subjectivity, but there isn't another film in which the subjective is observed as objectively. *He* may think of his life as miserable, but we see him as a successful comedian with Diane Keaton/Annie as his girlfriend and enough self-confidence to share his failings with us. Compared to Charlie's dismal, often scary life, Alvy's situation seems enviable, though he never stops complaining about it.

Alvy frequently offers explanations and rationalizations for his quirky behavior: His statement that "as long as there is one person suffering, I can't relax" seems vastly exaggerated, but he may feel so vulnerable that he needs to wall himself off from the reality of other people, especially if they are in pain.

Alvy's identity and boundaries are clearly porous: He can't shut out the pompous comments of a Columbia University instructor in a movie line during an argument he and Annie are having about their sex life, and when the instructor starts in on Samuel Beckett, Alvy gets into a major, albeit imaginary, confrontation with him.

His subjective life keeps invading the objective realm—a condition most of us have learned to avoid. Often, his hyperactive and compulsive inner monologue spills into what he actually says, or we hear him mutter the way our own unconscious does when we fail to shut it out. His words are audible to us even when no one on the screen can hear them, yet enhance rather than undermine the credibility of the scenes.

The explicit subjectivity of the film allows Allen to use any and every device—imaginary moments, animation, subtitles, direct comments to the camera, and split-screen images. We are not at all surprised when Alvy transforms into a rabbi at the Halls' Easter dinner or appears as a small cartoon figure dwarfed by a large Wicked Queen from *Snow White*. Both are persuasive renderings of his inner reality.

Just as Alvy's inner and outer experience blend into each other, there is no sharp dividing line between his past and present. In *Take the Money and Run*, the past is a mere joke without relevance to the action. But *Annie Hall* is one of the few comedies in which it plays a central role—as it does in most close relationships. We may not like it, but we are largely products of the past.

Alvy was clearly a misfit in childhood, but during a vengeful return to his grade school classroom it is the other children who become deviants and face a future as laughable adults. What he says and shows us is obviously untrue, but his hostile recollections and reductive evocation of his classmates—whose conforming normality made little Alvy look and feel like an outsider—are immediately familiar. In childhood, many of us think we don't belong and nurture fantasies of revenge against those who make us feel excluded.

Since the film is verbal rather than physical, it has the surface of high comedy, but what we are laughing about most of the time is the substance of low comedy: aggression and sex. Both are less likely to intrude on our lives in an active form than as forbidden wishes and impulses, and *Annie Hall* comes closer to approximating our actual experience than comedies that allow them physical expression.

In the film, as in the stream of consciousness in twentieth-century fiction, moments and scenes follow each other without chronology or logical connection. In life, too, our feelings and associations move so rapidly backward, forward, or sideways that keeping track of what is going on within us is difficult. When we actually try to focus on it, we run the risk of losing contact with the world around us.

But we never lose touch with Alvy, and his constant back and forth between outer and inner reality creates no problems or bumps. We are enough like him to follow even his fantasies and dreams, and have no trouble jumping across gaps in time. Though our own objective and subjective reality is different from his, we accept the mix as a rendering of our experience. The facts of his life are accurately observed, and we recognize that the intrusion of subjectivity approximates what would happen to us—if we could allow our inner world the free play Allen allows his.

The film is like an analytic session. Alvy tells us both his fantasies and the facts, though, as in all stories, the facts are highly selective and distorted by his subjective perspective. The narrative sequence is freely associative but permits us to understand his associations, something we could never do if we were listening in on an analytic session.

As in Freudian therapy and stand-up comedy, the link between scenes is often just a word. When his second wife won't have sex with him, Alvy says he is going to take a cold shower, and the next cut takes us to Max and Alvy coming out of the shower at a tennis club.

Some transitions are made by disjunction. After Annie asks Alvy whether he is always funny, the cut is to an utterly unfunny comedian, and at the end of the wish-fulfilling episode in the movie line, Alvy's comment—"Boy, if life were only like this!"—segues to the opening title of *The Sorrow and the Pity.*

Like Alvy, but unlike the other figures, Annie is rendered with her subjectivity. She often blurts out her subtext—"That was stupid! . . . What a jerk I am!" She is as accessible to us as Alvy, and we have no trouble believing these two belong together. His ethnic urban background, verbal facility, wit, and smattering of literary and philosophical references give him an appearance of sophistication, while she appears to be an eager empty slate on which he can inscribe what he wants her to be.

Though both keep spilling what they think and feel, and we get to know them from the inside, they don't rupture the surfaces of credible behavior. Like Charlie, they live in a hyperreality in which elements of their inner lives are acted out. There are even moments when Alvy's subjectivity merges with Annie's into the intersubjectivity of people in love—a heady state that seems to transport us back to the oneness of early childhood. Their intersubjectivity isn't always positive. The first time they are together, Annie blurts out, "You are what Grammy Hall would call a real Jew"—a comment that blends perfectly with Alvy's conviction that all non-Jews are anti-Semites.

Occasionally, the intersubjectivity appears to extend to others. When Alvy sees Grammy Hall staring at him at the Easter dinner, he transforms himself into an image of what *he* imagines *she* sees—an Orthodox Jew with long black sidelocks and a fur hat. The coincidence of Alvy's paranoia with Grammy Hall's suspicion constitutes a disjunction for them, but a connection for us.

Like *Citizen Kane* and *Raging Bull, Annie Hall* has a loose, unconventional form. Individual scenes are frequently played in uninterrupted takes, like the bedroom discussion between Alvy and Allison Porchnick in which he uses the Kennedy assassination to avoid sex. Like *Citizen Kane*, the film combines single-take scenes into a montage structure of the narrative. Moreover, no film since *Citizen Kane* has moved as effortlessly back and forth in time. Both are precluded—one tragically, the other nostalgically—and both orient us at the outset by revealing how the story will end.

Since *Annie Hall* was clearly restructured in the cutting room, we may assume the original script did not have a traditional plot, or a radical resequencing of the scenes would have been impossible.[5] Its free form, planned or unplanned, makes for a generative interface between the loose, episodic presentation of stand-up and the sequential structure of traditional story.

Take the Money and Run is no less free in form and was evidently restructured in the cutting room, but its underlying reality is other movies, whereas *Annie Hall* is grounded in experiences that resemble our own. The unpredictable, often fragmented narrative and dialogue render a central aspect of our reality. Though we are barely aware of it, we, too, often experience ourselves and others as fragments—not in a continuum.

The disconnect between scenes and the way the dialogue darts and skips unexpectedly is expressive of Alvy's daily life and, indeed, of his identity. He is so fragmented that he threatens to fly apart, but—like the movie—he is held together by the tensile bond of needs, fears, and hostility that remain hidden in most of us but are openly displayed in Alvy.

The free form allows Allen to render many moments in an accurately observed realistic style, while leaving out everything inessential. Because the film is made coherent by his subjectivity, he can, like poetry, eliminate anything that isn't important to him or us. Except for Annie, others don't interest him and he doesn't bother with them. The film moves from intensity to intensity, with few flat spots. No doubt, whatever didn't work in the editing was simply cut—something most films can't afford, since they are sequenced along clear narrative and emotional lines, and gaps would make them difficult to follow.

The radical elisions, economy, and speed allow for constant, nonmechanical surprises. At Alvy's first meeting with Allison Porchnick, he makes a series of condescending comments that reduce her, as she puts it, to a "cultural stereotype." Her reaction to him is unexpected— she finds him "cute"—and we have no problem accepting that they are married the next time we see them. The process of getting to know and care for each other is skipped.

The fragmented rendering of the figures is predicated on our awareness that we don't really know anyone, including ourselves, and that people behave, feel, think, and speak in ways that often strike us as utterly surprising. Only our need for predictability prompts us to overlook the discontinuities and fractures.

Figures in the film appear and disappear, and encounters follow each other randomly. Since the narrative is not pegged to chronology, cause and effect play a marginal role: important things happen in one scene but don't necessarily have an effect in the next, and effects are often shown before their causes.

Because the narrative isn't obliged to a plot, it simply follows the evolving and devolving relationship of Alvy and Annie, with the fragmented time structure allowing what would otherwise be the fairly predictable unfolding of their romance to become surprising and so more realistic—both in their experience of it and in ours.

There is no progression. Like most relationships, the story evolves in a spiral—a series of scenes that repeat the same essential pattern at different times and in different settings. We discover the central figures and their situation much as we discover people and situations in daily life, and get caught up in the process and texture of their relationship. The jokes and gags are thrown away and don't interrupt the flow of talk that, in *their* romance, constitutes the flow of life. What happens to and between them is ordinary and familiar, but is made intense and extraordinary by the constant intrusion of Alvy's and, at times, Annie's inner life.

Allen has said, "I hate reality. . . . Unfortunately it's the only place where we can get a good steak dinner."[6]

Though *Annie Hall* would be incoherent without the connective tissue of Alvy's subjective life, it would lose its bite without Allen's sharp observation of external reality.

Just as Alvy himself becomes real in the disconnect between Annie and himself, his subjectivity is substantiated by the discrepancy between his wishes and fears and the accurately rendered world around him. Moreover, he countermands his own feelings and needs with his often jaundiced self-observations. Though we are drawn into his and Annie's romance, we seldom lose our objective perception of them and their world. As in *Citizen Kane* and *Raging Bull*, we find ourselves deeply engaged with the central figures, but not imprisoned in them.

Annie Hall is at once Allen's most consciously subjective film and the most carefully observed. Its sharp psychological *and* social accuracy makes the inner realm visible without violating the familiar surfaces of our lives.

Though the poverty in Chaplin's films is substantiated and real, Charlie's feelings about the blind girl are those of an adolescent, and her feelings for him derive from an illusion. But the feelings of Alvy and Annie are real to us. We have an unusual sense of intimacy with them as a couple, and may know them better and see them more clearly than we know and see ourselves. Their failings, conflicts, fears, and vulnerabilities are recognizably our own, and when we laugh about them we are clearly laughing about ourselves.

While Chaplin and Keaton generated a credible but often highly subjective world around Charlie and Buster, the world of Annie and Alvy is the one we live in, and the persuasive rendering of both their internal *and* external life may make *Annie Hall* the most realistic of film comedies.

The films Allen has made since *Annie Hall* are either governed by traditional realism, with its claim to an objective viewpoint, or—like *Zelig* and *The Purple Rose of Cairo*—fantasies.

In his realist work, he is in full control. Once the script is written, its structure—shaped largely by familiar narrative conventions—is no longer in doubt or play. Conversely, the stories based on fantasy are free of the physical limitations that govern our lives: anything is possible. Both lack the tension between subject and object that informs *Annie Hall*—the ceaseless contradictions that make Alvy Singer and his world persuasive and surprising.

A successful artist who owes his success and identity to his discon-nected state is tempted to withdraw behind walls that shield him from the continuous challenges of ordinary life and leave him less vulner-able to the conflicts and self-doubt that once assailed him. Unless he suffers serious external or internal reverses, he isn't likely to leave the fortified, comfortably furnished space his success affords him. It may, however, have been conflict and self-doubt that were the source of his originality and sharpened the edges of his work.

Allen's films after *Annie Hall* are no longer rooted in his immediate, uncomfortable experience. Some moments and scenes are textured persuasively, but most situations are built on generalizations or ab-stractions. The precision and telling detail of *Annie Hall* give way to predictable shticks, and the plots that structure the narrative tend to be formulaic.

Perhaps the protective walls Allen erected around himself cut off his work from the profusion, energy, and chaos of ordinary life. For reality, alas, is more than a good steak dinner we can consume in se-clusion or with a few friends.

In an interview, Allen comments on the conflict between the comic—derived from disjunctions—and the "pretty," based on easy harmonies.[7] Since the comic figure is usually up against it and fighting for his survival, he can hardly afford harmony or consistency. Com-edies, like our lives, are often messy and unpretty, with but intermit-tent moments of harmony.

Annie Hall is comfortably open to the welter of city life, with many scenes set on streets that resist a unified design. The camerawork of Gordon Willis, who gave *The Godfather* and several of Allen's later films their harmonic look, is not, here, primarily determined by visual considerations, and Santo Loquasto, the art director who color-coor-dinated Allen's work after *Annie Hall*, had not yet joined the team.

But though the images have an unkempt, documentary look, many are informed and transformed by our awareness that Alvy and Annie are no longer together. The shot of the house under the roller coaster is charged with nostalgia as well as a spirit of fun, and the final shot of upper Broadway is transfigured by a palpable though nonemphatic sense of loss. The images are both more persuasive and more evocative than the visual harmony of his later work.

Annie Hall is among the rare films that combine comedy with genuine feelings, even if they don't run deep. We believe in Alvy and Annie's love for each other, though—as in *Twelfth Night*—we are not asked to invest our own feelings in theirs.

Annie is persuasive in part because she isn't just funny. When she calls him in the middle of the night to kill a spider in her bathroom, there is a shot of her huddled on her bed, crying. The sudden intrusion of her tears on a light-hearted moment substantiates her as a person; she doesn't exist simply to make us laugh. Though inarticulate at the outset, she learns to express herself eloquently through music, and Allen shows his respect for her feelings, talent, and hard-won self-esteem by keeping the camera on her throughout her second club performance.

We noted Allen's comment that when he wants to be funny, he hits his occipital bone with a mallet—"I do it for the money." But before he learned how to turn his alienated state to good account it was likely a source of distress. All that remains of it in *Annie Hall* is his insecurity and anger, but they enrich and deepen our response to the film. For in trying to make a relationship with Annie, Alvy is not just driven by biology but by our shared need to bridge the gap that divides us from each other.

There is an anecdote about a college student named Rinehardt, who had no friends and would stand under his own dormitory window in the evenings, calling, "Rinehardt! Hey, Rinehardt!"

Like Alvy and Charlie, he is both funny and sad.

D

The absurd or surreal has been a central feature of Allen's humor from the start. Like many artists, he clearly didn't buy into the assumptions on which our institutions are built, and once the links that make sense of the world fall away, what we call "reality" begins to look absurd.

Allen's joke about the bigot, who was a bed wetter and went to his Klan meetings in a rubber sheet, makes no claim on reality, but gains its edge from the ridiculous—just as the cartoon figures and situations in *Take the Money and Run* are brought to life and made pertinent by the disjunctures in the action. Virgil Starkwell tries to play his cello by blowing into it, and when he asks his wife how he should dress for the bank robbery, she says, "What are the other guys wearing?" Virgil's parents are so ashamed of him, they hide behind Groucho moustaches and glasses, and his father tells an interviewer, "He was an atheist. I tried to beat God into him, but he was very tough. How would you like to see my stamp collection?"

Though the films of Chaplin and Keaton are full of surprises and, in this sense, render the discontinuities or gaps in our experience, Charlie and Buster themselves make sense, and so does the world they inhabit.

The Marx Brothers and their world don't.

Groucho: "Either this man is dead or my watch has stopped."[8]

Groucho: "Did you hear anything?"

Chico: "No. Did you say anything?"

Groucho: "No."

Chico: "Maybe that's why I didn't hear anything."

Groucho: "Maybe that's why I didn't say anything."[9]

Connections in their films are deliberately destroyed, words no longer link to objects or meaning, and speech becomes a series of riddles with nonsensical solutions. Groucho's appalling puns, Chico's misuse of English, and Harpo's misreadings make a hash of verbal communication. But, like their absurd physical provocations and reactions, they make sense in a topsy-turvy world, where cause and effect have become uncoupled.

After *Duck Soup*—considered by many to be their finest film—failed at the box office, Paramount dropped their contract, and Irving

Thalberg signed them for MGM. But he insisted that henceforth their movies must have a story line that would satisfy rather than violate audience expectations. The disjunctions that were the basis of their comedy would have to be framed in a purposeful narrative that didn't fragment and undermine itself.

The absurdities on which they thrived confused not just American audiences. Benito Mussolini deemed them so threatening to the order and discipline he was trying to impose that he banned their movies in Italy—surely a greater absurdity than anything in *Duck Soup*.

But what seemed incomprehensible and pointless to audiences in the 1930s matches the experience of later generations.[10] The absurd or surreal has become central to our existence, and their nonsense makes sense to us. We have no trouble jumping across the gaps, since our own lives are continually fractured by discontinuities. Though the Marx Brothers and their situations are utterly unreal, we recognize our own increasingly fragmented experience in their disjunctions and laugh.[11]

Perhaps a time will come when we feel about the world at large as we once did about our small communities—at home with what happens and connected to others by shared values. But in the foreseeable future we are likely to live in a state of exacerbated disconnection or alienation—in close proximity to strangers with very different histories and different values, speaking different languages, and believing in different gods. As we noted, moreover, in a context of continuous change we can't even count on knowing or being predictable ourselves.

Many, disconnected and alone, withdraw into themselves, lose contact with the world, and become truly strange.

> *The New York Times* reported that a sixty-eight-year-old woman on the East Side had stuffed the dead body of her eighty-seven-year-old husband into a suitcase, which she kept on the living room floor. When the police asked her why, she said, "He always wanted to go to Arizona."

> Sirhan Sirhan, who shot Robert Kennedy, told the parole board, "If Robert Kennedy were alive today, he would not countenance singling me out for this kind of treatment."

A lawyer in a death penalty case asked a potential juror, "Can you participate in a trial in which the results might be death by lethal injection?"

"Yeah," the man said. "If it was on a weekend."[12]

During a visit to Tel Aviv, Igor Stravinsky was asked by an Israeli to write a concerto for shofar and orchestra.[13]

An English friend had lunch with the queen at Buckingham Palace on the day a new coin was issued. She told him she thought she looked awful on it.

Though estrangement is a central component of our experience, it is so distressing that most of us can only deal with it in the safe arena of fiction. We noted that the disjunctions in jokes and most comedies occur in situations that are clearly unreal.

What happens in *Annie Hall*, however, is at once surreal *and* persuasive. Much of the time, it originates in Alvy and Annie's inner life. Their first conversation is surreal on the surface, but makes perfect sense subjectively:

Alvy: "D'you want a lift?"

Annie: "Do you have a car?"

Alvy: "No. I was going to take cab."

Annie: "Oh. Well—I have a car."

Their exchange is no less absurd than a scene between Groucho and Chico, but we believe it might happen just this way.

When the man from "the cast of *The Godfather*" asks Alvy for his autograph, he starts out saying it's for his girlfriend, then tells him to make it out to Ralph.

Alvy: "Your girlfriend's name is Ralph?"

Man: "He's my brother."

He makes no sense, but is perfectly credible.

Had Alvy Singer arrived in Chippewa Falls in an earlier time, he would have likely passed through town as a peddler instead of sitting at the Easter dinner as Annie's boyfriend. But when her brother, Duane—on the one occasion he speaks—confesses he is tempted to drive into the headlights of oncoming cars, he turns out to be even more of an alien. Perhaps he sees Alvy as a fellow outsider with whom his secret is safe, but the misfit Jew, hearing that a mainstream Goy is wracked by self-destructive compulsions, feels an urgent need to "get back to Planet Earth."

CHAPTER TEN

Connected but Free

A

Some years ago, when I offered some grapes to a houseguest, he reproached me for buying fruit that all right-thinking folk were boycotting in support of a strike. Properly shamed, I left the room—but found when I returned that he had eaten the whole bunch. I was delighted to call him a hypocrite, only to be told, with what seemed to him infallible logic, that once the offense of purchasing them had been committed, no further harm was done by enjoying them.

Human existence is a web of contradictions that our communal structures and rules reconcile for us. We learn the rules early and absorb them so thoroughly that we remain largely free of conflict, unaware of the paradoxes—most obviously between culture and nature—that make us human. As we noted, only those who can't submit to communal structures—often because they were excluded by them—live nakedly exposed to the opposites and are pulled back and forth between them.

Yet all of us—though we barely know it—are boxed in by a set of demands that double bind us and leave us with a residue of tension.

So the community calls on us to be connected *and* separate, obedient to rules, yet self-determined, open and responsive to others, yet independent of them.[1]

To obey both imperatives and remain in balance between them, we shift ceaselessly—and for the most part unconsciously—back and forth between opposites.

Like the community, consciousness both separates and connects us—reminding us that we are part of natural life, yet apart from it.

It serves the community most significantly by dividing us against ourselves. For as we noted, we are ourselves the most effective guardians of the inner realm, where potentially destructive impulses have their origin.

The self-division fostered by our families early in life becomes second nature to us. But while we effectively learn to contradict ourselves, we try to avoid situations in which we are openly pulled in two directions at once. Getting caught between opposites makes us intensely uncomfortable, especially if we are divided against ourselves.

Explicit contradictions generate ambivalence and ambiguity that undermine our sense of identity and the clear direction we need to get through the day. We are, indeed, so dependent on certainties and consistency—both in others and ourselves—that we ignore inconsistencies. We avoid them even when they are of no consequence—like the grapes my houseguest was boycotting but felt free to eat.

Though our structures, institutions, and laws appear to negotiate the contradictions for us and allow us to ignore them, they can't actually resolve them.

Consciousness often says, "Yes, but—" or "No, but—," reminding us that things may not be as we want them to be, whereas our communal structures tend to suppress the "but." They may also assign it to the contrarian voice of a devil, who can assume any shape—including that of a political or religious perspective that differs from our own.

Stories, too, are structures, but since we consider them fictions, they offer us an opportunity to face the paradoxes of our existence without confusing and discomforting us.

We noted that both comic and tragic figures are often caught in a double bind. When we laugh or respond empathetically, we acknowledge that we recognize their situation and experience.

Like the community, stories send us a double message. They focus on the individual *and* invalidate him; preserve order but undermine it; stop time, yet show it moving relentlessly forward. Though we know what will happen from the start, they catch us up in the illusion that the figures can change their fate even as the precluded ending robs them—and by inference all of us—of the very freedom we have assigned them.

Since we don't believe in stories but keep returning to them, we may sense they have something to tell us.

Perhaps contemporary culture proclaims our freedom and individuality so insistently because our experience often suggests the opposite. Today, our individuality can seem little more than a tag—like differences in the clothes we wear and the cars we drive—and our freedom may extend no further than a choice between an overwhelming variety of brands in the marketplace.

Most of us survive with our confidence and sense of freedom intact by remaining within a small arena, where what we are and do allows us to think we make a difference. But we are haunted by the suspicion, if not the awareness, that the free individual may be little more than a construct decreed by the community and made plausible by our existence as separate biological creatures.

B

When Buster shadows the villain step for step, we laugh because he is naive, even though we know it demands great skill and perfect timing.[2]

Comedy pulls us in two directions at once. We root for the clown but want him to get in trouble—the worse, the better—and would be disappointed if he escaped it. We enjoy what appears to hurt or frighten him, and often laugh at situations that would be upsetting or sad in life.

We are at once close and distanced, involved and detached, know what will happen yet are surprised by *how* it happens, disbelieve it yet recognize it to be true to our experience.

Low comedy may shock us with its coarse content, but—like Freud's sexual jokes—is often elegant in execution.

Many comic figures embody contradictions. Native American clowns were called *Contraries*, and the costume of European jesters was motley, a patchwork of contrary colors. Towsen says, "Harlequin was . . . a chameleon who could be comic or sad, masculine or feminine, gentle or vulgar,"[3] and Chaplin deliberately made Charlie a figure of contradictions.[4] Moreover, this incompetent, penniless nobody is played by a world-famous millionaire, and his childlike, often instinctual behavior is countermanded by his highly refined control over his body and his absolute control over his films. As a prototypical outsider who makes a community of us, Charlie embodies the paradox we face as individuals—separate yet inextricably tied to the whole. Kierkegaard calls the pull of opposites in the comic "painless contradiction,"[5] and Girard says, "In laughter, for a few brief moments, we seem to have the best of two incompatible worlds."

Comic situations, jokes, gags, and wit often depend on paradox.

Duke Ellington said that if he could bring just two things to a desert island, he'd take the Bible and Lena Horne.[6]

A fellow physicist said of Paul Dirac, "There is no God and Dirac is his prophet."[7]

Yogi Berra reportedly said, "If you come to a fork in the road, take it."

The good news/bad news format of many jokes gives expression to our double-edged reality:

> A Vatican official came to see the pope in a state of great agitation.
> "What is it, my son?"
> "Holy Father, I have good news and terrible news."
> "Tell me the good news first."
> "Our Lord has returned."
> "Wonderful! And the bad news?"
> "The call came from Salt Lake City."

Baudelaire says, "The duality of art is one fatal consequence of the duality of man."[8] It renders a constant of our experience we cannot afford to face in life.

By pulling us in two directions at once, the comic stretches us and makes us tense, often to the edge of discomfort, then breaks the tension with a surprise that appears to resolve the contradiction.[9] The physical paroxysm of laughter swamps our bifurcated awareness and makes us whole.[10]

When we say, "I died laughing," people rightly assume we enjoyed the experience, for it frees us of the obligation to remain conscious and inherently self-divided beings, riven by implicit or explicit inconsistencies.[11]

The state of wholeness or fusion is brief but valued so highly that anyone who disrupts it by trying to understand or explain *why* we are laughing is resisted and resented.

C

Laughter not only releases tension but, by disabling our awareness, obscures the fact that we have been turned into its helpless victims—a condition potentially fraught with fear.

In life, we learn to guard our boundaries and abandon them only with family and lovers. Since intense experiences threaten to invade and fuse us, we avoid them in all but safe situations. The intensity of children makes us smile, but in day-to-day adult relationships "cool" may always be the preferred temperature, especially among men.[12]

In life, sympathy and empathy allow us to be in touch with others. We have a sense of what they are going through without feeling invaded or compelled to share their experience. We feel connected, but remain comfortably separate.

In fiction and music, however, we gladly submit to being intensely involved or even overwhelmed. We abandon our self-awareness and our control over what is happening to us, as well as our identity.

For the duration of a movie, we expect to identify with the central figures, become immersed in their world, and share their experience. We are at least dimly aware that in less explicit, less dramatic form it stands for our own experience, though communal life obliges us to keep it largely out of sight.

Implicitly or explicitly, most stories are governed by a point of view that renders or at least approximates the way we, too, perceive reality. But since fiction is safe, our identity can become fluid and extend even to figures we would avoid in life—to Lear and Raskolnikov.

Like music, stories are ultimately harmonic. They reconcile conflicts, differences, and dissonances. Boundaries between the figures and us become indistinct without making us anxious.

In Jean Vigo's *L'Atalante*, a young woman from the provinces finds herself stranded in Paris. When she tries to buy a train ticket that will take her back to her husband, a pickpocket steals her pocketbook. An elderly man, seeing her panic, falls into an epileptic fit, while out on the street an angry mob chases the thief—a starved-looking young man, who is filmed through the staves of an iron fence by a rapidly moving camera that charges the image with anxiety.

Within a few brief moments we have been transported into the subjective experience of three people, linked by fear. Their intersubjectivity includes us, and though in life it would make us intensely uncomfortable, we find it exhilarating in art.[13]

Within a story, the line between inner and outer realm often blurs. Alvy Singer at the Easter dinner sees himself as he fears Grammy Hall sees him.

Van Gogh paints both the object and his feelings about it. By merging object and subject, his image renders not only what the eye registers but a unifying combination of the double, often divided nature of our experience. This makes it more complete—and so more "real" or "true"—than a realist image that is focused on physical accuracy and claims to eliminate the response of the painter.

While van Gogh found relationships in life painfully difficult, his portrait of the postman Joseph Roulin is at once a substantiated rendering of the man and a clear expression of the painter's tender, deeply respectful feelings about him.

Though in life we keep trying to draw a line between what is outside us—we call it reality—and our thoughts, feelings, wishes, and fears, we often fail. Even the scientist cannot easily separate learned habits of thinking from his observations. As Werner Heisenberg says, we build our assumptions into our instruments, and so into our experiments.

The camera reproduces what we believe about reality. But despite its seeming objectivity, a meaningful photograph will—like a painting by Van Gogh—render both the object *and* the point of view or feelings of the photographer. What makes it persuasive to us is that it conforms to our assumptions: the subjective element is present, but we are not made *aware* of it. Unlike painting today, a photograph *implies* the subjective instead of stating it openly—much as we try to keep our own subjectivity out of sight in daily life.

Were we to claim that a painting by van Gogh renders what we actually see, people would think us mad. Fortunately, our own reactions to the same scene in life would not be nearly strong enough to intensify and purify the colors, or sweep everything into a whole—unified by the swirling energy of the creation itself. But on the canvas, as in fiction, we and the world can become safely one. Fragments cohere: the artwork reconnects or harmonizes what must, in life, be carefully kept apart.

As Baudelaire tells us, in art we can recover the original unity of object and subject: "What is pure art according to the modern idea? It is the creation of the vocative magic, containing at once the object and the subject, the world external to the artist and the artist himself."[14]

Surely, the "vocative magic" isn't confined to the "modern," but has been central to our experience of art from the beginning.

Occasionally a filmmaker will find a story in which an accurate rendering of the physical world, abetted by our faith in the photographic image, meshes perfectly with the subjective experience of the central figure.

In Robert Bresson's *A Man Escaped*, the physical and psychological survival of the central figure is fused: each is derived from and depends on the other. The brutal facts of his imprisonment and his imminent execution join the inner and outer realm seamlessly and make the fragments of his experience—everything he and we see and hear—cohere into a whole. The bare furnishings of his cell and the way he uses them to enable his escape are physical proof of his inner commitment and faith. And the final image of a young man the Germans were about to execute walking into the early dawn outside the prison wall becomes a tranquil but powerful affirmation that blends human courage with something other—perhaps no more than chance or luck—an image suffused with what we no longer dare call spirit.

Bresson's film has the objective reality of a document and the subjective force of a great poem.[15]

In popular work, too, object and subject are fused. But here the fusion comes easily—without the barely contained, sometimes violent tension between subject and object, or self and other, that energizes the paintings of van Gogh.

In popular stories, not only the world around the figures—like the weather—but the structure and outcome of the narrative are largely determined by their feelings and wishes. The writers and directors of our movies know that their primary job is to meet the emotional needs and daydreams of the audience. That's where the money is.

To some extent all art is wish fulfilling. Like children, most of us go to stories for reassurance, and we don't expect to see Snow White die or the Wicked Queen enjoy the rewards of her machinations, though in life that is often what happens.

But while traditional stories, like sentimental works, focus on and often derive from the inner realm, they don't allow our desires and wishes to dominate the physical, economic, social, and psychological realities of human existence. Like scientists, traditional storytellers will not knowingly let their wishes and feelings disregard the objective limitations of our situation to please themselves or their audience.

In genre narrative, familiar and predictable figures prompt our unconflicted identification with the hero, along with an unambiguous rejection of the villain. But Lear, Ahab, and Charles Foster Kane don't elicit a response from us that is simple and basic enough to make all of us alike. Their stories don't cater to the common denominator of popular fiction—our comfortable sense that we *are* like the central figure and can therefore *like* them. Lear, Ahab, and Kane are *not* like us. We may, indeed, dislike them.

But once we put ourselves in their situation—one in which their wishes and will are of no avail—differences between them and us cease to matter. The structure of stories *makes* us alike and allows us to find common ground even with those we would reject in life by showing them both in their grandeur *and* with their mortal limitations.

D

As differences were not perceived until we evolved into conscious beings, we may say the creation was once whole.

> Osip Mandelstam said his poems began as a hum that gradually transformed into words.

> Greek drama is thought to have evolved when a single figure stepped out of a choral song, followed by a second and third actor, each speaking as individuals.

Like our existence, the arts at once derive from the whole *and* separate from it.

Arthur Schopenhauer calls music a departure from the *Grundton*—a single sound deep at the core of undivided, unconscious nature.

Johann Sebastian Bach believed that "the connection of number and word and musical pitch" stood for "the mystical oneness of things."[16]

Music comes closest among the arts to inducing a sense of perfect harmony—a harmony we *seem* to recall, though we cannot actually have experienced it, for consciousness would have disrupted it the moment we became aware of it.

Music may be the most immersive art because it is largely nonrepresentational and doesn't depend on cognition.[17] It can enter us without passing through the mind and make us feel instantaneously whole and connected.[18]

All of the arts, as Walter Pater says, aspire to this same sense of harmony. Stories rupture it at the beginning—*without* a disruption there *is* no story—but most return to it at the end. Even jokes end in a kind of harmony, though it is often spurious and merely camouflages an underlying disjunction.

Significantly, comedians whose lives and work are rife with conflict and contradictions are often also musicians, or deeply engaged with music.

Chaplin composed much of the melodic material for *City Lights*, *Modern Times*, and the reissue of *The Gold Rush*, and during his early days in California he played the violin for hours. The Marx Brothers made their first appearances as singers; the Swiss clown Grock played a large number of instruments; Sid Caesar was a saxophonist and Peter Sellers a drummer before they became comedians. Jimmy Durante, Danny Kaye, and Noel Coward shifted back and forth between comedy and music, and Woody Allen plays the clarinet in a jazz group.

When Chaplin was young and unknown, he appeared in a Paris music hall, and after one performance a man in the audience asked to meet him. He introduced himself as a composer, complimented Chaplin, and told him, "You are instinctively a musician and dancer." The encounter meant little to Chaplin, who hadn't heard the music or name of Claude Debussy.[19]

Nietzsche says that tragedy was born out of music. But comedy *begins* in a disconnect and *ends* by taking us back into harmony—with low comedy taking us even further down: to the *Grundton* of the wholly natural or instinctual.

Like all of the arts, music can soothe and heal. In mid-nineteenth-century America, Quaker hospitals for the insane used music therapy to make their patients feel as whole as possible.

The paintings of schizophrenics are often harmonious and balanced, suffusing their art with a unity and tranquility that elude them in life.

The anthropologist Mary Catherine Bateson describes an evening she spent with villagers in a remote part of New Guinea. Everyone was outdoors and the mood was festive, when a man suddenly jumped up and filled the darkness with threats. Bateson was told he had killed his wife in a psychotic rage, but no one in the crowd laid a hand on him. Instead, someone shouted, "Come on, Selan, how about the Funny Group?" Others joined in, and he was cajoled into playing his harmonica. Then someone did a comic dance for him, and after another outburst of rage and threats he was himself coaxed into playing the clown. He calmed down and was taken to his house, where a guard was set for the night.[20]

A combination of music, dance, and comic turns defused a dangerous confrontation.

The connection between comedy and dance goes back at least to Attic Greece, when the wedding that concluded most comedies was celebrated with singing and dancing.[21]

The tension between Astaire and Rogers generated by the plot resolves in dance sequences that interrupt the narrative and effectively stop time. When the dance ends, the plot picks up and the tension between them rebuilds.

We delight in watching Charlie in the boxing ring of *City Lights* synchronize his steps perfectly with both his opponent and the referee, or pirouette in a berserk ballet along the assembly line in *Modern Times* while squirting his fellow workers with oil.

The resolution of Chaplin's stories and scenes is often as graceful and "musical" as his physical moves and his choreographic staging. At the end of *The Gold Rush*, when Charlie and Big Jim are sailing home as new millionaires, a press photographer persuades him to pose on deck in his discarded tramp outfit. Stepping away from the camera for a better picture, Charlie tumbles down into steerage and disappears inside a large coil of rope. It is fortuitously placed next to Georgia, the dancehall girl he has loved without hope. Two ship's officers appear in search of a stowaway, spot him in his ragged outfit, and arrest him, giving Georgia—who has no idea he has struck it rich—a chance to pay for his passage and prove that she cares for him. Just then Charlie's valet appears with his new finery, his status as a millionaire is revealed, and the valet is instructed to prepare a cabin for the bride-to-be. The resolution takes less than two minutes, and ends the story in perfect harmony.

Comedies and fairy tales share not only unexpected reunions and happy endings but also moments of enchantment that are, as the word implies, linked to music.

Dream sequences in Chaplin and Keaton allow them to perform extraordinary and sometimes magical feats—in *The Kid*, all of the residents on a ghetto street sprout wings and fly—without violating physical reality. The figures are transposed into a realm where dreams and spells, like those that transform the figures in *A Midsummer Night's Dream*, can work their magic and free us of our limits.[22]

E

The world of early childhood is undifferentiated and whole. In cartoons and fairy tales, as in childhood play and the paintings of Van Gogh, objects come to life and shapes are infinitely malleable. Charlie, in *The Adventurer*, turns a pair of salt and pepper shakers into binoculars, and Harpo consistently transforms words back into objects. One thing readily becomes another, and the transformations blur the distinctions we must make in life. They return us to an undivided state, just as low comedy short-circuits our civilized reactions and takes us back to a primitive, unconflicted time.

Surely the deepest pleasure we take in the comic derives from our sense of wholeness—with our laughter connecting us to ourselves and everyone else who is laughing and freeing us briefly of the obligatory separation, distinctions, and self-division that consciousness imposes.

The fusion of self and other—the unbroken connection between the world within and the world around us—has the beguilingly effect of returning us to childhood. As Freud says, the pleasure—he calls it the euphoria—that the comic evokes in us is "nothing other than the mood of . . . our childhood, when we were ignorant of the comic . . . incapable of jokes and . . . had no need of humor to make us feel happy in our life."[23]

We are back in the Garden of Delight—in Paradise.

For young children, magic shows hold no interest or surprises. Their reality is so changeable and fragmented that the tricks of the magician with their unexpected connections and disconnections hardly register. Cause and effect have, as yet, no meaning or place in their experience, and nonsense makes as much sense to them as sense. They might well not be surprised to see someone making sunshine out of cucumbers, or find anything odd and amusing in an encounter between a mouse and an elephant:

"My, you're a small!" said the elephant.
"I've been sick," said the mouse.

By releasing us into the realm of nonsense, the comic frees us of the burden of making sense. It allows us to cast off the rules and restrictions that reason and order impose, and inverts the sequences and hierarchies we have been taught to respect. W. S. Gilbert and Bergson call it topsy-turvydom.

In comedies as in fairy tales, the last may end up first, the fool turns out to be wise, and the simpleton or child wins out. Not accidentally, topsy-turvydom resembles the Kingdom of Heaven, where, too, the last shall be first and the hierarchies of importance that govern our lives are turned upside down.

An up-ending of the familiar is a frequent element in wit, from the subtle to the crude.

> "'Tis better to have loved and lost than never to have lost at all."

> Stuck in a hopeless movie production, the Hollywood actress asked, "Who do I have to fuck to get off this picture?"

F

Comedy as we know it is thought to have evolved from the rites of Dionysus, a fertility god with both male and female attributes. He was also the god of wine and music, and the revels associated with him constituted a period of license in which social distinctions were blurred and the forbidden was allowed.

Alcohol, music, and dance were integral to the occasion, as they are at similar celebrations in our own day. Boundaries become indistinct both between and within us; the control of the will or ego is loosened and individual participants are fused into a quasi-community.

The link between these celebrations and comedy is clear.[24] Both are collective and democratic; grave issues are temporarily forgotten and unreason rules, though it is often informed by the deeper reason of nature or instinct. Both are distinct from daily life and tolerate behavior that would be censured were it not enacted in a clearly separate and safe arena; and both rejoin what daily life must keep apart. They reaffirm the oneness of the creation.

Even the inversion of the established order in topsy-turvydom has a parallel in some celebrations and rituals. In the days before Lent, the medieval church allowed monks to appoint one of their own as the Lord of Unreason, who parodied the mass, worshiped an ass, and chanted the Liturgy of Folly.

At first glance, comedy and tragedy appear to be opposites. Comedy is focused on love, sexuality, and the continuum of life, with figures who are ordinary and often pleasure loving, while tragedy centers on a unique individual who is fated to die.[25]

But beneath the surface there is a fundamental likeness between a tragic hero who—for the duration of the action—*thinks* he is special, and the comic figure who knows from the start that he isn't. Both comedy and tragedy end with a loss of difference. The figures are either married or buried. Love and death alike rejoin them to the whole.

Nietzsche called the theater "epidemic," for it swallows the individual in the collective.[26]

G

The basic facts of our existence—our connection to the creature world and our irrelevance in the infinity of time and space—are so reductive of us and our concerns that we must be shielded from them if the community is to survive.

Shielding us has ever been a core function of the rituals that arise wherever we encounter the incomprehensible and limitless. The gods they honor make the impersonal forces that engender life more accessible—if not to our will, at least to prayer.

Our gods have always had attributes of the "nothing" beyond the human, though most reconstitute it in anthropomorphic form. Even so, we cannot look at them with the naked eye: their reality would turn us to stone. God said to Moses on the mountaintop, "You cannot see my face, for man cannot see me and live,"[27] and Perseus could slay the Medusa only by looking at her reflection in the shield of Athena.

Ritual allows us to face the gods—or the forces that govern and limit human existence—in mediated, metaphoric form, much as the commonplace rituals of daily life help us transform the void of time into a reassuring, ordered structure—a human domain in which we and what we do matters.

Like ritual, stories make the nonhuman accessible and less frightening by rendering it in forms that are repeated and become predictable. They allow us to face it in a circumscribed, structured context.

Though the original encounter between the founder of a faith and the divinity is often terrifying, the rituals that evolve from it and are celebrated by a priesthood make the sacred safe for us.

For the artist, however, an encounter with raw energy—the "real" under the surface of our day-to-day reality—may remain terrifying. For van Gogh, the stars in *Starry Night* are not distant and twinkling, as in our night sky, but huge balls of fire. The star nearest us not only generates life but also incinerates it, and we wisely avert our eyes. It is the painter's curse/gift that he must live in the presence of that energy and transmute it into a safe, secondary experience for us—not unlike the heroes of old, who were fated to kill monsters to save the community.

No one in their right mind would volunteer to face the sacred or "real" without the mediation of art or ritual, while those who find themselves beyond the structures and assumptions that protect the rest of us can neither choose their fate nor reject it. Jonah and Jesus tried and failed.

At a public meeting, C. G. Jung—who, like Freud, recognized the unconscious as a form of primeval energy—was asked how one might get in touch with it. His answer was "Don't!" He had seen his patients in the asylum ravaged by it, and his own encounters with it were not freely chosen.

In the Greek myths, the gods are center stage and though, in the tragic theater of Aeschylus and Sophocles, they have largely moved off stage, they continue to command the action. In Euripides, the psychological forces and aberrations that take the place of divinities leave the figures no freer to make their own fate. As Jung was to say of our own time, the gods had become psychological diseases.

In Aristophanes, the gods are ridiculed, and we noted that the supernatural is absent in most comedies. But effectively, the forces of nature and the instincts that govern them *are* gods.

Moreover, comic stories render our helplessness and lack of control more explicitly than other fictions. Nowhere else is the role of chance as crucial and undisguised. Though the outcome is benign, chance in the comic is the equivalent of fate in tragedy. As Eric Bentley says:

> What do the coincidences of farce amount to: Not surely to a sense of fate, and yet certainly to a sense of something that *might* be called fate if only the word had less melancholy associations.[28]

Coincidences often determine the ending of both comic and tragic stories. The messenger with the reprieve arrives too late for Cordelia but in time to save the hero in *The Beggar's Opera*.

Since the Enlightenment, fate and chance have been banished from narrative, derided as "the long arm of coincidence," and considered a mark of poor workmanship. Yet comedy continues to let them determine the narrative. As we noted, we can face our reality as long as we don't have to believe it.

The surprises that make us laugh constitute an intrusion from the realm beyond our control, a milder form of the *astonishing*—a word derived from a root meaning "thunderstruck." In our secular age, surprises in fiction may well be a residue of what we once deemed the intervention of nonhuman powers.

In life, too, fate often seems to strike suddenly, perhaps because, like the figures in stories, we must ignore the forces that determine us until they assert their role in unexpected, sometimes devastating ways. They surprise us for, in order to live our lives with a measure of confidence, we have to remain blind to them as long as possible.

The surprises in fiction, jokes, and riddles give expression to the sense of uncertainty that is forever gnawing at us. We, in the West, honor it when it appears as doubt, since it may spare us error. But its source is at the core of our being—in fear and consciousness.

When uncertainty appears as naked fear or as an utter lack of trust it will either undermine us—or generate a surge of energy that can help us survive.

H

In both ritual and art we can confront the fearful safely and become wholly immersed in whatever is on the screen, page, or canvas without endangering our identity.

The willing surrender of control in ritual—"Thy will be done"—has an equivalent in the willing suspension of disbelief and identity in fiction: an emptying out, a temporary and conscious surrender of consciousness. In art and religious ritual, the "believer" in the audience or congregation becomes open, porous, credulous. All differences and distinctions are submerged.

Proust, on his first visit to Venice, wrote to a friend, "My dream has become my address." In life, however, no dream can long remain our address, just as we cannot live in a fiction. At story's end we must leave it behind, as we must leave childhood, for to remain wholly connected to ourselves and others, as we are for the duration of the story, is seductive but ultimately annihilating. We would cease to be.

In life, total immersion is safe only in brief, entirely private moments of intimacy and in a secluded area like home. Elsewhere, when another person's experience and feelings threaten to become our own, our identity and command over ourselves are undermined. Even the briefest moments of fusion are apt to be confusing.

At the end of *The Garden*, Andrew Marvell invokes both the destructive and seductive powers of fusion:

> Annihilating all that's made
> Into a green thought in a green shade.

As Rilke says, the beautiful is but the edge of the terrifying.[29]

Ritual is a time-out—regular, predictable, reassuring. It takes no perceptual risk and requires none on our part; the sacred is contained and tamed. Though a sermon is not a verbatim repetition, it uses familiar texts and is based on assumptions shared by the congregation. When the minister tells a story, he makes clear, familiar points, confirming what we believe.

Like rituals and prayers, stories are repeated and their outcome is predictable. From Greek and Nordic myths—in which human beings had little agency and were like flies to gods—to our superheroes, who appear to command the outcome, we know absolutely how the story will end.

Lévi-Strauss tells us that cultures amplify their core assumptions in countless myths that, through repetition, keep confirming the values and assumptions we live by—the predicates of our communal structures. We may indeed need our stories to assure us that what we believe is valid, since life doesn't always bear it out.

But before stories reach their reassuring conclusion we expect them to shake us up and even to frighten us. Whereas ritual makes no attempt to render the texture of our lives with its uncertainties and surprises, stories embed the impersonal forces or gods in our *experience*—where they are, in fact, ever present but usually camouflaged by the sheltering assumptions of the community.

Our existence has changed radically over time. But in religious ritual the powers that govern us remain fundamentally the same over long periods of time, whereas story presents them in their ever-changing forms.

Beginning in the Middle Ages and at an accelerating pace during the Renaissance and the Industrial Revolution, our stories have—like all the arts—alerted us to the new, instead of simply confirming the old. Yet the preclusive structure of narrative hasn't changed for millennia: it continues to report the unchanging. The subtext of every fiction confronts us with the limitations of the human will, though in shifting shapes that reflect the changing conditions of our existence.

What is old in stories seems new to us, for the gods in them appear in their contemporary guise—as biology, chance, obsessions, and economics.

While the outcome of the old stories is known and, in this sense, reassuring, from a contemporary perspective they make no sense. We don't believe Oedipus must kill his father and marry his mother. But though no gods preside over *The Trial*, Kafka's K has as little control over his fate as Laius, Jocasta, and Oedipus. From our vantage point, his story would seem as pointless as the myth. But of course it isn't.

The end of every story is guaranteed, but the guarantee is purchased with the freedom of the figures. They have no control over their lives and, by implication, neither do we—a premise every community must deny. Though popular movies seem to confirm what has been instilled in us from childhood on, they actually tell us the opposite.

Within the known and apparently reassuring structure of fiction, we are willing to face the possibility that life doesn't connect in the patterns we have been taught to trust and that our seemingly solid systems are riddled by ambiguities and contradictions.

Comedies leave us feeling carefree, but the coincidences that often determine and resolve them are not reassuring. The happy ending of the fairy tale relieves us of tension: the hunter appears in time to save Little Red Riding Hood. But only by dismissing what happens as wish fulfillment can we ignore that she survives by sheer happenstance. Had the hunter—like the angel who saves Isaac from death—arrived a moment later, she would have died.

The import of stories is clear, but for good reason we cannot deal with it.

In daily life, we tend to assume that what happens on the surface is often window dressing or camouflage. When a situation matters to us, we try to understand the underlying and often determining factors— what someone *really* means or wants but leaves unspoken. Yet when we read or watch stories, we cling to its surfaces—especially if they mirror our own circumstances. We fail to see that it is the validity of the *structure* that keeps fiction relevant and alive.

Very likely it is the troubling uncertainties and contradictions implicit in all stories that make them persuasive and allow us—despite radical differences between the circumstances of the figures and our own—to recognize our experience in theirs.

Even closed systems, like traditional religion, cannot altogether spare us an awareness that our lot is uncertain and that even the most convincing answers and solutions are time bound.

We noted that jokes and riddles often seem to resolve at the end, yet they do so at the surface only, in sleights of verbal play that tie a graceful ribbon around a package that cannot be neatly wrapped.

Indeed, fictive situations may continue to engage us *because* they are insoluble. Once Oedipus has answered the riddle of the Sphinx, he must find the killer of the king whose throne and bed he occupies, and though failing to find the answers spells disaster, so does finding them. The myth is itself a riddle without a solution.[30]

Anton Chekhov says the reality of a story—and, we may add, of jokes and riddles—lies not in the answer but in a correct posing of the question.[31]

In life, we face riddle after riddle, even if most of us settle for a temporary answer that sees us through our brief sojourn.

There *are* no permanent answers—only permanent questions.

Though we enjoy the uncertainty stories induce in us, our fear of it runs so deep that—despite the unreality of the artwork and the frame separating it from us—we need the reassurance of a known outcome. The situations are clearly fictive yet activate our fear of what *might* happen that lurks under the armor of our confidence. Without the certain end we would become uncomfortable. It makes little difference to us whether the figures live or die as long as our knowledge of *their* future makes us feel secure in our own.

Unlike stories, rituals don't contradict themselves or leave us in doubt. But whenever circumstances rupture the domain that our community has enclosed and systematized with its explanations and laws, we find ourselves facing the unknown. When Acts of God or disasters strike "from the stars," the priest is reduced to saying we cannot understand the ways of God. We are left with a mystery—or in uncertainty—just as we are by the stories of Oedipus, K, and Chaplin.

We may believe the Judeo-Christian God is just and cares about us, but in his impact on our lives he is often hard to tell apart from the unpredictable, callous gods of Greece. The difference may be in our attitude to the divinity, rather than in the effect of the divinity on us.

I

As long as physical necessity ruled our days, the void of time—or eternity—was the domain of gods. It stretched far beyond us and our brief span on earth. Today, however, empty time yawns *within* our lives, as leisure.

Though we treasure the time we are free to fill as we wish, it constitutes a threat. Unlike a cat, we are not at ease doing nothing, and we try to avoid *boredom*—a word derived from the Anglo-Saxon meaning "to pierce, bore, drill." Emptiness drills into us, and we keep it at bay—meeting friends, fishing, or writing books—to ward off the limitless, nonhuman reality that threatens us with irrelevance. The diversions, entertainments, and arts that protect us against empty time have assumed central importance in our lives, and stories that once confirmed our core beliefs now serve—no less significantly—as distractions.

Until the nineteenth century, popular narratives were rooted in folk and fairy tales. Their underlying meaning was not substantially different from the plays and novels that served a privileged minority. All stories were subject to the nonhuman forces that were believed to govern us.

But once progress in science and industry enabled us to think we might control what was once called destiny, popular stories were transformed, most significantly in the United States. Instead of figures determined by nonhuman powers—like those in fairy and folk tales—they centered on men and women who appear to be in charge of their lives.

Since our freedom and empowerment are the assumptions on which we, in the West, have built our lives, they are disseminated, or amplified, in popular fictions from the earliest Westerns to our superheroes. They feature individuals who achieve what they set out to do in actions that require courage and perseverance. The stories not only fill our leisure time but assure us that since the will of the figures is effective, what we as individuals are and do matters.[32]

Audiences, however, are well aware that fictions are produced by writers and moviemakers who don't always believe what they tell us. Many do it for the money, and we buy into their fictions because we would *like* to believe them, not necessarily because we do.

But since we keep returning to stories despite a wide choice of other diversions, there would seem to be something in them that we *do* believe and need—over and above the convenience of remaining passive while the figures act, or act out, for us.

Most likely what draws us in is the very structure of narrative, the preclusive plot that popular stories seem to countermand. We conveniently ignore the fact that the heroes of both Westerns and *Rambo* are victims of a precluded narrative, just like Oedipus and King Lear. The differences are on the surface only, but they make *Rambo* palatable to us even as we dismiss the Greek myth.

Our continued interest in stories and their instant availability suggest that at a deeper, largely unconscious level we believe and fear their ancient claim—one made openly by myth and tragedy but that is today implied, or buried, in the structure of *Rambo*.

In popular stories, the core meaning of narrative is camouflaged so successfully that we can take from them what we need—the reassuring illusion that our will is effective—and ignore what is actually happening. The illusion they purvey—that we matter as individuals and determine our own lives—is, as it were, undermined in the dark.[33]

Freud says we don't know why we laugh. In a meaningful parallel, we don't know why we go to stories—and don't *want* to know.[34]

What appears to be a paradox—we don't expect the *storyteller* to believe the story even though we lend ourselves to it—suggests that we would rather not believe it. We may indeed take comfort from being manipulated by him, since we feel at ease with a human being in charge. The apparent artifice hides a truth we can afford to face only if we don't have to believe it.

Societies use their stories, as they do their institutions and laws, to preserve themselves, and since societies differ, so do their stories. Yet all of them share the same preclusive structure.

A narrative may appear to depend on human scheming, like *Double Indemnity*, or be loosely structured by the flow of time, like *The Remembrance of Things Past*. No matter whether the plot is manipulated by a moviemaker or originates in a religious belief, the underlying form remains identical. No story can free its figures and endow them with control over the events, whether they lock into each other consequentially, like the myth of Oedipus, or are jumbled together by happenstance, like *Tristram Shandy*.

The core implication of narrative can be countermanded only by having *nothing* happen—substituting pure description for storytelling and ignoring the impact of time on our existence. Once something happens—anything at all—it has clearly occurred before it is told. Within the structure of the story, it becomes "fated," whether by gods, chance, genetics, or whatever determining force the community credits.

J

An understandable and widely held view has it that troubling ourselves with things we cannot change is pointless. Yet they continue to hover at the edge of our awareness, and keep reminding us of our limits.

Though we have substituted human agency and a commitment to social and economic justice for our one-time faith in divine power, we know we didn't create the forces that govern the universe and generated life on earth. And though we have learned to channel our instincts, cure diseases, alleviate pain, and postpone death, we continue to be enthralled to impersonal systems, both within and beyond us.

Our sense of control is based on the assumption that our surroundings and the immediate future are predictable. Our institutions and the social and physical sciences persuade us that we can foresee the consequences of our actions. In turn, our communities—with their laws, penalties, and rewards—expect *us* to be predictable.

But our record in gauging the outcome of all but short-term endeavors is spotty. While surrendering to uncertainty would paralyze us, only our obligatory faith in freedom and control spares us from seeing that what befalls us—individually and communally—is not always what we planned *or* deserve. Moreover, many events have so many causes that our actions and interventions are often based on incomplete or invalid information.

Today the acceleration of change and the almost instantaneous impact of distant events must leave us wondering whether our own future and that of the species are up to us—though some are confident that computers will master all complexities and allow us to arrive at ever greater certainty and truly informed decisions.[35]

K

We seem to have wandered far afield. But we observed that the comic poses a more immediate challenge to our autonomy than the most foreclosed story.

We have all at times laughed unwillingly, in circumstances that were damaging to us or others, and even a poor joke can *make* us laugh.

Yet our laughter, though it makes us briefly helpless, often leaves us exhilarated.

Charles Lamb says comedy lets him wear his "shackles more contentedly for having respired the breath of imaginary freedom."[36]

But the sense of freedom that laughter induces *isn't* imaginary. Though most comic situations and figures are framed as fiction and perceived as unreal, our reaction to them is *physically* real. Laughter shakes up our bodies, frees them of muscular tension, and releases us from the stress of controlling and containing ourselves.[37]

We are so habituated to the stress that we barely note it—we call it our default position—but being briefly free of it comes as a relief.

By freedom we usually mean the freedom to control our circumstances and relationships. But what if the comic frees us from the *illusion* of freedom and control?

Coming face to face with the possibility—or fact—that we are not free and separate may *constitute* a kind of freedom. It releases the energy we need to deny what we half-know and fear. Facing it in an as-if setting relieves us briefly of the obligatory illusions and self-deceptions that see us through the day.

By lending ourselves to the comic—or, indeed, to any story—we happily surrender our claim to self-determination.[38] In exchange, we find relief from the pressure of maintaining our identity, importance, and free will—the stress of responsibility, guilt, and shame.

Within the safe arena of fiction, our lack of freedom grants us license to abandon the constraints of reason, order, and sense. As Freud tells us, we shake off the bonds of civilization, indulge forbidden impulses, and break the rules of the community.

Our pleasure in the comic is made possible by our very helplessness. We are free to enjoy it because have been *victimized* by laughter. We are no longer in charge.[39]

Though our lives matter within the community—and within the metaphysical system it may have projected into space and eternity—science today assumes that the order beyond the human is unconscious and pays us no mind.

Yet, significantly, it is in the sciences that we find both a willingness to acknowledge our limitations *and* the very confidence and faith that once empowered the humanities and the arts but are notably absent in them today.

Perhaps admitting that we are *not* free—or that our freedom is severely limited—is liberating and gives a foundation to our lives on which we can build.

L

At the end of Keaton's *Steamboat Bill, Jr.*, a storm blows away not just the town but the story itself. Buster succeeds in proving his worth by saving his father and girlfriend. But it hardly matters. The concerns that preoccupied the figures and generated the narrative are swept away. Money, status, success or failure, and even human relationships have become irrelevant. The storm that turns the figures, who thought of themselves as moving of their own accord, into tiny particles at the mercy of nonhuman powers, allows us to escape our own economic, social, and psychological constraints.

When Kierkegaard says that "humor is the last stage of existential awareness before faith," perhaps he means that in our laughter we submit to an impersonal force that is—in its effect on us—not altogether different from the gods we once worshipped.[40]

When we "break up" or "die laughing," we are wiped out as individuals and become part of a whole—connected to everyone and everything. We are transported back to a time when both we and the world were one.

Almost as soon as consciousness divides us, we try to put the world back together—in families, communities, friendships, unified field theories, and poems. As we noted, connections and a sense of wholeness would seem to meet our deepest need and be the source of our deepest pleasure.

The comic invokes at once an unwanted truth and a state of wholeness. In our laughter we are released from the contradictions and self-division that are the price of being human.

We are free yet belong—free *and* connected—free, but not alone. As in art and ritual, the opposites are in balance and the severed parts rejoined.[41]

The German mystic Meister Eckhart said, "God is at home and we are in the far country."

Our laughter allows us to go briefly home, and when we return to the far country of our contradictory, often lonely existence we feel a little freer and lighter in spirit.

But the last word should surely go to a Fool—

> A long time ago the world begun,
> With hey, ho, the wind and the rain;
> But that's all one, our play is done,
> And we'll strive to please you every day.[42]

Notes

Chapter 1: Surprised

1. The Teddy Roosevelt story was told by Winston Churchill to Dr. Charles McMoran Wilson, known as Lord Moran.

2. John Coltrane in Nat Hentoff's Liner Notes, "John Coltrane, Giant Steps," Atlantic Records, 1959.

3. René Girard, "Perilous Balance: A Comic Hypothesis," in *To Double Business Bound: Essays on Literature, Mimesis and Anthropology*, reprinted in *Comedy: Meaning and Form*, ed. Robert Corrigan (Scranton, PA: Chandler Publishing Company, 1965), 121–73, 128.

Charles Baudelaire says, "I said that laughter contained a symptom of failing; and, in fact, what more striking token of debility could you demand than a nervous convulsion, an involuntary spasm comparable to a sneeze and prompted by the sight of someone else's misfortune? And can you imagine a phenomenon more deplorable than one failing taking delight in another? But there is worse to follow. The misfortune is sometimes . . . a failure in the physical order. To take one of the most commonplace examples in life, what is there so delightful in the sight of a man falling on the ice on the street, or stumbling at the end of the pavement, that the countenance of his brother in Christ should contract in such an intemperate manner, and the muscles of his face should suddenly leap into life like a timepiece at midday? The laugh has gone forth, sudden and irrepressible. It is certain that if you cared to explore this situation, you will find a certain unconscious pride at the core of the laugher's thought. That is the point of departure. 'Look at me! I am

walking upright. I would never be so silly as to fail to see a gap in the pavement or a cobblestone blocking the way.'" Charles Baudelaire, *The Essence
of Laughter: And Other Essays; Journals and Letters* (Chicago: Northwestern
University Press, 1991), 315.

4. Milton Berle, in *The New Yorker*, October 18–25, 1999.

5. W. B. Yeats, *The Autobiography of William Butler Yeats* (New York:
Macmillan, 1965), 326.

6. Henri Bergson, *Laughter: An Essay on the Meaning of the Comic* (New
York: Dover Publications, 2005). "We do not see the actual things themselves; in most cases we confine ourselves to the labels affixed to them."
"Generalities, symbols, or even types form the current coin of our daily
perception." 164–65.

7. Thomas Kuhn describes a psychological experiment in which subjects
were asked to identify a series of playing cards—many of them normal, but
some anomalous (e.g., a red six of spades or a black four of hearts). Significantly, "the anomalous cards were almost always identified, without apparent
hesitation or puzzlement, as normal. The black four of hearts might, for example, be identified as the four of either spades or hearts." Thomas S. Kuhn,
The Structure of Scientific Revolutions (Chicago: University of Chicago Press,
1962), 252–53.

Jason Zweig, in a study of investment biases, *Your Money & Your Brain:
How the Science of Neuroeconomics Can Help Make You Rich* (New York: Simon & Schuster, 2007), 57–58, says, "Humans have a phenomenal ability to
detect and interpret simple patterns. That's what helped our ancestors survive the hazardous primeval world, enabling them to be predators, find food
and shelter and eventually to plant crops in the right place at the right time
of year. But when it comes to investing, our incorrigible search for patterns
leads us to assume order exists when it often doesn't."

8. In many situations sensory pleasure derives from a mix of repetition
and surprise. Even cooking often depends on unexpected combinations of
textures and flavors.

9. Jim Holt, *Stop Me If You've Heard This: A History and Philosophy of
Jokes* (New York: W. W. Norton and Company, 2008), 100. The complete
joke reads, "What's the big deal? We only killed him for a couple of days."

10. Adapted from *I Killed: True Stories of the Road from America's Top
Comics*, compiled by Ritch Shydner and Mark Schiff (New York: Crown
Publishers, 2006). The joke conforms perfectly to Freud's definition of
smutty humor by exposing the female genitals verbally while letting them
remain hidden from sight.

11. Tennessee Williams says, "I am the opposite of the stage magician. He gives you illusion that has the appearance of truth, I give you truth in the pleasant disguise of illusion."

12. The great Swiss clown, Grock, responded to comic situations by exclaiming "Nit moeglich!"—"Impossible!" But it is possible. The impossible happens all the time, though we don't much want to know it.

13. Freud twice mentions the connection between jokes and riddles, but he pursues the link no further.

14. Riddlelike wit is not always meant to make us laugh. Einstein said he wasn't sure how World War III would be fought, but he knew what we would be using in World War IV: rocks. Walter Isaacson, Einstein: His Life and Universe (New York: Simon and Schuster Paperbacks, 2007), 494.

15. He refers to "the odd feature jokes have of being able to manifest their full effect only when they are new . . . and come . . . as a surprise." In our view, of course, surprise isn't an "odd feature," but the core of the joke. Freud also mentions surprise as one of the ways hostile and obscene jokes mask their intentions. Sigmund Freud, The Joke and Its Relation to the Unconscious (New York: Penguin, 2003), 147–48.

16. Milton Berle, More of the Best of Milton Berle's Private Joke File, ed. Milt Rosen (New York: William Morrow and Company, 1993), 419–20.

17. John Gregory Dunne, "The Old Pornographer," The New Yorker, November 8, 1999.

18. Duck Soup (film), directed by Leo McCarey, 1933.

Chapter 2: Freud

1. Originally, a clown denoted a boorish, clumsy country fellow—someone not fit for company, and an idiot was a private, disconnected person.

2. "Now it may be observed that young children do not laugh aloud for some months. The first occasion of doing this seems to be surprise, which brings on a momentary fear first, and then a momentary joy in consequence of the removal of that fear, agreeably to what may be observed of the pleasures that follow the removal of pain." David Hartley, "Of Wit and Humor," in Observations on Man, fifth edition, part I, chapter 4, paragraph I, London, 1810, cited in The Philosophy of Laughter and Humor, ed. John Morreall (New York: State University of New York Press, 1987), 41.

3. Freud, The Joke and Its Relation to the Unconscious, 216.

4. In children we sometimes hear what seems like the laughter of pure delight, laughter in the joy of being. But even children most often laugh

when they have mastered something, escaped a threat, or made a connection or joke.

5. Freud makes the point that if the obstacle to the tendentious joke is external, we don't laugh as hard as when internal obstacles stand in the way and are overcome, or circumvented. Clearly, the external threat constitutes less danger. Freud, *The Joke and Its Relation to the Unconscious*, 113–14.

6. Antoinette Baker, "A Time to Laugh; A Study in Laughter: Its Psychology and Its Role in Analysis" (PhD dissertation in Kristin Mann Library at the C. G. Jung Foundation, New York, 1980), 42.

7. As cited in Freud, *The Joke and Its Relation to the Unconscious*, 230.

8. "Instinctively, and because one would rather be a cheater, than be cheated, in imagination at all events, the spectator sides with the knaves." Bergson, "Laughter," in *Comedy*, introduction and appendix, Wylie Sypher (Garden City, NY: Doubleday Anchor Books, 1958), 111.

9. Clowns at the Spanish court were often dwarfs, and in circus sideshows the physically misshapen, weird, and freakish are offered for our entertainment.

10. Seinfeld said this in a 2002 documentary film titled *Comedian*.

11. His references to the theater are limited to Johann Nestroy, a Viennese comedian and playwright, whose farces, although they included music and dance, depended largely on the spoken word.

12. Harry C. Carr, "Mack Sennett—Laugh Tester," *Photography* (May 1915): 71, quoted in Albert Bermel, *Farce: A History from Aristophanes to Woody Allen* (New York: Simon and Schuster, 1982).

13. Freud calls the region in the psyche where repressed materials reside the "preconscious" rather than the unconscious. The preconscious holds materials that were once conscious. *The Joke and Its Relation to the Unconscious*, 199.

14. Since he is investigating the role of the unconscious, or preconscious, Freud limits his discussion to the origin and technique of jokes, and he isn't primarily concerned with their effect on us. But there is a clear connection between the source of the joke and the reason we laugh, and since our study has a different focus, it moves back and forth between them.

15. Harold Lloyd says, "The old formula for comedy drama was . . . 'a laugh, a tear and a laugh.' The recipe for thrill pictures is a laugh, a scream and a laugh. Combine screams of apprehension with stomach laughs of comedy and it is hard to fail." Harold Lloyd, *An American Comedy* (New York: Dover Publications, 1971), 84.

16. Adapted from Freud, *The Joke and Its Relation to the Unconscious*, 53.

17. Adapted from Freud, *The Joke and Its Relation to the Unconcious*, 56.

18. When a ten-year-old girl, accused of being bossy, says, "I'm not bossy. I'm a leader," we laugh both at her self-justification and at her hurt feelings.

19. John H. Towsen, *Clowns* (New York: Hawthorn Books, Inc., 1976), 38.

20. Towsen, *Clowns*, 83.

21. Towsen, *Clowns*, 168. Two of the Hanlon brothers, to publicize their appearance in Baltimore, "climbed to the top of a towering monument. With thousands of spectators watching . . . from the street below, they performed dangerous acrobatic stunts on [a] balcony ledge. . . . The slightest miscalculation would have sent them plummeting to their death. After finishing [their] act, they sprinkled the crowd with thousands of fake dollar bills that read, 'Go see the Hanlon-Lees!'" Towsen, *Clowns*, 178.

22. Freud, *The Joke and Its Relation to the Unconscious*, 97. The sentence is so central to his discussion that he italicizes it.

23. Freud stresses significant parallels between the techniques used by jokes and by dreams. Both circumvent the censor—the introjected, judgmental voice of society. But they do so for different reasons; the distressing content of the joke would keep us from laughing, while in the dream it would keep us from sleeping.

24. Brett Butler in *The Comedy Thesaurus*, ed. Judy Brown (Philadelphia, PA: Quirk Books, 2005), 265.

25. There is some doubt that this actually happened during a broadcast, but the example remains valid.

26. Immanuel Kant, *Kritik der Urteilskraft*, part 1, section 1, paragraph 54, cited in Freud, *The Joke and Its Relation to the Unconscious*, 8.

27. "A man will not laugh . . . unless there is an actual threat to his ability to control his environment and the people in it, even his own thoughts and his own desires. A man will not laugh, however, if that threat becomes too real. The conditions necessary for laughter are therefore contradictory. The threat must be both overwhelming and nil." René Girard, "Perilous Balance: A Comic Hypothesis," in *Comedy: Meaning and Form*, 121–73.

With regard for the comic, even the most incisive comments are not necessarily valid. For the stand-up comedian, the threat is subjectively or psychologically real—he may be rejected—but for Buster Keaton and Harry Houdini, doing their death-defying physical stunts, the threat is objectively real.

28. Freud's use of the word *witzig*—translated as "witty"—describes humor that is verbally and intellectually sophisticated. Great clowns are often no less subtle or complex, but they are only occasionally "witzig."

29. Dugas is quoted by Freud in *The Joke and Its Relation to the Unconscious*, 141. Martin Grotjahn succinctly summarizes Freud's central

observation: "Laughter occurs when repressing energy is freed from its static function of keeping something forbidden under repression and away from consciousness." Martin Grotjahn, *Beyond Laughter: A Summing Up* (New York: McGraw-Hill, 1957), 255–64, reprinted in Corrigan, *Comedy*, 270–75, 270. Freud himself ascribes the pleasure we derive from *all* forms of the comic to a saving in psychological energy or effort, what he calls "the economy of expenditure." By allowing the expression of socially unacceptable drives, tendentious jokes clearly save us the energy we need to keep them bottled up.

30. Robert R. Provine, *Laughter: A Scientific Investigation* (New York: Penguin Books, 2001).

31. Theodor Lipps, cited by Freud, *The Joke and Its Relation to the Unconscious*, 148.

32. Our tendency to identify with and root for the underdog may be attributed to it. Rooting for your home team when it is favored to win is a clear exception.

33. Maintaining our balance is a continuous and, for the most part, unconscious process—equilibrating between pairs of opposites.

34. Freud's view of pleasure as the avoidance of distress, or "unpleasure," is reminiscent of Arthur Schopenhauer's definition of happiness as the absence of unhappiness. The joke pleases us by sparing, or saving, us discomfort.

35. Freud says that in addition to the person making an aggressive joke and the person who is the target, there must be a third party—an uninvolved spectator who would be distressed if the aggressive or sexual implications were out in the open but who is free to enjoy them when they are camouflaged.

When we watch a comedy on stage or screen, we are presumably in the position of Freud's third party—witnessing a tendentious comic performance while safe from attack. We may, however, find ourselves the indirect target. Molière's Monsieur Jourdain, like the circus clown, and Chaplin's Charlie make us laugh because we share their laughable qualities—albeit in a less extreme and less visible form.

36. Jeffrey Sweet, ed., *Something Wonderful Right Away: An Oral History of the Second City and the Campus Players* (New York: Avon Books, 1978), 193.

37. Of course, the conclusion of a story, like the end of a game, is an arbitrary stopping point. Like life, the story could go on even though the central figures are dead. *Hamlet* could segue into the story of Fortinbras or Horatio, just as our own stories become the stories of our children.

38. Girard points out that the audience experiences the equivalent of a thrill ride. We are on a psychological roller coaster—we feel endangered but know we are safe.

Chapter 3: Different and Scary

1. Sigmund Freud, *Das Unbehagen in der Kultur*, standard edition, volume 21(Germany: Fischer Taschenbuch Verlag GmbH, 2001), 122. Though some are uncomfortable calling aggression "instinctual," we can hardly ignore the fact that many creatures depend for their survival on hunting and eating others, or that the propagation of the species is often linked to fierce battles between males.

Recent research into cooperative and altruistic behavior in the animal kingdom need not blind us to socially destructive components in our biology.

2. Will Rogers regarding W. C. Fields, quoted in Carlotta Monti and Cy Rice, *W. C. Fields & Me* (New York: Warner, 1973), 54.

3. Lord Rutherford quoted in "Crash Course," by Elizabeth Kolbert, *The New Yorker*, May 14, 2007.

4. Personal communication, Burton Benedict.

5. The humor of politicians tends to be reductive to the point of cynicism. Since they can't openly admit what they know about their profession, humor serves as a safety valve.

Mark Hanna said, "There are two things that are important in politics. The first is money, and I can't remember what the second one is."

Obliged to show a friendly face in public, they are often scathing in private. Lyndon Johnson said that watching George Romney run for public office was like seeing a duck trying to fuck a football.

6. Jay McInerney, *Story of My Life* (New York: The Atlantic Monthly Press, 1988).

7. *History of the World, Part I* (film), directed by Mel Brooks, 1981.

8. "The passion of laughter is nothing else but sudden glory arising from some sudden conception of some eminence in ourselves, by comparison with the infirmity of others, or with our own formerly: for men laugh at the follies for themselves past, when they come suddenly to remembrance." Thomas Hobbes, *Human Nature*, chapter 8, paragraph 13, in *The English Works of Thomas Hobbes*, volume 4, ed. Sir William Molesworth (London: Bohn, 1840), and also cited in *The Philosophy of Laughter and Humor*, ed. John Morreall (New York: State University of New York Press, 1987), 20.

9. Freud, *The Joke and Its Relation to the Unconscious*, 216–17. "The feeling of superiority is not *essentially* related to comic pleasure." Freud, *The Joke and Its Relation to the Unconscious*, 192.

Theories of comedy often claim that laughter *does* or *does not* derive from a sense of superiority. "Laughter comes from the idea of one's *own* superiority. A Satanic idea if ever there was one! And what pride and delusion! For it is a notorious fact that all the madmen in the asylums have an excessively over-developed idea of their own superiority: I hardly know of any who suffer from the madness of humility. Note, too, that laughter is one of the most frequent and numerous expressions of madness." Charles Baudelaire, "On the Essence of Laughter" (1855), in *The Mirror of Art*, ed. and trans. Jonathan Mayne (New York: Phaidon Press Ltd., 1955), reprinted in Corrigan, *Comedy*.

10. Merle Miller, *Plain Speaking: An Oral Biography of Harry S. Truman* (Berkeley: Berkeley Publishing Corporation, 1973).

11. Walter Isaacson, *Einstein: His Life and Universe* (New York: Simon & Schuster, 2007), 292.

12. I was told this anecdote by Elie Wiesel, but I have not found it in print.

13. The original observations of three- and four-year-olds were made by Martha Wolfenstein. I was referred to it by an unpublished PhD thesis by Antoinette Baker. Baker, "A Time to Laugh," 42.

14. This is surely what Rainer Maria Rilke meant when he says, "The beautiful is nothing but the onset of the terrifying." Rainer Maria Rilke, "Die Erste Elegie," in *Die Duineser Elegien*, vol. 1 of *Sämtliche Werke, Herausgegeben vom Rilke-Archiv in Verbindung mit Ruth Sieber-Rilke, besorgt durch Ernst Zinn* (Frankfurt am Main: Im Insel Verlag, 1962), 717. The harmonic, uncontra-dicted whole is an evocation of the absolute connection we lost in infancy. In later life it is the edge of the terrifying since it threatens our extinction as individuals.

It has been said that our saddest songs are the most beautiful, but perhaps our most beautiful songs are the saddest. They invoke a state of fusion that can be actualized for brief moments only—a lost paradise that is suffused with its own evanescence and a melancholy tranquility in both art and life.

15. Translating "Das Unheimliche" as "The Uncanny" doesn't convey the frightening, shudder-inducing, otherworldly sensation of the German. The word appears frequently in the fairy tales collected and retold by the Brothers Grimm. *Eerie* may be both more accurate and more suggestive.

16. Sigmund Freud, *The Uncanny* (London: Imago Publishing Co., Ltd., 2003), 220. Freud cites the ancient fear of being buried alive that, in his view, speaks to the buried or repressed instinctual life in all of us (244). It haunted people well into the nineteenth century, perhaps most fearfully those who remained close to childhood, the time before they were conscious. When Hans Christian Andersen slept away from home, he left a note on the bedside table declaring he wasn't dead. It is surely significant that Baude-laire, in his essay "On the Essence of Laughter," makes several references to nineteenth-century tales of terror. He senses the connection, though he

doesn't explore it. Towsen, in *Clowns*, gives innumerable examples of the mix of horror and comedy in nineteenth-century vaudeville performances.

17. Surprises in horror films often spring from a sudden confrontation with gross injury. It is frequently inflicted on scantily clad young couples at their most vulnerable and unaware of their surroundings—when they are engaged in sex.

18. Performers often say that without an element of anxiety their performance suffers.

19. Walter Benjamin, "The Storyteller," in Walter Benjamin, *Illuminations*, ed. Hannah Arendt (New York: Schocken Books, 1969), 94.

20. *Play It Again, Sam* (film), directed by Woody Allen, 1972.

21. *Richard Pryor: Live in Concert* (film), directed by Jeff Margolis, 1979.

22. Sam was the name of Minnie Marx's kind but ineffectual husband and the Marx Brothers' father.

23. Henny Youngman in *The Comedy Thesaurus*, ed. Judy Brown (Philadelphia, PA: Quirk Books, 2005), 14.

24. A version of this appears in *W. C. Fields & Me* by Carlotta Monti with Cy Rice, 216: "I'd sooner be dead in Los Angeles than alive in Philadelphia." Philadelphia was notoriously unreceptive to vaudeville entertainers.

25. I first read this "joke" in an early account of the camps. Though Curzio Malaparte used it in his novel *The Skin*, he clearly did not originate it. It seems worth noting that the Jew, like figures in many myths and fairy tales, saves his life by answering a riddle.

26. Freud, *The Joke and Its Relation to the Unconscious*, 97.

27. Freud, *The Joke and Its Relation to the Unconscious*, 93.

28. Though civilization has gradually distanced the contact between us from touch, smell, and taste to the more remote seeing and hearing, the sexual organs remain primarily organs of touch, not of sight. If what we are looking for is a genuine and close connection to another person, in a lasting relationship the skin is more likely to produce it than our eyes. In our culture, with its extreme emphasis on sight, refining the sense of touch, which depends on proximity, might have a salutary effect on marriage. In the intimate realm, our concern with the way we look can be disruptive and worse.

29. After the scheduled performance, tent shows traveling the Midwest sometimes invited men to step up to the stage, where—no doubt for an additional fee—female performers exposed themselves by squatting.

30. Freud, *The Joke and Its Relation to the Unconscious*, 95.

31. Joshua Halberstam, *Schmoozing: The Private Conversations of American Jews* (New York: The Berkeley Publishing Group, 1977), 148.

32. Justin Kaplan, *Mr. Clemens and Mark Twain: A Biography* (New York: Simon and Schuster, 1966), 323.

33. Carol Montgomery in *The Comedy Thesaurus*, ed. Judy Brown, 86.

34. Adapted from Lizz Winstead in *The Comedy Thesaurus*, ed. Judy Brown, 86.

35. Freud, *The Joke and Its Relation to the Unconscious*, 93.

36. Richard Feynman, *"What Do You Care What Other People Think?" Further Adventures of a Curious Character* (New York: W. W. Norton, 1981), 11.

37. Adapted from Myron Cohen, *The Haunted Smile: The Story of Jewish Comedians in America*, by Lawrence J. Epstein (New York: Perseus Books, 2001), 168.

38. Anita Milner tells the same joke about a husband in *The Comedy Thesaurus*, ed. Judy Brown, 248.

39. Like so much in art, effective jokes thrive on detail. Six minutes is more specific and persuasive than the generic five minutes.

40. Adapted from Cohen, *The Haunted Smile*, 159.

41. An exception is a scene in Lina Wertmüller's *Swept Away* (1974), in which a naked, generously proportioned woman was filmed from behind as she crawled all over a man in bed. It was laughable but cruel and exploitative.

42. *The Comedy Thesaurus*, ed. Judy Brown, 365.

43. *Radio Days* (film), directed by Woody Allen, 1987.

44. Adapted from Graham Farmelo, *The Strangest Man: The Hidden Life of Paul Dirac, Mystic of the Atom* (New York: Basic Books, 2009), 393.

Chapter 4: Disconnected

1. The incest taboo is found in every culture and, according to depth psychology, safeguards our emerging identity during the protracted stay in the family that makes our development into civilized beings possible.

The Westermarck effect traces the taboo to a purely biological origin. Nonhuman primate species "spurn individuals with whom they were closely associated in early life. Mothers and sons almost never copulate, and brothers and sisters kept together mate much less frequently than do more distantly related individuals." Edward O. Wilson, *Consilience, The Unity of Knowledge* (New York: Alfred A. Knopf, 1998), 174.

2. Freud, *The Joke and Its Relation to the Unconscious*, 93.

3. What we call the human spirit may be a transmutation of raw survival instinct. Since a part of our biology has transformed into psychology, matter could be said to have become "spirit."

Needless to say, dephysicalization in no way justifies degrading and exploiting our bodies or those of people we deem less worthy.

4. Freud quotes Karl Groos: "Recognition is everywhere . . . connected with feelings of pleasure" and continues with "Aristotle saw the basis of the enjoyment of art in the delight we take in recognition." Freud, *The Joke and Its Relation to the Unconscious*, 116.

5. Baudelaire, *The Essence of Laughter and Other Essays*, 313.

6. Freud, *The Joke and Its Relation to the Unconscious*, 3.

7. Freud, *The Joke and Its Relation to the Unconscious*, 165.

8. Isaacson, *Einstein: His Life and Universe*, 67.

9. This observation is sometimes attributed to Buster Keaton.

10. A student pointed out that just before the final scene Charlie is, for the first and only time in the movie, without his cane. When some newsboys pull on the underwear that sticks out of his pants, he doesn't fight back, as he did in an earlier incident with them.

11. Bergson, "Laughter," 63.

12. Psalms 2:1–4 and 37:12–13.

13. Here, as elsewhere, Freud believes a saving in the expenditure of our energy to be the source of our laughter.

14. Freud, *The Joke and Its Relation to the Unconscious*, 220.

15. John Lahr observes that "the mission of [Noel] Coward's laughter . . . was not to confront suffering but to avoid it at any cost," but an undercurrent of loss and melancholy lends charm to his best musical work. John Lahr, "Charm's Way," *The New Yorker*, September 9, 1966.

16. With the exception of Falstaff, it is the figures living above stairs that have feelings, but since they don't run deep, they don't violate the comic texture. Malvolio suffers pain when his love for Olivia becomes a source of comic sport, but we are not expected to empathize.

17. Girard points out that the comic process resembles tickling. It hovers at the uncertain interface between aggression and affection, attacks playfully, teases, both hides and shows itself. Unless it makes us intensely uncomfortable, our response to tickling is laughter.

Chapter 5: Bergson and High Comedy

1. Henry Bergson, "Laughter," 65.

2. Bergson, "Laughter," 174.

3. Bergson, "Laughter," 147.

4. Scapegoating of someone different is often a source of childhood laughter. But in the process of becoming socialized, we proceed to hide part of

ourselves and, in this sense, become—secretly—different ourselves. We end up laughing not at the other but at the other in ourselves.

5. Though he draws examples from Molière, he doesn't refer to his farces, or to the farcical figures in his plays.

6. Whereas, in Bergson's view, high comedy tries to conform the uncivilized, unaccepting, nonconformist, and "abnormal" in all of us by exiling it, low comedy gives it room to express itself. Our laughter acknowledges that we are, secretly, as different and weird as the comic figure.

7. Freud points out that the joker in a group is often a neurotic personality with ambivalent feelings about the group. Since he is able to turn them into jokes, they make him a welcome member of the group.

8. Chaplin said this in a conversation with Alistair Cooke when they were working on an unproduced screenplay.

9. Bergson, "Laughter," 164.

10. Bergson, "Laughter," 156.

11. Conversely, he notes that "every resemblance to a type has something comic in it." Bergson, "Laughter," 154.

12. Both Chaplin and Keaton began their work on the set with a group of performers who improvised in response to a given situation. Significantly, improvisation is not known to have been used in tragedy, with its focus on the experience of an individual figure.

It is worth noting, however, that an artwork often begins in improvisation, whether by the painter facing the canvas, the composer at the keyboard, or the storyteller among his listeners. The work can begin with a "doodle."

13. Bergson calls it "classic comedy" ("Laughter," 107); elsewhere he refers to it as "high-class comedy."

14. "As though wearing the ring of Gyges with reverse effect, he becomes invisible to himself while remaining visible to all the world." Bergson, "Laughter," 71.

15. This holds true though Molière performed in his own plays.

16. Shakespeare no doubt intended to make Shylock a laughingstock. As Wiley Sypher says about the Elizabethan audience, "A Christian without money arouses our sympathy, a Jew without money is funny." However, Shakespeare's emerging sympathy for—and perhaps identification with—the scorned outsider spoils the easy fun. Wylie Sypher, "The Meanings of Comedy" in Comedy, ed. Wylie Sypher (New York: Doubleday and Company, 1956), 243.

17. Bergson, "Laughter," 55.

18. Significantly, in daily life the less privileged are often more intolerant of deviance and more sensitive to peer pressure than the privileged, who,

perhaps by virtue of specialization, are accustomed to seeing and tolerating differences.

Though, in the theater, the audience of low comedy sides with the very figure that high comedy scapegoats, in daily life the poor are quick to ridicule and exile anyone who separates from others by thinking he is better, or higher up on the social ladder.

What we so often laugh at is the opposite of what we see and show all day.

19. The tragic theatre has disappeared as well. With all of us theoretically equal and aware of our own miniscule role in events, it becomes difficult to sustain the intensity of feeling tragedy requires; it seems to arrogate an importance to the individual that is out of keeping with reality.

20. Even a privileged education no longer assures, or requires, the verbal sophistication on which high comedy depends.

21. Quoted by Sypher, "The Meanings of Comedy," 193–258.

22. Bergson, "Laughter," 79.

23. Freud, too, extends his approach from the tendentious joke to the comic in general. But his premises, like low comedy itself, have wider-ranging validity.

24. In "Das Unheimliche," Freud points out that it is the essence of our instincts to repeat.

25. Bergson, "Laughter," 97.

26. He mentions contradiction only in passing: "Every comic effect, it is said, implies a contradiction in some of its aspects" ("Laughter," 177). Elsewhere in his essay, he refers to "the equivocal nature of the comic. It belongs neither altogether to art nor altogether to life" ("Laughter," 148).

27. We noted that popular stories like *Back to the Future* invoke double-bind situations but don't see them through. They don't resolve them, like tragedy, through death, through the intervention of natural or supernatural forces, or through coincidence.

28. Bergson, "Laughter," 66.

29. Bergson, "Laughter," 66.

30. His approach to comedy rests on the same assumptions as the plays of George Bernard Shaw, who wanted his comedies to change us.

31. Bergson is right to say that art is descriptive rather than prescriptive, even if the description transforms our perception and may, when we are exposed to it repeatedly, alert us to fundamental realities of our existence and so affect our lives.

32. Bergson, "Laughter," 145. See also 111.

33. Bergson, "Laughter," 111.

34. Bergson, "Laughter," 67.

35. Implicit in Freud's *The Joke and Its Relation to the Unconscious* is an essentially tragic view of the human situation, since we are caught between biological imperatives and the demands of civilization. In Bergson, comedy simply serves to preserve the community.

36. Bergson, "Laughter," 111.

37. Einstein says, "Human beings in their thinking, feeling and acting are not free but are as causally bound as the stars in their motions."

"I am a determinist. Everything is determined, the beginning as well as the end, by forces over which we have no control. It is determined for the insect as well as for the star. Human beings, vegetables, or cosmic dust, we all dance to a mysterious tune, intoned in the distance by an invisible player."

"I am compelled to act as if free will existed, because if I wish to live in a civilized society I must act responsibly."

Isaacson, *Einstein, His Life and Universe*, 391–92.

38. E. M. Forster, *Aspects of the Novel* (New York: Harcourt Brace, 1954), 164.

39. Jacques Monod, *Chance and Necessity: An Essay on the Natural Philosophy of Modern Biology*, trans. Austryn Waynhouse (New York: Alfred A. Knopf, 1971), 112–13.

40. Bergson, "Laughter," 86.

41. Bergson, "Laughter," 170. He draws the untenable conclusion that because comedy isn't centered on the individual it isn't an art form. He fails to recognize that the great comedian is as specific in his work and as interested in detail as the painter and novelist. In his effort to differentiate comedy from drama and art, Bergson says that drama "lays bare a secret portion of ourselves," and that what interests us in the dramatic "is not so much what we have been told about others as the glimpse we have caught of ourselves" (164). This, of course, is precisely what we have found to be true in many comedies and jokes.

Chapter 6: Blind and Helpless but Alive

1. How differently a poet, W. H. Auden, sees the world: "Art can have but one subject; man as a *conscious* unique person" (my emphasis).

2. Apparently some early communities had similar sunrise rituals.

3. A useful side effect of the comedian's claim to blindness or ignorance is that in life an unaware person is clearly nonmanipulative. Since what he says or does seems genuine and spontaneous, a performer who claims to be unaware gains in credibility.

4. We may say that in relation to their own context of fate, the figures in every story can be deemed naive.

5. *The Immigrant* (film), directed by Charlie Chaplin, 1917.

6. Towsen, *Clowns*, 141–44.

7. Francis M. Cornford, *The Origin of Attic Comedy* (Ann Arbor: University of Michigan Press, 1993).

8. The helpless, beleaguered husband/father is a common motif in television serials, and may reflect a psychological reality of many male relationships to women inside the home, as well as a comforting, compensating picture of a society long dominated by men.

9. Robert Lewis Taylor, *W. C. Fields: His Follies and Fortunes* (New York and Scarborough: New American Library, 1967), 247.

10. *The Diaries of Kenneth Tynan*, ed. John Lahr (London: Bloomsbury Publishing, 2001).

11. Charles Chaplin, *My Autobiography* (New York: Pocket Books, 1966), 299.

12. Joseph Telushkin, *Jewish Humor: What the Best Jewish Jokes Say about the Jews* (New York: Quill, William Morrow, 1992), 98.

13. Adapted from Steve Lipman, *Laughter in Hell: The Use of Humor during the Holocaust* (Northvale, NJ: Jason Aronson, 1993), 178.

14. Perhaps we burst into laughter and spontaneous applause at the end of a rapid run on the piano or violin in part out of relief that the performer has made it to the finish line. When a football player, carrying the ball, spins and twists his way past his opponents, we see the same mastery and may feel the same exhilaration.

15. Adapted from Kenneth Maxwell, *The Sex Imperative: An Evolutionary Tale of Sexual Survival* (New York: Plenum Press, 1994).

16. Marlon Brando, *Songs My Mother Taught Me* (New York: Random House Value Publishing, 1997), 126.

17. Adapted from Leo Rosten, *The Joys of Yiddish* (New York: Pocket Publishing, 1970).

18. Telushkin, *Jewish Humor*, 67–68.

19. Carol Burnett, *One More Time: A Memoir* (New York: Random House, 1986), 99–100.

20. Taylor, *W. C. Fields*, 63.

21. Taylor, *W. C. Fields*, 95.

22. Taylor, *W. C. Fields*, 214.

23. Monti and Rice, *W. C. Fields & Me*, 94.

24. The stand-up comedian resembles an athlete rather than a filmmaker. When the tennis player hits the ball across the net, his or her opponent is

more immediately up against it than Charlie or Buster. The tennis ball can't be returned multiple times, with only the best one counting.

Understandably, those who need to believe that what they are watching is literally true prefer athletic games and automobile races, where the participants are in actual psychological or physical danger.

25. Michael Moschen in Mark Levine, "The Juggler," *The New Yorker*, December 7, 1998, 14.

Chapter 7: Childhood

1. Hal Roach says, "One of the big secrets of successful comedy is relating it all to childhood. Laurel and Hardy built their whole routine around that." Freud says, "It would appear very tempting to relocate the specific characteristic of the comic . . . to the revival of the child in us, and understand the comic as the 'lost laughter of childhood' regained. . . . The comic is always on the childhood side." Freud, *The Joke and Its Relation to the Unconscious*, 217. He also quotes Bergson: "There is something childish in most of our joyful feelings" (Bergson, *Laughter*, 215).

2. Chaplin says, "I had thought of possible voices for the tramp—whether he would speak in monosyllables or just mumble." Chaplin, *My Autobiography*, 420.

Animated cartoons do not have to face the problem of speech, and there is no radical break between those of the silent era and sound. The distorted speech of cartoon figures and their blithe freedom from all physical limitations keeps them in the realm of childhood.

3. In Chaplin's spoken narration for the 1942 reissue of *The Gold Rush*.

4. Lita Grey, *My Life with Chaplin: An Intimate Memoir* (New York: Grove Press, 1966).

5. Charles Baudelaire, *Selected Writings on Art and Literature*, trans. P. E. Charvet (New York: Viking, 1972).

The complete quotation reads, "Genius is no more than childhood recaptured at will, childhood equipped now with man's physical means to express itself, and with the analytical mind that enables it to bring order into the sum of experience involuntarily amassed."

6. Freud says the joke is made, whereas the comic happens. But he notes that the joker often has no control over the joke; it appears, uncalled, out of his preconscious. In this sense, some jokes can be said to happen. There are even people who cannot resist making puns when they are inappropriate and unwelcome.

7. Tom Nolan, *Three Chords for Beauty's Sake: The Life of Artie Shaw* (New York: W. W. Norton and Company, 2010), 45.

8. H. Leivick, "Introduction to *The Golem*," in *Three Great Jewish Plays in Modern Translations* (New York: Applause Theater Book Publishers, 1986).

9. A. A. Milne, who wrote endearing stories and poems for his son Christopher that generations of parents have read to their own children, was a deeply alienated father. Poems like "What shall we call our dear little dormouse?" were alternate connections—the only way he could express his affection and tenderness.

10. Monti and Rice, *W. C. Fields & Me*, 32.

11. Monti and Rice, *W. C. Fields & Me*, 33.

12. Monti and Rice, *W. C. Fields & Me*, 227.

13. Harold Hayes, in John Keats, *You Might as Well Live: The Life and Times of Dorothy Parker* (St. Paul, MN: Paragon House, 1986).

14. Taylor, *W. C. Fields, His Follies and Fortunes*, 280.

15. Monti and Rice, *W. C. Fields & Me*, 227.

16. Nietzsche says that staring into an abyss can turn you into one.

17. Arthur Marx, *Son of Groucho* (New York: David McKay Company, Inc., 1972), 128.

18. Marx, *Son of Groucho*, 98.

19. Marx, *Son of Groucho*, 166.

20. Marx, *Son of Groucho*, 94.

21. Marx, *Son of Groucho*, 172.

22. Joe Adamson, *Groucho, Harpo, Chico and Sometimes Zeppo: A Celebration of the Marx Brothers and a Satire on the Rest of the World* (New York: Simon & Schuster, 1983).

23. I believe I ran across this in an introduction to a collection of farces by Georges Feydeau and Eugene Labiche.

24. Heinrich Heine says, "I cannot relate my own griefs without the thing becoming comic." In *End Game*, Beckett says, "Nothing is funnier than unhappiness."

25. *New York Times*, February 14, 2000.

26. Epstein, *The Haunted Smile*, 221.

27. Taylor, *W. C. Fields, His Follies and Fortunes*, 104–5.

28. Children who are barely or intermittently recognized grow up with a highly uncertain sense of themselves.

In "The Madness of Spies," John le Carré describes the paranoia afflicting some who work in the espionage services. He doesn't spell it out, but the fact that they are fundamentally disconnected from everyone they know, and can trust no one, would seem to be at the root of their anxiety and their often tenuous hold on reality. *The New Yorker*, September 29, 2008.

29. Hegel, in Alexandre Kojève's interpretation, says, "The human *reality* is nothing but the fact of the recognition of one man by *another*." Alexandre Kojève, *Introduction to the Reading of Hegel: Lectures on the Phenomenology of Spirit*, assembled by Raymond Queneau (New York: Basic Books, 1969), 41.

30. In most societies, the privileged are expected to earn their right to be *not*, like everyone else, by becoming members of the community but by distinguishing themselves. They are groomed to stand apart—to be in a fundamental way disconnected. At the age of eight, boys of the English upper class were sent from comfortable homes to schools, where all feelings and sensory pleasure were denied them; they were poorly fed, hazed by fellow students, and flogged for infractions.

In an extreme but not unrelated case, the king of Prussia forced his teenage son to watch the beheading of his closest friend, a young man with whom he had shared a deep emotional and physical relationship. The boy became Frederick the Great.

31. Early in life we must be given the illusion that we are separate and free, even though the community must maintain an unshakable grip on us.

Today, with our sense of connection increasingly tenuous, we strive urgently to rejoin the whole though we haven't actually left it; we have merely been marginalized. We are no more separate than we ever were; we just feel more isolated.

The very urgency of our need for connection—Americans are joiners—makes us more vulnerable to the feelings and opinions of others. This, in turn, prompts some to withdraw into a hard shell of apparent independence.

32. Very likely, a democracy open to talent and effort makes for insecure, anxious citizens. Moreover, our commitment to starting the world over—to living without the past—dooms us to a permanent identity crisis and contributes to our anxiety.

33. Our freedom and the uncertainty that comes with it may be imposed on us by a capitalism that clearly constitutes economic freedom for those with the requisite drive and skills, but may often be of marginal benefit to society at large.

34. His third wife said about him, "Nobody understands Buster Keaton." He doesn't seem to have understood himself.

35. Rudi Blesh, *Keaton* (New York: McMillan Publishing, 1971), 151.

36. The account was written by William Pittenger, who took part in the raid into the South as a Union soldier.

37. Tom Dardis, *Keaton: The Man Who Wouldn't Lie Down* (New York: Charles Scribner's Sons, 1979), 139.

38. Bernard C. Meyer, *Houdini: A Mind in Chains; A Psychoanalytical Portrait* (New York: Dutton, 1976), 119. "Like Poe, he sought to master his fear by recreating it under his own authorship."

Chapter 8: Making It Real

1. John Constable, who describes painting as "another word for feeling," paid careful attention to the material world of things and creatures.

2. Igor Stravinsky said about one of his compositions that he wanted it to be "like a nose."

3. If the object further proves his existence by drawing attention to him, so much the better. But making it to prove his existence is the primary objective.

4. See Bruno Bettelheim, *The Empty Fortress: Infantile Autism and the Birth of the Self* (New York: The Free Press, New York/Collier-McMillan Limited, 1967).

"According to Piaget (1954) the concept of the permanence of the object is so central an issue because it is 'only by achieving belief in the object's permanence that the child succeeds in organizing space, time, and causality'" (Bettelheim, 445).

"The autistic child cannot bear it if the object does not always appear in the same place, or events do not occur in the same order. Is it not reasonable to assume that this is so because he cannot believe in the persistence of an object if its place is not the accustomed one? Might this not reflect the ultimate effort to establish the constancy of objects that he needs for his security?" (Bettelheim, 447).

"On the basis of our experience with autistic children, we may say that as long as the child is not convinced of his own existence as a constant, he cannot believe in permanence of any kind. . . . At the root of the child's wish that nothing should change in the external world is his desperate wish that nothing should change in or about himself, since he is convinced that any change would be catastrophic. It is based on his conviction that he is helpless to preserve his integrity in the face of change, of his not being a self with an inner consistency that will survive outer change" (Bettelheim, 447–48).

5. In the battle scenes at the end of *The Seven Samurai*, the death of combatants is made credible by a torrential rainstorm. When the warriors fall, their bodies splash into water; some are dragged through it by their horses,

plowing up a plume of spray. Though their death is no more persuasive than death in Westerns, the impact of their bodies on water is immediate and sensory. A battle staged in a dust storm has nowhere near the same immediacy.

6. Robert Altman's fluid, empathetic staging of the scenes close to the battlefield gives way to jazzy editing that ends the film as a service comedy. At screenings, audiences—unaccustomed to the mix of graphic gore and broad comedy and put under tension by it—clearly welcome the brainless farce of the football game. They, too, need rest and relaxation.

7. John Belushi as an enormously fat Elizabeth Taylor devouring a whole chicken while being interviewed about the movie *Cleopatra* will strike us as funny only as long as we are familiar with both the actress and the movie's disastrous production.

8. Adapted from Myron Cohen, cited in Jim Holt, *Stop Me If You've Heard This*, 106–7.

9. Charles Chaplin, "What People Laugh At," *American Magazine*, November 28, 1918, 36.

10. Our word *reality* is derived from Latin *res*, meaning "thing."

11. Graham Farmelo, *The Strangest Man: The Hidden Life of Paul Dirac, Mystic of the Atom* (New York: Basic Books, 2009).

12. Walter Kerr, "Around the Globe, Shakespeare Remains a Mirror for Mankind," *New York Times*, September 12, 1976, sec. 2. The entertainer's need for public affirmation may be an adult equivalent of the child's need for attention and can override all other considerations. Maurice Chevalier was but one of many performers who entertained the Germans during their occupation of France.

13. Dana Goodyear, "Man of Extremes: The Return of James Cameron," *The New Yorker*, October 26, 2009.

14. The continuous and emphatic stress on individual freedom in our society suggests it is in grave doubt. Our popular stories appear to reinforce what we desperately *need* to believe.

15. Goodyear, "Man of Extremes."

Chapter 9: *Annie Hall*

1. Eric Lax, *On Being Funny: Woody Allen and Comedy* (New York: Charterhouse, 1975), 91.

2. "If one has occasion as a doctor to make the acquaintance of one of those people who . . . are well known in their circle as jokers . . . one may be surprised to discover that the joker is a disunited personality, disposed to neurotic disorders." Freud, *The Joke and Its Relation to the Unconscious*.

3. Ralph Rosenblum and Robert Karen, *When the Shooting Stops . . . the Cutting Begins: A Film Editor's Story* (New York: Viking Press, 1970), 273. Whatever the motives behind their account, I am inclined to trust it. Artists like Allen, who insist on total control, can be uneasy admitting their own uncertainties.

4. Welles no doubt knew that he served as a model for Charles Foster Kane. He realized that in his climactic destruction of Susan Alexander's room he revealed himself. After shooting the scene he said, "I really felt that." In later years he obscured his own relationship with the figure of Kane by dismissing their shared psychological roots as "dollar book Freud."

Welles, like Allen in his work before *Annie Hall,* was far more comfortable showing himself masked. His rendering of Kane as an old man when he himself was twenty-five is powerfully persuasive, while his rendering of Kane as a young man is sometimes awkward.

5. Given the high cost of making movies, the difficulties Allen encountered in the cutting room would spell disaster for most productions.

6. Stig Bjorkman, ed., *Woody Allen on Woody Allen* (New York: Grove Press, 1993), 50.

7. Lax, *On Being Funny: Woody Allen and Comedy,* 105.

8. *Monkey Business* (film), directed by Norman McLeod, 1931.

9. *A Day at the Races* (film), directed by Sam Wood, 1937.

The Surrealists, whose paintings, sculptures, and texts thrive on disjunction, were well aware of the comic element in their work. On a visit to Hollywood, Salvador Dali called the Marx Brothers American surrealists. Conversely, a newspaper account of the 1936 International Surrealist Exhibition in London called the artists "the Marx Brothers of art."

10. Despite the unreality of the figures and situations in *Monty Python's Flying Circus,* the randomness and incongruity are immediately relevant and real to us, though they at first confused audiences who watched the show on the BBC.

11. When I saw Renoir's *Rules of the Game* in the early 1960s, I was delighted when the aviator veers his car off the road in a self-destructive impulse for which the film had not prepared me. At the time I failed to realize that this was how a great deal of my own life actually happened—disjointed, coming out of nowhere, seemingly causeless. I laughed at the scene without understanding why.

I had been raised on Enlightenment assumptions in Europe, and when I came to the States, they were reinforced by American positivism, with its faith in cause-and-effect relationships and the efficacy of the human will. I never doubted them consciously, though much of my own experience made no sense, and none of it was subject to my will. From childhood on I had effectively been a tumbleweed, blown this way or that, from home to home, country to country, and continent to continent.

Perhaps the meaningless was so threatening that to survive I had to ignore the implications of my experience. Since my physical survival was not at stake, I could live in an alternate reality—unlike those who were sent to the camps, who could not shut out what was happening any more than they could escape it physically.

Not until the failure of my work combined with a personal crisis to undermine my assumptions was I forced to face what I had *actually* experienced.

12. Adapted from a collection of courtroom exchanges by Rodney R. Jones, Fort Bragg, California.

13. Robert Craft, *Stravinsky* (New York: Alfred A. Knopf, 1972), 176.

Chapter 10: Connected but Free

1. Our childhood family prepares us for life in the community by both sheltering us and enjoining us to separate.

As adolescents, unable to channel our biological energies into existing communal structures and assumptions, we are apt to become a battleground of opposites. Indeed, adolescence may have evolved in response to rapid change; it gives the young, who once moved directly from childhood to being adults, a time to challenge assumptions and institutions that no longer meet the conditions in which they will have to survive.

Though the community must maintain an unshakable grip on us, we must be given the illusion that we are separate and free.

Today, with our sense of connection increasingly tenuous, we strive urgently to rejoin the whole, though we have never actually left it; we have merely been marginalized. We are no more separate than we ever were; we just feel more isolated. Indeed, the very urgency of our need for connections makes us more vulnerable to control by the community.

2. *Sherlock, Jr.* (film), directed by Buster Keaton, 1924.

3. Towsen, *Clowns*, 67.

4. Chaplin, *My Autobiography*, 144.

5. Soren Kierkegaard, *Concluding Unscientific Postscript*, trans. David F. Swenson (Princeton, NJ: Princeton University Press, 1941), 459–68. Cited in *The Philosophy of Laughter and Humor*, ed. John Morreal (New York: State University of New York Press, 1987).

"The tragic and the comic are the same, insofar as both are based on contradiction; *but the tragic is suffering contradictions, the comical, painless contradictions*" (Kierkegaard, 83).

"The comic is present wherever there is a contradiction, and wherever one is justified in ignoring the pain" (Kierkegaard, 85).

See also Girard: "We are ambivalent about everything we call our 'self,' our 'ego,' our 'identity,' our 'superiority.' All this is both the ultimate prize we are trying to win, the most precious treasure to which we keep adding tirelessly, like busy ants, and the most frightful burden we are desperately eager to unload, preferably on the back of someone else.

"Since we can never unload that burden permanently, we are constantly looking for temporary relief; laughter provides some. In laughter, for a few brief moments, we seem to have the best of two incompatible worlds. Our feeling of control and autonomy is increased as we see others lose theirs and slip into the pattern. And as we, ourselves, beginning to come 'loose,' the feeling of rigidity and tension that goes with self-control is relaxed." Girard, *In Perilous Balance*, 130.

6. Jeremy Bernstein, *The Life It Brings: One Physicist's Beginnings* (Boston: Houghton Mifflin, 1987), 2.

7. Graham Farmelo, *The Strangest Man: The Hidden Life of Paul Dirac, Mystic of the Atom* (New York: Basic Books, 2009).

8. Charles Baudelaire, *Oevres II* (Paris: La Pléiade, n.d.), cited in Georges Poulet, *Studies in Human Time*, trans. Elliott Coleman (New York: Harper & Brothers, 1956), 276.

9. As we noted, Baudelaire says that without the double or contradictory element in the comic there would be no convulsion or laughter. Baudelaire, *The Essence of Laughter and Other Essays*.

10. There is some evidence that laughter, by allowing us to feel whole, not only enhances our sense of well-being but also may help us heal when we are ill.

11. Inasmuch as acknowledged aggression and sexuality leave us less self-divided, even tendentious jokes can induce a sense of connection and wholeness.

12. The humor of American men is sometimes so understated and unemphatic that the listener can't be sure it is meant to be funny. Both Mark Twain and Will Rogers made jokes that work by indirection, as seen in this example from Twain: "A man who carries a cat by the tail learns something he can learn in no other way."

13. Stories and art are most often generated by those who seek intense, fusing experiences in life—possibly because, like adolescents, they are in danger of flying apart.

14. Charles Baudelaire, "The Painter of Modern Life," in *The Painter of Modern Life and Other Essays*, trans. Jonathan Mayne (London: Paidon Press, 1964), 9.

Bergson approaches the same core issue, though without the existential urgency of the artist: "What is the object of art? Could reality come into contact with sense and consciousness, could we enter into immediate communion with things and ourselves, probably art would be useless . . . for then our soul would continually vibrate in perfect accord with nature" (Bergson, "Laughter," 157–58).

15. As is surely apparent from the fervor of these comments, *A Man Escaped* has been of deep personal significance in my life.

16. Jan Swafford, *Johannes Brahms: A Biography* (New York: Alfred A. Knopf, 1997), 124.

17. In popular movies, as in nineteenth-century melodrama, music ensures that our experience aligns perfectly with the feelings of the central figures and those of everyone in the audience.

18. Unlike narrative, music may be the most immersive because it generally doesn't have a direct or mimetic relationship to reality; the harmony is not contradicted by what we know to be otherwise. Even so, the first performance of *The Rites of Spring* caused a near riot, and Beethoven said he composed to allay the confusion or dissonance of his experience. No doubt some contemporary listeners rejected it because it didn't sound harmonious to them.

19. Chaplin, *My Autobiography*, 115.

20. Mary Catherine Bateson, *With a Daughter's Eye: A Memoir of Margaret Mead and Gregory Bateson* (New York: Harper Perennial, 1994), 159.

21. Significantly, there is no dancing and little music in tragedy, though some may feel that opera qualifies as a form of the tragic.

22. As in fairy tales, the figures in Shakespeare's late comedies are the victims of magical spells. But in these plays the dark matter that is at the core of both narrative forms tends to rise to the surface. The stories end happily but are not always funny.

23. Freud, *The Joke and Its Relation to the Unconscious*, 226.

See also Freud: "It would appear very tempting to relocate the specific characteristic of the comic . . . to the revival of the child in us . . . and understand the comic as the 'lost laughter of childhood' regained" (Freud, 217). He quotes Bergson: "There is something childish in most of our joyful feelings" (Freud, 215). We noted that the exhilaration of being in love may have its source in the promise of perfect union and communion, of becoming one with another. In *In the Shadow of Young Girls in Flower*, Proust speaks of "that extension and possible multiplication of self which we know as happiness."

Francis Cornford notes that in Attic Comedy "the Golden Age is an extraordinarily frequent motif." "The reign of Zeus stood in the Greek mind for the existing moral and social order; its overthrow, which is the theme of so many comedies, might be taken to symbolize . . . the breaking up of all ordinary restraints . . . or the restoration of the Golden Age of Justice and Loving kindness which lingered in the imagination of poets, like the after-glow of a sun that had set below the horizon of the Age of Iron." Francis M. Cornford, *The Origin of Attic Comedy* (London: E. Arnold, 1914).

It invokes a time we might think of as the childhood or, indeed, the infancy of the race.

24. See also Bakhtin on carnivals in Mikhail Bakhtin, *Problems of Dostoevsky's Poetics*, ed. and trans. Caryl Emerson (Minneapolis: University of Minnesota Press, 1984), 176–77.

25. It has been said that farce is a tragedy in which the figures are not actually made to suffer. Some tragic situations are not unlike comic ones, but with a bad ending, and some comic situations are like tragic ones that end well.

Apparently some satyr plays were comic versions of the material treated in the tragic trilogy that preceded them. We may assume they complemented tragedy's focus on elevated, highly differentiated individuals.

26. Frederick Nietzsche, *The Birth of Tragedy* (Whitefish, MT: Kessinger Publishing, 2004), 28.

27. When God spoke to Moses from the burning bush, "Moses hid his face; for he was afraid to look upon [Him]."

28. Eric Bentley, "Farce," in *Comedy: Meaning and Form*, ed. Robert W. Corrigan (San Francisco: Chandler, 1965), 196.

29. Rainer Maria Rilke, *Duineser Elegien* Die erste Elegie (my translation).

30. In *Einfache Formen* (Tübingen: Max Niemeyer Verlag, 1958), André Jolles says, "Myth is an answer that comprises a question" (129).

31. *Letters of Anton Checkov*, selected and ed. Avraham Yarmolinsky (New York: Viking Press, 1973), 88.

32. This may be the reason our movies are popular all over the world. They demonstrate, as Peter Gay says about America, "the Enlightenment in practice." But beneath our exceptionalism and optimism there is, in the American psyche, a less confident and perhaps more realistic sense of the role we play in determining our lives. The men who fought in World War II, Korea, and Vietnam became self-described "luck freaks," and many of those spared on the battlefield knew that circumstance and chance had determined their lives. Lincoln, reflecting on his years in office, wrote, "I claim not to have controlled events, but confess that events have controlled me," and Sherwood Anderson said late in life, "My luck held."

33. We are like children at the edge of night, who need the reassurance of stories that include the terrifying but rob it of its numinous power by giving it a definite shape—one we have encountered in other stories, in which it was eventually made harmless.

34. Though a story reminds us that we are not free, it could be said to empower the storyteller, conferring a sense of agency on him. But stories traditionally have their own logic and force the storyteller's hand. They cannot be changed at will or by whim. Moreover, the storyteller may be *obliged* to tell it, just as Freud's joker cannot always keep the tendentious joke from bubbling out of his unconscious.

35. Those who earn their living by teaching literature at our elite institutions are caught in a bind. Since they work in communities charged with educating future leaders, they are bound to insist on the freedom and efficacy of our will even more urgently than society at large. Any challenge to this basic assumption, even in fictive form, constitutes a grave threat.

Since fiction is part of their livelihood, they cannot dismiss it as meaningless, and yet must invalidate its core meaning. For the preclusive plot affirms a deeply traditional view of the human situation. It takes us back to the very assumptions the Enlightenment swept away.

Postmodernists in the academy solve the problem by labeling the basic structure or plot of narrative a mere convention—one a knowing storyteller won't use and a knowing audience no longer requires. When it *is* used, it serves as an artificial construct, a manipulation of events that in no way reflects our existence. To the postmodernist, the frank manipulation of story and audience seems more honorable and to the point than fictions that actually *believe* what they tell us. It empowers the human will, dismisses impersonal forces, and reflects the way we see ourselves and our situation today.

Putting the storyteller in charge has led to a comfortable convergence between the postmodern view of narrative and fictions explicitly manufactured for the marketplace. As I Lay Dying and Strangers on a Train are thought to differ in the complexity, vitality, and detail of their rendering, but at their core—the structure or plot—neither story is deemed "real" or credible.

Not surprisingly, the relationship of the postmodernist to narrative has a parallel in our relationship to magic. Both were once in the service of religious ritual. Even today, the moment in the Mass when the bread and wine transubstantiate into the body and blood of Christ is, for the believer, at once miraculous and utterly real.

Though most of us in the West believe that science accounts for what were, for millennia, deemed manifestations of the supernatural, magic continues to astonish and please us. But what used to fill us with awe we now watch with delight at the dexterity of the magician and his skill at deceiving us.

36. At a conference on Storytelling in the New Millennium, attended mostly by people who design software for video games, I was struck by their consistently positivist perspective. They were confident that we are masters of our fate and convinced that their games—unlike traditional stories— empower the players to determine the plot and outcome, though in every instance they had merely been given a choice between several fixed alternatives.

37. From an essay on Restoration comedy by Charles Lamb.

38. Freud points to the liberating effect of humor. Tendentious jokes save—or free—the energy we usually need to repress the hidden material released by the joke.

We noted that until recently comedians were acrobats and jugglers who did the seemingly impossible. Watching them exceed our physical limitations with apparent ease must have given the audience a sense of freedom— just as a joke or witticism allows us to leap across an unbridgeable gap and feel airborne. The French word for "witty" is *spirituel.*

39. The comic constitutes one of the few occasions when someone who *makes* us feel or do something—the comedian makes us laugh—gives us pleasure.

40. Kierkegaard, *Concluding Unscientific Postscript,* 459–68.

Without further commentary by Kierkegaard, and with no more than a liberal arts familiarity with his philosophy and biography, I can only guess at his meaning.

Perhaps he sees the source of the comic in the discrepancy between God's power and our own utter lack of it, and in our uncertain relationship to him. If this interpretation is valid, it is but a small step from Kierkegaard's existential anxiety to our own view of uncertainty and surprise as the core of the comic.

41. The contradictions are not resolved, but are buried in our laughter. It seems possible, moreover, that we are briefly relieved of them by the contradictions in the comic experience itself.

42. William Shakespeare, *Twelfth Night.*

It seems appropriate to end the book on a personal note. From 1939 to 1945, I lived at Bunce Court, a coeducational boarding school in England that sheltered and gave a sense of existence to refugee children without families or homes.

Our plays were directed by Wilhelm Marckwald, an exiled German man of the theater, who also stoked the school furnace and did the heavy work in the garden.

From this gifted, kind, sane, and deeply modest human being and artist I first learned that persistence might allow even second-rate talent to do decent work; after working on *Twelfth Night* for a year we were ready to perform just seven scenes, but we knew they were good.

In the small part of the Fool, it fell to me to end the evening with the song that closes the play. It has never left my memory—just as my deep sense of gratitude to the man who was the father I couldn't have has never left my heart.

Index